考研英语指南

总主编　梁为祥　李　刚
主　编　肖　辉　孙　瑾　王　婕

东南大学出版社
·南京·

内 容 提 要

本书是众多专家、教授集多年的教学经验并根据近年来考试内容的走向,以国家教育部颁发的《2009 年全国硕士研究生入学统一考试英语考试大纲〈非英语专业〉》为依据而精心编写的。本书的前两个单元重点介绍《大纲》的要求和考试内容的规范,并且从语言知识的角度细化了考试的内容和范围以及考生必须要掌握的基本知识。后三个单元主要紧扣考题的形式和内容进行了详细的讲解与分析,如:语言知识运用,阅读与理解(含翻译)以及写作等。在每个部分都配有大量的讲解分析题和练习题,以此引导考生如何去掌握语言基本知识以及如何去做好每一题目,从而达到提高考生的语言能力和水平。

图书在版编目(CIP)数据

考研英语指南/梁为祥,李刚主编. —南京:东南大
学出版社,2009.9
 ISBN 978 - 7 - 5641 - 1828 - 0

Ⅰ. 考…   Ⅱ. ①梁…②李…   Ⅲ. 英语—研究生—
入学考试—自学参考资料   Ⅳ. H31

中国版本图书馆 CIP 数据核字(2009)第 157257 号

出版发行:东南大学出版社
社　　址:南京四牌楼 2 号　邮编:210096
出 版 人:江　汉
网　　址:http://press.seu.edu.cn
电子邮件:press@ seu.edu.cn
经　　销:全国各地新华书店
印　　刷:南京京新印刷厂
开　　本:787mm×1092mm　1/16
印　　张:13.5
字　　数:329 千字
版　　次:2009 年 9 月第 1 版
印　　次:2009 年 9 月第 1 次印刷
书　　号:ISBN 978 - 7 - 5641 - 1828 - 0
定　　价:25.00 元

本社图书若有印装质量问题,请直接与读者服务部联系。电话(传真):025 - 83792328

前　　言

　　《考研英语指南》是根据教育部有关部门最新颁布的考研英语《大纲》规定的考试功能和作用以及内容要求的原则而编写的。要求考生要达到的知识、能力和水平目标是全面的、完整的、系统的。根据"大纲"的规定和要求，将本书的内容规划为语言知识和语言技能两大部分。第一部分为语言知识，包括语法知识：语法知识涵盖时态和语态，虚拟语气，非限定动词，主从复合句和某些连词的用法，倒装，强调，否定，反意疑问句，插入语，形容词和副词及其比较结构和特殊用法，句子的完整性和一致性。第二部分为语言运用能力，包括阅读能力和写作水平。其中词汇知识涵盖词义辨析，词语搭配，习语和固定词组的意义，语篇连接。此部分均以完形填空的方式体现词汇的各种用法，并且进行详细的解析。其后还设计了一些练习题，供考生练习提高。阅读理解部分根据试题的设计，分为 A、B、C 三节。每节都简述考题要点和典型试题分析，同时对试题范例的答案进行详细的解析，引导考生如何准确地做好每一道题目。最后精选练习题，让考生做自测。

　　根据《大纲》的要求，写作内容包括 A、B 两节（英语应用文和英语短文）。英语应用文写作主要是考查学生运用英语撰写不同类型的应用文的能力，包括私人和公务信函，备忘录，摘要，报告等。在此部分，对于每一种文体的应用文都设计有：写作要点和范文。

　　英语短文写作主要是要求考生能够通过短文写作提高英语表达能力以及掌握短文写作要领。在此部分，对于每一种文体的短文都有不同的设计和要求。譬如：在设计每一篇范文时，都有写作特点和要领，提供主题句或写作提纲，规定情景，图表以及范文和点评等，最后配有写作练习，便于学生练习提高。

　　为了编写出一本紧贴《大纲》的要求，而又能体现"新选材、新题型、新理念"的高质量的考研新教材，以便更加满足非英语专业考生的需求，东南大学、中国药科大学、南京财经大学等高校的英语专家、教授进行了认真的探索，并直接参与编写工作。由东南大学外国语学院梁为祥教授和李刚副教授担任总主编，肖辉、孙瑾、王婕担任主编。在编写和出版过程中，得到了东南大学出版社史建农编辑的大力支持与配合，在此表示感谢。

　　由于编写工作时间仓促，书中难免会出现不妥和谬误之处，真诚地希望广大读者批评指正。

作　者

2009.6

总主编 梁为祥 李 刚

主 编 肖 辉 孙 瑾 王 婕
副主编 （以姓氏笔画为序）

王鉴莺 李 涛 汪 佩
陈 怡 赵 娜 徐 黎

编 委 （以姓氏笔画为序）

王鉴莺 李 涛 李 刚
肖 辉 孙 瑾 王 婕
陈 怡 胡孔旺 汪 佩
赵 娜 徐 黎 戴 磊
梁为祥

目　　录

第一单元
最新考研英语大纲要点（非英语专业）

I. 新大纲要求

1. 语法

要求考生应熟练地运用基本的语法知识。目的是鼓励学生用听、说、读、写的实践代替单纯的语法知识学习，以求考生在交际中能更准确、自如地运用语法知识。

2. 词汇

考生应能掌握 5 000 个左右的词汇以及相关词组。

重点与范围：考试词汇见"大纲"，相关词组见后面的词组表。

词汇表的动态特征：在一定时段内，词条也有一定的变化，而这些变化一定与社会生活的变化密切相关，但变化不是很大的。

考生扩大词汇量是必要的，同时还要注意词汇的多义性以及使用的语境，尤其是注意词汇的搭配用法以及同义词之间的区别。因此，要系统记忆，灵活掌握。比如说，词根、词缀知识可以帮助迅速掌握词汇。在记忆词汇中，应该根据"共核"，来考虑构建自己的词汇范围以及词组，对那些不太了解的词汇要多查词典，特别是原版词典，不能只满足中文释义，还要掌握词汇的发音和具体用法。不要死背硬记，要在使用中记忆。结合例句，结合文章来记忆。这样的句子及文章的"周边"信息能为记忆提供"联想"或"刺激"，从而可以深化词汇的记忆。同时记忆词汇更是为了使用。

3. 阅读

要求学生读懂选自各类书籍和报刊的不同类型的文字材料（生词量不超过 3%），还要读懂与本人学习、工作有关的文献，技术资料说明和产品介绍等。

对所读的材料应具备下面的能力：

1）掌握文章大意、信息和概念性含义；

2）对文中的内容进行判断、推理和引申；

3）根据上下文来判断词义以及结构之间的关联；

4）理解作者的意图、观点、态度并加以分析、区别。

要求考生：读懂，理解，速度，解题。并对英语词汇、短语、词组、句型等习惯表达方式，尤其是对语言知识和语言运用技能更好地掌握。

在记忆词汇过程中，能够掌握好 1,000 至 1,500 个核心词汇，阅读起来就很流畅。

提高阅读技能也很关键。文章阅读完以后，稍稍回想一下读过的内容，然后再去做题目。在阅读过程中，考生应多接触各类的英语文章，了解各种文体、题材的文章。

4. 写作

考生应该写出不同类型的应用文，包括私人和公务信函、备忘录、摘要、报告等，以及一般描写文、叙述文、说明文和议论文等。写作时应能做到以下几点：

1）语法结构、拼写、标点正确，用词得当；

2）遵循文章的特定文体格式和要求；

3）安排好文章结构，使其内容统一、连贯；

4）恰当地选用语域。

5. 其他方面知识要求

听力测试已改在各校复试中进行，听力题型也由各校自行确定，要求考生加强听力训练。

Ⅱ. 试卷结构要点

从 2009 年起，考研英语笔试试卷内容和结构确定为：试题分三大部分，共 52 道题，包括英语知识运用、阅读理解和写作。

1. 英语知识题

此部分涵盖词汇、表达方式和语言结构。共 20 小题，每小题为 0.5 分，共计 10 分。

在一篇 240—280 单词的文章留有 20 个空白，每道题给出四个选项，从其中选一个最佳答案。填入空白后，使文章语意正确。

2. 阅读与理解题

此部分由 A、B、C 三节组成，考查考生理解文章的能力。共 30 小题，每小题为 2 分，共计 60 分。

A 节（20 小题）：测试理解短文的主旨、具体信息、以及根据上下文推断生词意义等能力。从每道题的 4 个选项中，选择一个最佳答案。

B 节（5 小题）：测试考生对文章的连贯性、一致性以及文章的理解能力。此部分有三种备选题型，从中选择一种进行考查。

备选题型有：

1）一篇有 500—600 单词的文章，其中有 5 段空白，文章后有 6—7 段文字，从中选择能分别填入文章中 5 个空白处的 5 段。

2）在一篇 500—600 单词文章中，各段落的原有顺序已打乱，要求考生根据文章内容和语言结构将所列段落（7—8 个）重新排序，其中已给出 2—3 个段落在文章中的位置。

3）在一篇约有 500 单词的文章中，在其前或后有 6—7 段文字或 6—7 个概括句或小标题。带有对文章某一部分的概括、阐述或举例。要求从这 6—7 个选项中选出最恰当的 5 段文字或 5 个标题填入文中的空白处。

C 节（5 小题）：考查考生理解较难英语文字材料的能力。要求阅读一篇约 400 单词的文章，并将其中 5 个画线部分（约 150 个词）译成汉语。

3. 短文写作题

此部分由 A、B 两节组成,考查书面表达能力,总分为 30 分。

A 节:考生根据提供的情景能写出 100 词(不含标点符号)的应用性短文,总分为 10 分。

B 节:根据所提供信息,考生能写出 160—200 词的短文(不含标点符号)。总分为 20 分。

近几年来,写作部分分值的增加就是要强调重视写作,加强写作训练。应用文写作是平时工作、生活中常见常用的内容。具体写作内容和方法已在写作部分体现出来。

第二单元
最新考研语法要点

Ⅰ. 语言和语法

"英语知识运用"是测试考生在全面理解一篇短文的基础上弄清楚本文的语法，词汇，语言结构及篇章等，然后从四个选项中选择一个最佳答案，并符合原文的意思和结构。

此部分内容特点：

1. 短文长度一般在 240—280 个词汇之间；

2. 文体和题材：多为说明文，议论文；内容涉及科技、经济、历史、文化、教育、社会生活等；

3. 测试方法：文中留 20 个空白，即 20 个小题，每小题分数值为 0.5 分；每小题给出 4 个选项，从中选一个最佳答案；

4. 在 20 道小题中，通常有 12—15 道题是测试词汇题；词语的搭配；习语用法（固定词组）等；其中 5—8 题是测试语法结构和篇章结构。

下面分三个方面点出其要点：

Ⅱ. 语法结构

全面掌握好英语语法知识对于考生阅读理解英文文章至关重要，具体复习范围如下：

1）动词的时态

一般现在时	一般过去时	现在进行时	过去进行时
现在完成时	过去完成时	一般将来时	过去将来时

2）动词的语态

主动语态和被动语态

3）虚拟语气

在英语中，虚拟语气的使用也很重要，要抓下列几个要点进行复习消化：

（1）由 if 引导的从句：一种从句是真实条件句；另一种是非真实条件句，通过虚拟语气来表达。

① 非真实条件句：表示与现在事实相反时，从句中一般用过去时，主句中用 would/should/could + 动词原形，be 动词的过去时为 were，如：

If I were free, I would go there.

② 非真实条件句：表示与过去事实相反时，从句中用过去完成时，主句中用 would/should/could + have done，如：

If it hadn't rained yesterday, we would have gone sightseeing.

③ 非真实条件句：表示与将来事实相反时，从句中用 should do or were to do 结构，主句中用 would/should/could + do，如：

If we should fail again, we wouldn't lose courage.

④ 错综复杂的虚拟语气（主句和从句分别表示两个时态），如：

If I were you, I would have gone the theatre.（从句是对现在情况的假设，主句是对过去情况的假设）

All this would have been impossible in the past.（"in the past"实际上等于"if it had been in the past"，称之为"含蓄条件句"）

⑤ 含有 if 引导的虚拟条件句，"if"常被略去，将从句中的系动词或助动词置于主语之前，构成倒装句。如：

Had you followed(= If you had followed) her advice, you would have succeeded.

（2）用句子的其他形式表示虚拟语气。如：

But for(= If it had not rained) we should have had a pleasant journey.

（3）从句中 should do 句型

① 有些形容词、动词和名词（表示要求、建议、提议、命令、意愿等）后跟有主语从句、宾语从句、同位语从句、表语从句时，从句中谓语动词要用虚拟语气，即 should + do 形式。如：

It is essential that we should overcome the financial crisis at present.

常见的形容词有：essential, appropriate, imperative, advisable, desirable, important, necessary, vital, urgent, insistent, keen, preferable, natural 等。

常见的名词有：suggestion, proposal, insistence, desire, preference, resolution, requirement, motion, demand, advice, instruction, order, request, recommendation 等。

② 由 lest, in case, for fear that 引起的从句，其谓语动词用 should + do 的形式表示虚拟语气，如：

I demand stricter control of him lest he should make mistakes again.

（4）在特殊句型中的虚拟语气

有些单词或短语后面所引出的从句有几种情况：

① 如是现在的情况，要用一般过去时；

② 如是过去的情况，要用过去完成时；

③ 在"It is(high/about) time(that)…"和"I'd rather(that)…"等特定句型中，从句要用虚拟语气的过去时（即过去虚拟语气），如：

It is time(that) you started(= you should start).

④ 用在宾语从句中：用在 wish 后的宾语从句中，如：

I wish she hadn't gone on business.（对过去情况的假设）

I wish you would come again.（对将来情况的假设）

⑤ 用在状语从句中：用在"as if"或"as though"引导的方式状语从句中，从句中的谓语

动词通常用虚拟语气,如:

It looks as though it might rain.

⑥ 用在"If only…"句中:用来表示不可能或很难实现的愿望,用动词过去式(be 用 were),相当于"I wish"引导的句子。如:

If only he weren't so naughty.

If only he would accept my advice.

⑦ 助动词 would/should/could 等 + have done 结构,单句型表示虚拟语气,如:

I should have told you the truth. (本该告诉而没有告诉)

I should not have help him. (本不该帮助却帮助了)

I needn't have done the homework. (本没有必要做却做了)

4)非限定动词

由不定式、动名词和分词构成的三种形态,又称"非谓语动词",它有三种时态:

(1)完成时:非限定性动词所表示的动作发生在谓语动词的动作之前。如:

He seems to have known something about clone.

(2)进行时:谓语动词的动作发生时,它的动词的动作也正在进行。如:

She seems to be working out a plan.

(3)一般时:一般时所表示的动作,要么和谓语动作几乎同时发生,要么在它之后发生。如:

He saw her go upstairs. (几乎同时发生)

She is determined to work harder at English next term. (work 动作发生在 is determined 动作之后)

(4)三种形式(不定式、动名词和分词),所表示的一般时含义各有不同。

① 不定式:该动作与谓语动作同时发生或是在其之后发生。如:

He planned to go back home tomorrow. (在谓语动作之后发生)

I am waiting to hear her sing. (同时发生)

② 动名词:该动作与谓语动作同时发生,有时在谓语动作之前发生。如:

I remember writing a letter to him. (在谓语动作之前发生)

He is fond of drawing the scene from memory. (和谓语同时发生)

③ 分词:常表示存在的状态或进行中的动作。如:

A group of students came out of the reading-room, talking and laughing.

④ 个别动词(如 remember, forget, go on, stop)后跟不定式和动名词作宾语时,意义有明显不同。如:

Don't forget to take a pen with you. (别忘了带钢笔。)

He forgot taking his pen with him. (忘了带钢笔。)

注:一些动词词组和短语,如 look forward to, stand up to, object to, take to, be used to, adhere(keep/hold) to, strict to, sing to, dance to, fight to, sit down to, go down to, be superior to, correspond to, be inconformity to, be proper to, refer to, trust oneself to, be faithful to, be true to, be hurtful to, be due to, be grateful to, pay attention to, reply to 等,其后面的 to 为介词,故后面跟名词或动名词。

有两种语态：主要指它与其逻辑主语之间关系。

（1）主动态：如它的逻辑主语是动作的施动者,则它就用主动态。如：

I have many things to deal with. (句子主语兼作不定式的逻辑主语)

She only takes care of the old man, ignoring the children. (ignoring 的逻辑主语是 she)

Rainfall being plentiful, crops grow rapidly. (being 逻辑主语为 rainfall)

All things weighed and considered, her paper is better than his. (weighed 和 considered 的逻辑主语是 all things)

（2）被动态：如它的逻辑主语是动作的承受者,则它就用被动态。如：

It's a great honor for me to be invited to your party.

The English novel is said to have been translated in Chinese.

Being criticized helped him see things more clearly.

We were told of the girl's having been highly praised for her hard work.

This is one of the experiments being carried on in the laboratory of our school.

The work having not been finished in time, he was criticized.

5）某些特殊结构

（1）目的状语：so that…(为了,以便), in order that…(为了,以便), so as to(为了,以便)

（2）结果状语：so…that…(以至于……), such…that…(以至于,结果……), only to…(结果……), too…to(结果,以至于), so…as to(以至于)

（3）从句和主句的主语一致时,由 while, when, once, though, if,unless 引导的从句中可以直接用分词结构。

（4）从句和主句的主语无法一致时,可使用"独立主格结构",即分词拥有自己的主语。如：

Mary coming back, they discussed it together.

With night coming on, they went home.

（5）在情态助动词后不定式结构省略"to",如：will/would, shall/should, can/could, may/might, must, need, dare 等。

（6）与某些词搭配之后,不定式结构省略"to",如：had better, had best, would sooner, would rather, would just as soon, might just as well, cannot but, cannot help but, do nothing but, rather than 等。

（7）使役动词(have, make, let, tell, command, leave, bid 等)和感官动词(hear, listen to, feel, see, look at, watch, notice, observe, perceive 等)后面不定式结构省略 to。

（8）在 help(to 可用可不用)和 know 之后,不定式结构省略 to。

III. 如何使用主从复合句

英语从句有三种：

1）名词性从句

（1）引导这几种从句的关联词(connective)是一样的。

从属连词：that，whether(or not)，if(不与 or not 连用)，只能引导宾语从句,etc.

连接代词：who，whom，what，whatever，whose，which，etc.

连接副词：how，when，where，why，therefore，thus，etc.

使用 if 和 whether 的区别

（2）陈述句作主语时,引导词 that 不能省略。全句很长时,可用 it 作形式主语,that 引导真实主语(逻辑主语)置句尾。

（3）特殊疑问词(what，who，how，when，where，why)可跟不定式 to do,用作名词性短语,在句子中作宾语、主语等。

（4）系动词后接表语,引导表语从句的词有 that，because，what，why 等。

（5）同位语从句：引导词 that 置于各词之后,常用名词有：fact，doubt，idea，news，suggestion，information，message，problem 等。

（6）特殊句型结构：A is to B what C is to D。

2）定语从句

用来修饰主句中某个成分或全句,常见置于先行词(被修饰的词)后面。它由关系代词(who，whom，whose，which，as，that，but)和关系副词(when，where，why)来引导。

（1）当先行词为 something，anything，nothing，all，much，little，somebody，nobody，anybody 等时,或者先行词前面有 no，just，only，any 等词或 first，second，third 等序数词以及形容词最高级修饰时,引导词只用 that。

（2）先行词分别为人和物的并列短语时,也只用引导词 that。

（3）非限定性定语从句由引导词 which 引导,在 which 前用逗号分开;限定性定语从句由引导词 that 或者 which 引导,前不用逗号。

（4）as 引导非限定性定语从句时,先行词为一个句子,可以置于句首。尤其是先行词前面有 same，such 或 as。

（5）主句为否定式时,but 可作准关系代词,引导定语从句,这种情况的 but 相当于 that not。

（6）why 引导的定语从句时,先行词只能是 reason 或 cause。

（7）which 或 whom 引导的定语从句可作介词宾语。

3）状语从句

副词性从句归纳为九大类(见书)

Ⅳ. 掌握特殊句型

1）倒装句型

（1）用在存在句型中,在 there 后谓语动词(be 除外)是：stand，exist，seem，lie，remain，appear 等。

（2）在虚拟语气的条件句中,were，had，should 要倒装(if 被省略时)。

（3）副词 here，there，now，then，thus 等用在句首时,且谓语动词是 come，go 或 be 时,需要倒装。

（4）表示祝愿的句子,用倒装。如：May you succeed!

（5）大多数的疑问句和表示让步状语从句，用倒装。

（6）在 neither, nor, so, as 开头的句子，要倒装。

（7）在频度副词 often, always, once, now and then, many a time, every other day 和程度副词 such, so, thus 等开头的句子中，用倒装。

（8）away, down, on, up, out 置于句首时，句子倒装。

（9）形容词置于不定代词之后，用倒装。如：Anything new?

2）强调结构用法

（1）It is(was) + 状语 + that + 句子(主语从句，宾语从句)。

（2）It is(was) + 代词(名词 + 形容词) + that(who, whom, whose, whose, which) + 句子。

（3）What…is(was) + that 句型，强调 is(was) 后面的部分。

3）否定句型用法：一般否定，特指否定，全部否定

（1）一般否定：I do not agree with you.

（2）特指否定：Not every man can do it.

（3）全部否定：None of my friends smoke.

　　　　　　　Neither of these answers is right.

　　　　　　　All people here are not kind.

4）反意疑问句的用法

（1）在有些动词(think, believe, suppose, expect, figure, fancy, assume, imagine, reckon, seem, feel)等构成的句子中，反意疑问句的形式要依据后半部分而定。如：I think you can finish the work, can't you?

（2）当句子主语用不定代词(anything, everything, nothing, something 等)替代物时，主语用 it；当句子中的主语是替代人的不定代词(everyone, nobody, anyone, no one, somebody, anybody, everybody 等)时，主语用 they。如：

Everything is all right, isn't it?

No one wants to go, do they?

（3）陈述句主语为 such 时，反意疑问句中的主语单数用 it，复数用 they。如：

Such is his trick, isn't it?

Such are your excuses, aren't they?

（4）在 I wish 句子结构中，反意疑问句用 may I 结构表示。如：

I wish to realize my dream, may I?

（5）在 I am…句子结构，如是否定句，用 am I，如是肯定式，就用 aren't I。如：

I am not a doctor, am I?

I am a teacher, aren't I?

（6）在含有情态动词的句子中，反意疑问句有不同的用法。

① 在 need, dare 用作情态动词时，各有不同形式。如：

You needn't hand in your paper, need you?

He dare do it, daren't he?

② 在含有 must, may 的句子结构中，must 后动词的类属和时态不同，反意疑问句也不

同。may 可用 mightn't or can't or will(偶尔用),如:

Judging by the smell, the food must be good, isn't it?

She must have arrived by air, hasn't she?

I may come and borrow the book tomorrow, mayn't I?

You might bring me some paper, will you? （请求）

（7）当陈述句谓语部分含有 used to 时,疑问部分常有三种形式:

a. 反意疑问句用 didn't + 主语;

b. 疑问句直接用 usedn't + 主语;

c. "存在"句子结构中如含有 used to be,反意疑问句用 used there to be 或 wasn't
(weren't) there? 如:

He used to get up early, didn't he? Or he used to get up early, usedn't he?

There used to be peach tree in the garden, wasn't there?

（8）在 let's 引导的祈使句中,反意疑问句中一般用 shall we。如:

Let's have a meeting, shall we?

注:如不是 let's,而是 let us,一般用 will you。

（9）当陈述句的助动词为 ought to 时,其形式有两种: ought you(oughtn't you)或 should
you(shouldn't you)。

（10）none 的反意疑问句: none of 结构作主语时,其谓语动词的数和人称要与前面的陈
述部分一致。如:

None of his friends is interested, is he? （不可用 are they?）

None of his friends are interested, are they? （不可用 is he?）

None of his friends has come, has he? （不可用 have they?）

（11）neither...nor 的反意疑问句,由于本身表意为否定,故反意疑问句用肯定式。如:

The book is neither in Chinese nor in English, is it?

He can neither read nor write, can he?

5）插入语的用法

（1）单词插入语:通常是副词,位于句中或句尾。如:

It is, indeed, a great pity.

He is you, he knows a lot about the world, though.

（2）短语插入语:大多数为介词短语,也可以是不定式短语或分词短语, to be // the
fruth, of cause, in addition, after all, by any chance, by no means, to begin with, roughly
speaking, to a certain extent, to be exact 等。如:

His words, to a certain extent, are right.

（3）and + 副词等用作插入语。

and + 副词、介词、句子或 what 从句用作插入语。如:

He is a good writer, (and) what is better, a great statesman.

Ⅴ. 形容词和副词的比较级用法

1）形容词：用作定语、表语

（1）用作表语：afraid, alive, alike, asleep, aware, awake, alone, ashamed, alight 等词，并不能与 very 连用。well, ill, unwell, faint, healthy 等可用作表语，或用作定语，但只有意思发生变化时，才可以用。如：ill temper, faint hope。content, glad, sorry, pleased, satisfied, joy 等（表示感觉或反应），用作表语，只有意思有变化时可用作定语。如：glad day, a sorry situation。

（2）在句子中的位置：形容词修饰名词时，一般放在被修饰名词之前；几个形容词修饰同一个名词时，修饰顺序是：限定词→官能性的→描述形状性的→描述年龄或新旧的→颜色→描述国籍→出处→描写材料→表示用途和类别。如：

A beautiful old brown French handmade kitchen cupboard；

A new giant size cardboard detergent carton；

A tall pale thin man

2）副词的用法：有两种形式，一种与形容词同形；另一种形容词加后缀-ly。两者在表意和用法上有所不同。如：

hard（猛烈地，努力地，仔细地）/hardly（几乎不）

clean（完全地，彻底地，干干净净地）/cleanly（利索地，顺利地）

late（晚，迟）/lately（最近，近来）

most（最）/mostly（主要地，大多数地）

close（靠近，接近）/closely（细心地，严密地）

dead（的确，极其，正好，完全）/deadly（死一般地，非常地）

sharp（准时，急剧地）/sharply（急剧地，突然地）

slow（怠工地，慢地）/slowly（怠工地，慢地）

right（好地，立即地，直接地，恰好地，完全地）/rightly（正确地）

firm（稳稳地，坚定地）/firmly（坚定地，牢固地）

fair（公正地，公平地，恰好地）/fairly（不感情用事地，相当地，非常地）

easy（慢慢地，别急，轻松地）/easily（不费力地，容易地，无疑地）

wide（宽广地，张得开地，完全地）/widely（广泛地，很大地，到处地）

sure（当然地，的确地）/surely（当然地，一定地）

loud（声音大地）/loudly（大声地，花哨地）

deep（深深地，至深地，在深处地）/deeply（非常地，深深地）

near（接近，靠近地）/nearly（几乎地，差不多地）

round（转过来地）/roundly（狠狠地）

free（无约束地，松开地，免费地）/freely（直率地，大量地）

large（很大地，顺风地，夸大地）/largely（主要地，基本上地，大量地）

clear（一直地，完全地，避开地）/clearly（清楚地，清晰地，显然地）

short（简短地，不久地）/shortly（简短地，不久地）

cheap(便宜地,卑鄙地)/cheaply(便宜地,轻易地,容易地)

first(先,初次,宁可地)/firstly(第一,首先)

rough(粗暴地,简陋地)/roughly(粗暴地,大致地,大约地)

new(新,新近)/newly(新近地,最近地,重新,再一次)

last(最后地,上一次,最后一次)/lastly(最后一点,最后)

just(只是,仅仅,勉强地,刚刚,差一点就不,正好)/justly(公正地/应得地)

direct(径直地)/directly(直截了当地,正好地,马上,立刻)

fine(很好地,细小地)/finely(雅致地,极好地,仔细地)

much/very：much 或 very much 用来修饰动词,单独的 very 只可修饰形容词。在否定句中,一般只用 much,不用 very much。very 修饰现在分词(-ing),而 much 修饰过去分词(-ed),同时修饰形容词的比较级。

fairly/rather：fairly 修饰表示积极意义的形容词。rather 多用来修饰含有消极意义的形容词表示"相当"意思时,也可修饰表示积极意义的形容词,并且可与 too 连用,定冠词置于其前后皆可;fairly 不可与 too 连用,定冠词只能放在它之前。

3) 英语比较级结构：同级,比较级,最高级

(1) 同级比较：一般使用 as...as 结构

注意下列用法：

a. as the same as：在 same 前加冠词 the。

b. just, nearly, almost, quite,... + as...

c. as + many + noun + as/as + much + 不可数名词 + as/as + objective + a/an + 单数可数名词 + as

d. 表示倍数词(half, twice, times...) + as...as

e. 在 as...as 之间通常为表示数量、程度、性质的词,如 many, much, little, few, good, tall, short...

(2) 在比较结构中,含有 than 的比较用法：常用 more...than/more than 结构。注意下列情况用法：

a. 在 more...than/more than 前面可以加表示程度的副词 still, far, much, a lot, a bit... 修饰。

b. 同类事物比较时,用 other 把其排除在其他同类事物之外。

c. 一些含义特殊的形容词,如 empty, wrong, false, daily, unique, monthly, right, perfect 等,一般不用 more...than 比较结构。

d. 一些形容词本身与 to 使用,不用 than 表示比较。如：superior, prior, posterior, junior, senior...

e. 表示其他含义：no more than(仅仅,和……一样都不)/not more than(至多,不超过,不比……更……), the more...the more 这是常用的比较结构,意思是"越……越……"。

Ⅵ. 使句子的完整性和一致性的重要性

英语句子的完整性、一致性和连贯性对于英语表意来说,是十分重要的,要善于分析句

子的结构,找出它的主干部分,这是掌握好句子的前提。

1)句子的完整性

（1）判断句子中是否缺少主要成分——主、谓语;

（2）分析句子中是否有遗漏的成分或多余的成分,语言是否正确。

（3）分析句中的主、谓语是否齐全、恰当,可以结合实例进行分析、掌握。

2)句子的一致性:主要指的是句子中主、谓的一致性。

（1）主语与谓语动词要一致;

（2）连词 or, either...or, nor, neither...nor, not only...but also, and 等,连接两个名词或代词时,主语与谓语保持一致性;

（3）有些词或词组如 each, every, neither, either, a great deal of, many a, a series of, a set of, little, much 等,置于名词前,动词用单数形式;

（4）and 连接二个主语指同一事物时,谓语动词用单数形式;

（5）在句子的主、谓间有 as well as, with..., together with..., along with..., besides..., rather than..., in addition to, including..., plus..., however..., without..., accompanied by..., except..., except for...等时,只考虑主、谓保持一致性;

（6）定语从句的谓语动词应与先行词一致;

（7）在英语句子中,有些表示时间、重量、距离、数量、面积、价格、度量衡等的复数名词或短语作为一个整体看待时,谓语动词一般用单数形式。如:

Fifty years is not a long time.

Four thousand dollars is more than she can afford.（她付不起400美元）

Ten apples is enough.

An estimated two hundred persons was killed in the battle.

VII. 词汇的理解和运用

词汇是测试的重点之一,占总题量的三分之二左右。要求考生熟练地掌握词性、词义和搭配用法。根据每年考试的统计,大约3%左右的词汇是超纲词汇,这些超纲词汇是命题人要测试考生根据上下文来判断词义的能力,或根据词缀来判断词义的能力。

在复习过程中,除了要熟练掌握"大纲"中所规定的词汇外,还要掌握词汇搭配的词组或短语。

"名词 + 介词"搭配的短语

attend to(专心,致力,花时间)	attempt at(试图……)
attendance at(出席,参加)	attitude to/toward(对……的态度)
attraction to(对……的吸引)	attribute to(认为……归属于,把……归因于)
authority on(……的权威)	bargain with(与……讨价、还价)
candidate for(……的能力)	capacity for(……的能力)
care for(对……关心)	caution against(对……的防备)
collision with(与……冲突、碰撞)	compensation for(给……补偿)
comment on(对……的评论)	comparison with(与……比较)

key to(……答案)

leisure for(有空做某事)

likeness to(between)(相似,相像)

longing for(渴望,希望)

major in(专修……)

monopoly of/on(绝对控制,占有)

obedience to(对……的服从)

observation on(对……观察,评论)

opposition to(对……反对,反抗)

passport to(获得……保障)

pity for(对……表示同情)

precaution against(预防……的措施)

preparation for(为……作准备)

proficiency in(对……的精通)

reason for(为……理由)

reflection on(对……反思和回忆)

remarks of(对……评说)

replacement for(取代……)

reprimand for(对……谴责)

resistance to(对……抵抗)

responsibility for(对……负有责任)

search for(对……搜查)

success in(at)(在……方面成功)

sympathy for/with(对……同情)

trust in(对……责任)

want of(对……的缺乏)

wonder at(对……的惊讶)

lecture on(关于……的演讲,讲课)

liability to(易于……,趋向于……)

limit to(对……限制)

loyalty to(对……忠诚)

monument to(……的纪念碑)

mortgage on(用……抵押)

objection to(反对……)

operation on(做……手术)

passion for(对……的爱好)

perception of(对……理解,认识)

preface to(……前言)

preference for(对……偏爱)

pride in(为……自豪,骄傲)

prohibition of(对……禁止)

reference to(对……提及)

reliance on(对……依靠)

remnants of(遗存,遗迹,遗孤)

requirement for(对……要求)

research into/on(对……研究)

respect for(对……尊重)

reward for(对……回报)

sorrow for(对……遗憾)

suspicion of(对……怀疑)

traitor to(……的叛徒)

vicinity to(……的近邻)

witness to/of(……的见证人)

zeal for(对……热心)

"介词 + 名词"的短语

in accord with(与……一致,与……符合)

in the act of(在做……的过程中)

to advantage(有利地,有优点突出地)

in the aggregate(总共作为整体)

on the air(广播)

in answer to(作为对……回答)

for anything(无论如何)

on approval(供试用的,包退包换的)

in brief(简言之)

behind bars(在狱中)

in accordance with(依照,根据)

in addition(另外,加之)

in advance(在前面,优先,事先)

in the air(流传中,在传播中)

by analogy(用类推的方法)

in all(总共,共计)

to all appearance(就外表看来)

behind one's back(背着某人,暗中)

in the balance(在危急状态中)

beyond belief(难以置信)

beside oneself(极度兴奋)

for the better(好转,向好的方向发展)

in(full) blossom(正开着花)

above board(正大光明地)

by the book(按规则,依照惯例)

in business(经商,经营)

on the button(准确地,准时地)

in any case(无论如何,总之)

by chance(偶然,碰巧)

in character(与自身特点相符)

in chorus(一齐,一致,一起)

in common(共用的,共有的)

in comparison with(与……比较起来)

in confidence(私下地,秘密地)

in confidence(与……共同,连同)

by common consent(经一致同意)

in consequence of(由于,因……缘故)

in charge(负责,主管)

on the contrary(正相反)

by/in contrast(对比之下)

in control of(掌握着,控制着)

to the core(透顶地,十足地)

at all costs(不惜任何代价,无论如何)

in the course of(在……期间,在……过程中)

by courtesy of(承蒙……的好意)

to one's credit(在……名下,……值得赞扬)

in danger(在危险中)

in one's debt(欠某人债)

to a/the day(恰好,一天不差)

in default of(因缺少,在缺乏……时)

to some degree(有点,稍微)

on demand(一经要求)

in detail(详细地)

in disgrace(很不讨人喜欢)

at sb's disposal(凭某人处理)

in the distance(在远处)

in doubt(不能肯定地)

at best(充其量,至多)

in cold blood(残忍地)

across the board(包括一切地,全面地)

on board(在船/飞机上)

in bulk(大量地,大批地)

on business(因公,因事)

in case(万一,假如)

in no case(绝对)

by any chance(万一,也许)

under no circumstances(绝不)

in/under the circumstances(在这种情况下,既然如此)

by/in comparison(相比之下)

in concert(一齐,一致)

in connection with(关于,与……有关)

in conscience(公平地,凭良心)

in consequence(因此,结果)

in consideration of(考虑到,由于)

in conclusion(总之)

to the contrary(正相反)

in contrast to/with(与……对比起来,与……形成对比)

under control(在控制之下)

around/round the corner(临近)

at the cost of(以……为代价)

in due course(到时候)

under cover(秘密地,暗地里)

on cue(恰好在这时候)

in debt(负债)

to date(迄今为止)

to death(极,非常)

by degrees(逐渐地)

in demand(非常需要地,受欢迎地)

in depth(深入地,彻底地)

on a diet(节食)

in disguise(伪装,假装)

in dispute(在争论中,处于争议中)

beyond a doubt(无疑地,确实地)

in difficulties(在困难中)

in due course(到时候,到适当时候)

in effect(有效地,实际上地)

in earnest(认真地,坚定地)

at ease(安逸,不拘束地)

in embryo(在萌芽中)

of the essence(极其重要地,必不可少地)

in any event(不管怎样,无论如何)

in excess of(超过)

in exchange(交换)

to a certain extent(在一定程度上)

in the face of(在……面前,尽管,不顾)

in fact(其实,实际上)

in good faith(真诚地,善意地)

in favor of(支持,赞同)

on fire(着火)

on guard(警惕,防范)

on occasion(有时,不时)

in the flesh(本人)

in front of(在……前面,在……面前)

for/in fun(取乐地,娱乐地)

in future(今后,从今以后)

on the sly(偷偷地)

on one's own(独立地)

on purpose(故意地,有意地)

on the go(很忙)

in the habit of(有……的习惯)

in harmony with(与……一致,与……和睦相处)

at heart(内心里,本质上)

on schedule(按预定时间地)

on the spot(当场,在现场)

on time(准时)

in honor of(为了向……表示敬意)

on the house(由店家出钱,免费)

on the increase(正在增加,不断增加)

on the whole(总的来说,大体上)

out of breath(上气不接下气)

out of danger(脱离危险)

out of doors(户外)

in duplicate(一式两份)

in the end(最后,终于)

on earth(究竟,到底)

at a low ebb(处于低潮地,衰退)

in essence(本质上,实质上,基本上)

at all events(不管怎样,无论如何)

in the event(结果,到头来)

to excess(过度,过分,过量)

at the expense of(由……付费,以……为代价)

in the extreme(非常,极其)

as a matter of fact(实际上)

without fail(决定,一定)

at fault(有责任,出毛病)

on duty(值班,上班)

on foot(步行)

on hand(在手边)

on file(存档)

in force(有效地,生效地)

in full(全部地,不省略地)

in the future(在将来)

on one's honor(以……名誉担保)

on second thoughts(经重新考虑)

on sale(出售)

on a large scale(大规模地)

with good grace(欣然地)

in half(一半)

in haste(慌忙,匆忙)

by heart(凭记性)

on the side(作为兼职,额外)

on the stage(在舞台上,当演员)

over the hill(走下坡路)

on the hour(在整点时刻)

on impulse(一时冲动)

on the way(在途中,在路上)

out of balance(失去平衡)

out of control(失控)

out of date(过期)

out of fashion(过时)

out of order(发生故障)

out of sight(看不见)

out of step(步调不一致,不协调)

out of work(失业)

out of place(不适当地)

out of practice(久而不练,荒疏)

out of touch(失去联系)

"be+形容词+介词"的固定搭配词组

be anxious about(为……忧虑)

be concerned about(对……关心)

be excited about(对……感到激动)

be particular about(对……研究,挑剔)

be worried about(对……担心)

be angry at(对……愤怒)

be apt at(善于……)

be bad at(不善于……)

be quick at(对……很敏感)

be slow at(对……反应迟钝)

be acquisitive for(渴望)

be appropriate for(对……合适)

be convenient for(对……方便)

be famous for(以……闻名)

be good for(对……有益)

be liable for(对……负有责任)

be proper for(适合于……)

be responsible for(对……负责)

be vital for(对……极为重要)

be absent from(缺席)

be diverse from(不同于……)

be exempt from(免除……)

be isolated from(没有……危险)

be absorbed in(专心于……)

be concerned in(与……有牵连)

be disappointed in(对……失望)

be interested in(对……有兴趣)

be rich in(富有,富于)

be skillful in(精于……)

be ashamed of(因……而惭愧)

be capable of(能够……)

be characteristic of(表示……特征)

be confident of(确信……)

be certain about(对……有把握)

be enthusiastic about(热衷于)

be nervous about(因……不安)

be suspicious about(对……怀疑)

be amazed at(为……感到吃惊)

be annoyed at(为……烦恼)

be astonished at(对……惊愕)

be good/great at(善于……)

be ready at(易于……)

be accountable for(对……有义务说明)

be adequate for(适合于……)

be competent for(对……胜任)

be eager for(渴求……)

be fit for(合适于……)

be indispensable for(对……绝对必要)

be profitable for(对……有益)

be requisite for(对……必要的)

be thirsty for(渴望……)

be wild for(渴望……)

be distant from(远离……)

be divorced from(脱离……)

be free from(无……)

be separate from(与……分离)

be abundant in(富于……)

be deficient in(不足……)

be explicit in(对……直言不讳)

be lost in(沉湎于……)

be rigid in(在……严格)

be versed in(精通于……)

be aware of(知道……)

be careful of(留心,注意……)

be composed of(由……组成)

be certain of(对……有把握)

be considerate of(体贴……)

be conscious of(意识到……)

be decisive of(决定……)

be afraid of(害怕,担心……)

be doubtful of/about(对……有怀疑)

be fond of(喜好,喜欢)

be guilty of(有……罪的)

be incapable of(不能……的)

be independent of(独立于……之外的)

be indicative of(有……象征的)

be innocent of(没有……的)

be jealous of(妒忌……)

be representative of(可代表……的)

be proud of(以……自豪)

be worthy of(值得……)

be envious of(嫉妒……)

be ignorant of(对……无知)

be exclusive of(除……以外)

be keen on(喜欢,渴望)

be intent on(专心于……)

be severe on(对……严厉)

be contingent on(视……而定)

be founded on(以……为根据)

be soft on(亲切对待……)

be acceptable to(为……接受/通用)

be accessible to(可接近,为……理解)

be accustomed to(习惯于……)

be adaptable to(适应于……)

be additional to(附加于……)

be apparent to(明显,明了……)

be applicable to(适用于……)

be beneficial to(有益于……)

be alike to(与……相似)

be allergic to(对……过敏)

be equal to(等于,胜利)

be equivalent to(等于,相当于)

be grateful to(感谢……)

be harmful to(对……有害)

be helpful to(对……有益,有帮助)

be hostile to(对……有敌意)

be inaccessible to(达不到……)

be inadequate to(不充足……)

be indispensable to(为……所需要的)

be loyal to(忠于……)

be paralleled to(和……平行)

be preferable to(比……更好的)

be proportional to(与……成比例)

be relative to(和……有关)

be relevant to(和……有关)

be sensitive to(对……敏感)

be apt to(易于……)

be attractive to(对……有吸引力)

be blind to(忽略)

be approximate to(近似于……)

be devoted to(献身于……)

be loyal to(忠诚于……)

be confined to(限于……)

be obedient to(服从于……)

be prior to(在……之前)

be similar to(类似于……)

be superior to(胜于……,优于……)

be subject to(易受……)

be concerned with(关心,挂念,从事于)

be consistent with(与……一致)

be familiar with/to(熟悉……)

be identical with(与……相同)

be incompatible with(与……不相容的)

be angry with(对……人生气)

be burdened with(担负……)

be confronted with(面临……)

be faced with(面对……)

be satisfied with(对……满意)

be strict with(对……严格)

第三单元
完型填空题型指导

该部分是把考查学生综合运用语言能力作为重点。

I. 考查要点

1）要综观全文，读懂大意。

通过读懂全文，就可以了解文章的大意，或者至少了解文章主要讲些什么。这样，短文的主线就会沿着你的解题思路，使解题过程沿着正确的方向继续下去。

2）边读短文，边进行思考，初选试填。

一开始就要逐句仔细地阅读短文，根据文章内容和上下文连贯以及各方面的知识，利用语法、逻辑、词汇线索等来确定正确答案。

3）阅读短文时，前后照应，寻觅启示。

在试题中，假如某一个空白处的四个选项是同义词或存在着某些相似的部分，势必要仔细地思考，辨别其词义，并依照上下文的意思和所提供的线索，进一步去探询空白处前后的语义呼应关系，搭配关系，然后再确定最佳答案。

4）选项全部确定之后，再综观全文，核对答案。

填完所有答案之后，再仔细地认真地回读短文，核查一下答案在内容、表义、语言结构、前后搭配和连贯关系以及逻辑关系等方面是否与文章相吻合，是否合情合理，从而提高答案的正确度。

II. 范例及解析

Section I Use of English

Examples

Example ❶

Directions：

Read the following text. Choose the best word(s) for each numbered blank and mark A, B, C or D on the ANSWER SHEET 1. (10 points)

Can you change your name just because you feel like it? The answer appears to be "yes" in

Virginia and "no" in New York.

The Virginia __1__ involved two women who wanted to take their maiden names __2__, even though they were still married. The lower court in Virginia __3__ their request for change of name on the __4__ that Virginia law, like that of many states, allowed a married woman to __5__ her maiden name only after she was divorced. But the Virginia Supreme Court __6__ the lower court, saying that there was __7__ in the law that indicated that a name could only be changed after __8__. The court then pointed out that __9__ the ·10 law, a person is free to adopt any name __11__ it's not for a fraudulent purpose or to cheat creditors.

__12__, if you live in New York, you may well have a more difficult time changing your name. A woman named Cooperman went to __3__ to have her name changed to Cooperperson. She explained that she believed in the feminist __14__ and felt that the name Cooperperson could more properly __15__ her sense of human equality than could the name Cooperman. __16__ New York Supreme Court Justice John Scileppi did not agree with her reasoning and refused to __17__ the change-of-name request. He wrote that "the possibilities are __18__ endless and increasingly inane, and this would truly be __19__ the realm of nonsense." So Miss Cooperman will remain Miss Cooperman, __20__ she gets married or moves to Virginia.

1. A) law   B) rule   C) case   D) matter
2. A) away   B) back   C) out   D) off
3. A) denied   B) refused   C) declined   D) rejected
4. A) senses   B) meanings   C) reasons   D) grounds
5. A) rename   B) resume   C) change   D) assume
6. A) countered   B) objected   C) reversed   D) disapproved
7. A) nothing   B) anything   C) everything   D) something
8. A) marriage   B) separation   C) appeal   D) divorce
9. A) for   B) on   C) under   D) inside
10. A) common   B) general   C) ordinary   D) usual
11. A) now that   B) so long as   C) in case   D) for example
12. A) Hence   B) Though   C) Therefore   D) However
13. A) home   B) office   C) court   D) register
14. A) career   B) movement   C) affair   D) cause
15. A) reflect   B) react   C) expose   D) modify
16. A) Then   B) Yet   C) Furthermore   D) And
17. A) admit   B) accept   C) grant   D) approve
18. A) genuinely   B) deceptively   C) perfectly   D) actually
19. A) in   B) at   C) as   D) like
20. A) as   B) unless   C) when   D) after

答案与解析
1. 答案：C

解析：上下文推理题。law 表示"法律、法规"，即由惯例、约定或权力机构制定的行为规范或程序；rule 表示"规则、规定"，指权威性的成文的行为规范，尤指规范立法机构程序的规则和游戏、运动或比赛当中参加者必须遵守的规则；case 表示"案例、诉讼案"；而 matter 则表示"事件、问题"。根据上下文，本处是指弗吉尼亚州的一个案件。因此，正确答案应该是选项 C) case。

2. 答案：B

　　解析：词义辨析题。take away 表示"拿走"，take back 表示"收回"，take out 表示"带某人去某地"，而 take off 则表示"脱掉(衣服等)、起飞"。根据上下文，本处是指恢复婚前的名字。因此，应该选择选项 B) back。

3. 答案：A

　　解析：近义词辨析题。这四个动词都表示"拒绝"的意思，但是，它们之间略有区别。deny 表示"否认、拒绝"，指拒不给某人所求或所需之物、阻止某人获得所求或所需之物；refuse 表示"拒绝"，表示不愿意做、接受、给予或允许，通常暗示决心，且常带有"粗鲁"的意思；decline 表示"拒绝、谢绝"，指有礼貌地拒绝或婉言谢绝；而 reject 则表示"拒绝、抵制"，通常因为不令人满意、有缺陷或无用而抛弃，它暗示无条件的拒绝，语气最为强烈。根据句意，本处是指，法院拒绝了她们更改名字的请求。refuse、decline 和 reject 在语气和意思表达上都不符合句意。因此，正确答案应该是选项 A) denied。

4. 答案：D

　　解析：词义辨析题。sense 表示"感觉、判断力"；meaning 表示"意义、含义"；reason 表示"理由、原因"，常用于 reason for...结构中；而 ground 则表示"地面、场所"，其复数形式 grounds 表示"理由"，常用于结构 on the grounds that...(出于……原因)中。按照句意，这里应该选择"原因"一词。而根据结构，正确答案应该是选项 D) grounds。

5. 答案：B

　　解析：词义辨析题。rename 表示"重新取名、改名"；resume 表示"重新开始、恢复"；change 表示"改变、变化"；而 assume 则表示"假定、设想"。根据句意，本处是指恢复婚前的名字。因此，正确答案应该是选项 B) resume。

6. 答案：C

　　解析：近义词辨析题。counter 表示"反对、驳回"；object 表示"反对、拒绝"，与介词 to 连用，构成词组 object to；reverse 表示"撤消、取消"，指撤消或取消一个判决或法令；而 disapprove 则表示"不赞成"，与 of 介词连用，构成词组 disapprove of。本句是指，弗吉尼亚最高法院推翻了下级法院的判决。因此，正确答案应该是选项 C) reversed。

7. 答案：A

　　解析：上下文推理题。本句说的是，弗吉尼亚最高法院推翻了下级法院的判决，指出，法律中并没有规定人的名字只能在离婚的情况下才能更改。因此，正确答案应该是选项 A) nothing。

8. 答案：D

解析：上下文推理题。marriage 表示"结婚"；separation 表示"分居"；appeal 表示"请求、上诉"；而 divorce 则表示"离婚"。上文中说，弗吉尼亚的法律不允许已婚妇女更改名字。本句提到了一个例外情况，只有在这一情况下，已婚妇女才可以更改名字。我们知道，西方妇女的名字是随婚姻状况变化而变化的。那么，可以推想，如果一个妇女不想用丈夫的姓作为自己名字的一部分，只有在他们婚姻解体的情况下才有可能。因此，最符合题意的选择应该是选项D）divorce。

9. 答案：C

解析：词义辨析题。for 表示"为了……、因为……"；on 表示"在……之上、关于……"；under 表示"在……之下、考虑到……"；而 inside 则表示"在……里面"。此处是指按照法律的规定。因此，最符合题意的选择应该是选项C）under。

10. 答案：A

解析：结构搭配题。本题四个单词意思非常接近。common 表示"普通的"；general 表示"普遍的、一般的"；ordinary 表示"普通的、平凡的、不特别的"；而 usual 则表示"经常的"。但是，普通法 common law 是一个固定搭配。因此，正确答案应该是选项A）common。

11. 答案：B

解析：逻辑推理题。now that 表示"既然……"，引导原因状语从句；so long as 表示"只要……"，引导让步状语从句；in case 表示"以防……、如果……"，引导条件状语从句；而 for example 则表示"例如……"，用于举例。根据句意，"只要不是以欺骗为目的，人们可以用任何名字。"此处是一个让步状语从句。因此，正确答案应该是选项 B）so long as。

12. 答案：D

解析：逻辑推理题。上文中提到，住在弗吉尼亚的人可以更改名字，而本句说的是，住在纽约的人不能随意更改名字。很明显，此处是一个转折关系。hence 和 therefore 表示结果"因此"，不符合题意。though 和 however 表示转折"然而"，但是，though 不能放在句首。因此，正确答案应该是选项 D）However。

13. 答案：C

解析：上下文推理题。home 表示"家、住宅"；office 表示"办公室"；court 表示"法院、法庭"；而 register 则表示"登记、记录"。按照上下文的含义，一个人想要更改名字，得去法院申请。因此，正确答案应该是选项 C）court。

14. 答案：D

解析：词义辨析题。career 表示"事业、生涯"，指某人从事的职业；movement 表示"运动、活动"，指一定时期内为达到某种原则或政策而进行的一系列活动及事件；affair 表示"事务、事件"，指发生的事情；而 cause 则表示"目标、理想、事业"，强调极力维护或支持的目标、原则或运动。此处表示"女权运动"，是妇女为争取平等权利而进行的运动、从事的事业。因此，正确答案应该是选项 D）cause。

15. 答案：A

解析：词义辨析题。reflect 表示"反映、表明"；react 表示"起反应、起作用"；expose 表示"暴露、揭露"；而 modify 则表示"更改、修改"。本句的意思是，Cooperperson 这个名字更能反映出人权平等这一概念。因此,正确答案应该是选项 A)reflect。

16. 答案:B

解析:逻辑推理题。上文中提到,一个名叫 Cooperman 的妇女想把名字改成 Cooperperson。本句说,纽约最高法院法官 John Scileppi 不同意她的请求。这是很明显的转折关系。因此,正确答案应该是选项 B)Yet。

17. 答案:C

解析:近义词辨析题。admit 表示"容许、承认、接纳";accept 表示"接受、同意";grant 表示"同意、准予",含有"权威"的概念;而 approve 则表示"赞成、核准"。这里提到了纽约最高法院法官,他是权威。因此,选项 C)grant 最符合题意。

18. 答案:D

解析:词义辨析题。genuinely 表示"真诚地、诚实地";deceptively 表示"迷惑地、虚伪地";perfectly 表示"完全地、完美地";而 actually 则表示"实际上、事实上"。此处是指,实际上有很多可能性。因此,正确答案应该是选项 D)actually。

19. 答案:A

解析:结构搭配题。in the realm of 为固定的词组搭配,意思为"在……领域、在……范围"。因此,正确答案应该是选项 A)in。

20. 答案:B

解析:逻辑推理题。本句是让步状语从句,意思是除非她结婚或是移居弗吉尼亚州,否则,Cooperman 小姐只能叫 Cooperman 小姐。因此,正确答案应该是选项 B)unless。

Example ❷

Directions:

Read the following text. Choose the best word(s) for each numbered blank and mark A, B, C or D on the ANSWER SHEET 1. (10 points)

What makes the mind of man so superior to the brain of even the most intelligent animals? It is a secret that psychology knows nothing __1__, and religion has never properly explained.

Human brains and animal brains look very much __2__. They have the same general shape, structure and composition. As to size, the brain of a chimpanzee, one of the most intelligent animals, is smaller than __3__, but the brains of elephants and dolphins are actually __4__ than human being's. Size and shape __5__ cannot __6__ the vast difference. Then what does? Animals can __7__ with each other; many of them have highly __8__ senses of sight, touch and hearing. __9__, they don't use letters, words, sentences, grammar and syntax. They don't add and __10__, multiply and divide. They certainly can't __11__ algebra, geometry, trigonometry and calculus. Animal minds don't __12__ in abstractions and theories. But clearly our minds do. The theory of evolution has never __13__ explained the difference it sees man as just another __14__. There are other critical differences as well. The animal mind works __15__ the principle of instinct. Beavers don't go to engineering school to learn to build dams. They know how to do it __16__.

But human beings are vastly different. Their behavior is much more __17__ by free choice than by instinct. Their __18__ of possibilities is much greater. They learn, and grow, and experiment, and create. They even __19__ machines to do some of their __20__ for them.

1. A) of   B) about   C) on   D) over
2. A) like   B) likewise   C) alike   D) likely
3. A) man's   B) men's   C) the man's   D) the men's
4. A) smaller   B) larger   C) cleverer   D) more
5. A) alone   B) singly   C) separately   D) individually
6. A) work out   B) count in   C) account for   D) make of
7. A) touch   B) understand   C) contact   D) communicate
8. A) developed   B) trained   C) exercised   D) fostered
9. A) So   B) And   C) However   D) Furthermore
10. A) reduce   B) calculate   C) subtract   D) eliminate
11. A) appreciate   B) acquire   C) grasp   D) comprehend
12. A) deal   B) work   C) take   D) operate
13. A) implicitly   B) skillfully   C) adequately   D) absolutely
14. A) being   B) animal   C) creature   D) thing
15. A) in   B) from   C) on   D) by
16. A) instinctively   B) naturally   C) inwardly   D) tactically
17. A) steered   B) subdued   C) ruled   D) governed
18. A) limit   B) span   C) range   D) extent
19. A) renovate   B) invent   C) refund   D) invest
20. A) thinking   B) thought   C) intention   D) purpose

答案与解析

1. 答案：B

   解析：结构搭配题。在这四个选项中,只有选项 A 和选项 B 是固定的词组搭配:know of 表示"听说过、知道有(某人、某事)",而 know about 表示"了解有关……的情况"。本句的意思是,这一奥秘是心理学所不了解的。因此,正确答案应该是选项 B) about。

2. 答案：C

   解析：词义辨析题。like 通常用作动词,表示"喜欢",用作介词时,表示"像、如同"; likewise 是副词,表示"同样地、也";alike 是形容词,表示"相同的、相似的",不能用作定语修饰名词,但可以用作副词,表示"以同样的方式";而形容词 likely 则表示"可能的"。本句的意思是,人的大脑和动物的大脑很相似。因此,正确答案应该是选项 C) alike。

3. 答案：A

   解析：词义辨析题。man's 表示"人类的";men's 表示"人的、男人的";the man's 表示"这个人的";而 the men's 则表示"这些人的、这些男人的"。本句说的是,人类的大脑。

因此,正确答案应该是选项 A) man's。

4. 答案:B

解析:上下文推理题。此处谈论的是大脑的容量,选项 C) cleverer 和选项 D) more 不符合题意。上文提到黑猩猩的大脑比人类的大脑小,本句用了一个转折连词 but,将大象和海豹的大脑与人类的大脑进行比较。but 表示的意思是,后一种情况与前一种情况不同。既然黑猩猩的大脑比人类的大脑小,那么,大象和海豹的大脑比人类的大脑大。因此,正确答案应该是选项 B) larger。

5. 答案:A

解析:近义词辨析题。alone 用于名词或代词之后,表示"只有、仅仅";singly 表示"各自地、一个一个地";separately 表示"个别地、分离地";而 individually 则表示"分别地、独特地"。本句的意思是,只有容量和外形说明不了问题。因此,正确答案应该是选项 A) alone。

6. 答案:C

解析:词义辨析题。work out 表示"找到解答、解决";count in 表示"包括";account for 表示"解释、说明";而 make of 则表示"了解、理解"。本句的意思是,只有容量和外形说明不了其中的巨大差异。因此,正确答案应该是选项C) account for。

7. 答案:D

解析:词义辨析题。touch 表示"用手或手指接触、触摸";understand 表示"理解、懂得";contact 表示"通过捎信或打电话与某人联络、和某人建立联系";而 communicate 则表示"沟通,交流意见、感情、消息等"。选项 A 和 B 与题意不符,应该排除。动物不会通过捎信或打电话相互联络、建立联系,只会沟通和交流意见、感情、消息。因此,正确答案应该是选项 D) communicate。

8. 答案:A

解析:词义辨析题。developed 表示"发达的、发展的";trained 表示"训练的、锻炼的";exercised 表示"练习的、锻炼的";而 fostered 则表示"养育的、抚养的"。此处的意思是高度发达的。因此,正确答案应该是选项 A) developed。

9. 答案:C

解析:逻辑推理题。so 表示"因此";and 表示"以及";however 表示"然而";而 furthermore 则表示"此外"。上文说,动物可以相互交流,它们中还有许多拥有高度发达的视觉、触觉和听觉能力。而本句说,动物不能运用文字、不会语法。根据上下文推断,此处是转折关系。在这四个选项中,正确答案很明显,应该是选项 C) However。

10. 答案:C

解析:词义辨析题。reduce 表示"减少";calculate 表示"计算";subtract 表示"减去";而 eliminate 则表示"消除"。此处表示的是,加减乘除中的减法。因此,选项 A、B 和 D 都不符合题意,正确答案应该是选项 C) subtract。

11. 答案:D

解析:词义辨析题。appreciate 表示"欣赏、感激";acquire 表示"获得、学到";grasp 表示"抓住、掌握";而 comprehend 则表示"理解、领会"。选项 A 不符合题意,而选项 B 和 C 均指人通过学习获得或掌握知识,也不符合题意。这里说的是,动物是无法理解抽象科学的。因此,正确答案应该是选项 D) comprehend。

12. 答案:A

   解析:词义辨析题。deal in 表示"处理";work in 表示"插入";take in 表示"接纳、吸收";而 operate 不和 in 搭配,与 on 搭配,operate on 表示"动手术"。本句的意思是,动物的大脑不对抽象概念和理论进行处理。因此,正确答案应该是选项 A) deal。

13. 答案:C

   解析:词义辨析题。implicitly 表示"含蓄地、暗中地";skillfully 表示"巧妙地、技术好地";adequately 表示"充分地、足够地";而 absolutely 则表示"完全地、绝对地"。选项 A、B 和 D 均不符合题意。因此,正确答案应该是选项 C) adequately。

14. 答案:B

   解析:上下文推理题。being 表示"生物",尤指人,通常前面加定语修饰;animal 表示"动物";creature 表示"生物",尤指动物,也指人;而 thing 则表示"东西、物品"。句中的 another 一词提示所填单词在上文中出现过,并且此处是将人和动物进行比较。本句的意思是,在进化论中,人是另一种动物。因此,正确答案应该是选项 B) animal。

15. 答案:D

   解析:词义辨析题。in 表示"在……里面";from 表示"从……、来自……";on 表示"在……上面";而 by 则表示"通过……、按照……"。另外,in principle 和 on principle 是固定搭配,in principle 表示"基本上";on principle 表示"按原则地"。此处表示的意思是,根据……的原则。选项 A、B 和 C 均不符合题意。因此,正确答案应该是选项 D) by。

16. 答案:A

   解析:上下文推理题。instinctively 表示"本能地";naturally 表示"自然地";inwardly 表示"在内部地";而 tactically 则表示"战略上地"。上文中提到,动物的行为是出于本能。本句的意思是,它们本能地知道如何去做。因此,正确答案应该是选项 A) instinctively。

17. 答案:D

   解析:近义词辨析题。steer 表示"驾驶、掌舵";subdue 表示"征服、制服";rule 表示"依照规则、法则统治、治理";而 govern 则表示"统治、支配、决定、起决定影响"。本句的意思是,人类的行为是随意的,并不受本能的支配。选项 A 和 B 不符合题意,予以排除。而选项 C 强调受某种规则或法则的影响,也不符合题意。因此,正确答案应该是选项 D) governed。

18. 答案:C

   解析:近义词辨析题。limit 表示"界限、限度",主要指在数量、程度或时间上确定最大值,人或事物不可能或不可以超越它;span 表示"跨度、跨距",指两点或两端间的空间或距离;range 表示"范围",range of possibilities 是常用表达,指可能性的大小;而 extent 则表示"范围、程度",主要指事物延展的范围、高度或距离、某事物伸展的程度。因此,正确答案应该是选项 C) range。

19. 答案：B

　　解析：词义辨析题。renovate 表示"革新、修复"；invent 表示"发明、创造"；refund 表示"退还、偿还"；而 invest 则表示"投资"。选项 A、C 和 D 均不符合题意，只能是，发明机器。因此，正确答案应该是选项 B）invent。

20. 答案：A

　　解析：词义辨析题。thinking 表示"思想"，强调思考的人的行为或行动；thought 表示"想法、思想"，指思考的产物、具体的想法，特别是指经过思考和推理后得出的结论；intention 表示"意图、目的"，指某人想要追随的行动方向；而 purpose 则表示"意图，目标"，强调决心或决定的想法。此处是指抽象的思想、思考的行为。因此，正确答案应该是选项 A）thinking。

Example ❸

Directions：

Read the following text. Choose the best word(s) for each numbered blank and mark A, B, C or D on the ANSWER SHEET 1. (10 points)

　　Scientists have come up with the strongest evidence that children living near nuclear power stations could be at risk of getting cancer. The evidence has ___1___ confidence in an industry that has always claimed to put ___2___ first. According to the report, it is the children of those who work at nuclear sites who are likely to be ___3___ risk. Their fathers receive small ___4___ of radiation in the course of their work, and ___5___ the weakness to their children. It has been ___6___ to pay millions of pounds to the children who have suffered. And some families are seeking ___7___. The theory comes from Dr. Martin Gardner, who ___8___ the families of workers at the Sellafield nuclear power plant in Cumbria. He found that the children suffered more often than other children ___9___ leukaemia, a ___10___ cancer that attacks blood cells. Meanwhile the authority which sets safety standards ___11___ nuclear workers said it would ___12___ the new evidence to find out if the deadly theory is true.

　　Radiation is the strong energy ___13___ when tiny particles of certain types of materials break up. ___14___ it has been used for energy. Some people feared that science would not be able to ___15___ safely the massive forces of nuclear radiation. But radiation also ___16___ life-saving uses in medicine. It can be used like a gun to ___17___ diseased parts of the body. And in its most common form—X-rays-radiation can show what is going on ___18___ the body. Some are now saying perhaps male patients and ___19___ workers need greater protection ___20___ X-rays than had been thought.

1. A) rocked　　　　B) deprived　　　　C) roared　　　　D) trembled

2. A) emphasis　　　B) safety　　　　　C) balance　　　　D) danger

3. A) at　　　　　　B) in　　　　　　　C) on　　　　　　D) with

4. A) amounts　　　B) doses　　　　　C) shots　　　　　D) quantities

5. A) pass over　　　B) pass by　　　　C) pass away　　　D) pass on

6. A) ordered　　　B) spurred　　　　C) urged　　　　　D) needed

7.	A）money	B）repayment	C）compensation	D）payment
8.	A）surveyed	B）studied	C）looked	D）examined
9.	A）from	B）of	C）in	D）into
10.	A）deadly	B）harmful	C）dangerous	D）risky
11.	A）of	B）about	C）for	D）on
12.	A）check over	B）check in	C）check out	D）check up on
13.	A）aroused	B）released	C）flowed	D）discharged
14.	A）Although	B）Because	C）Ever since	D）So
15.	A）include	B）contain	C）possess	D）occupy
16.	A）created	B）invented	C）found	D）made
17.	A）knock over	B）knock down	C）knock off	D）knock out
18.	A）at	B）on	C）inside	D）outside
19.	A）healthy	B）feeble	C）sick	D）health
20.	A）to	B）on	C）from	D）of

答案与解析

1. 答案：A

   解析：词义辨析题。rock 表示"动摇"；deprive 通常与介词 of 连用，deprive sb. of sth. 表示"剥夺"；roar 表示"吼叫"；而 tremble 则表示"发抖"。此处动词后的宾语是 confidence，选项 B、C 和 D 都不能与 confidence 搭配。只能用 rock confidence，表示"动摇信任"。因此，正确答案应该是选项 A）rocked。

2. 答案：B

   解析：上下文推理题。本文说的是辐射的危害与用途。上文提到，有证据表明住在核电站附近的孩子有得癌症的危险。所谓危险，即安全问题。由此可见，选项 A）emphasis和 C）balance 不符合题意，予以排除。而核电站不会把危险放在第一位，只会把安全放在第一位，选项 D）danger 也应排除。因此，正确答案应该是选项 B）safety。

3. 答案：D

   解析：结构搭配题。at risk 是固定的词组搭配，表示"危险、冒险"。因此，正确答案应该是选项 A）at。

4. 答案：B

   解析：近义词辨析题。amount 表示"数量"，用于词组 a large amount of 中，修饰不可数名词；dose 表示"（药物等的）剂量、射线剂量"；shot 表示"皮下注射"；而 quantity 则表示"数量"，常用词组为 a large quantity of，主要用于修饰可数名词。此处答案很明显，应该是选项 B）doses。

5. 答案：D

   解析：词义辨析题。pass over 表示"忽略"；pass by 表示"不理会、忽视"；pass away 表示"去世"；而 pass on 则表示"传给某人"。本题的答案很明显，应该选择选项 D）pass on。

6. **答案：C**

解析：词义辨析题。order 表示"命令"；spur 表示"刺激、激励"；urge 表示"敦促、促进"；而 need 则表示"需要"。根据句意，已有人敦促将数百万英镑支付给了那些受害的孩子，选项 A 和 D 不符合题意，予以排除。spur 通常和介词 on 搭配，不合适。因此，正确答案应该是选项 C）urged。

7. **答案：C**

解析：词义辨析题。money 表示"钱"；repayment 表示"报答、偿还的款项"；compensation 表示"补偿、赔偿"；而 payment 则表示"付款、报酬"。此处指受害的家庭要求补偿。因此，正确答案应该是选项 C）compensation。

8. **答案：B**

解析：词义辨析题。survey 表示"调查"，即考察某一事件或现象，后面一般不跟人；study 表示"研究"，即研究并收集资料而得出结论；look 表示"看"，后面加介词 at；而 examine 则表示"检查"。此处是指，Martin Gardner 医生对一些案例进行研究，进而得出结论。因此，正确答案应该是选项 B）studied。

9. **答案：A**

解析：结构搭配题。suffer from 是固定搭配，表示"遭受……"。因此，正确答案应该是选项 A）from。

10. **答案：A**

解析：词义辨析题。deadly 表示"致命的"；harmful 表示"有害的"；dangerous 表示"危险的"；而 risky 则表示"冒险的"。句中有一个生词 leukaemia（白血病），但是，这并不影响本题的选择。本文说的是辐射对人的危害，并且本句提到了这一癌症会破坏血细胞。如果人的血细胞被破坏了，那么，人的生命一定会受到威胁，这种癌症一定是致命的。另外，cancer（癌症）不用 harmful、dangerous 或 risky 来修饰。因此，正确答案应该是选项 A）deadly。

11. **答案：C**

解析：词义辨析题。of 表示"属于……的"；about 表示"关于……的"；for 表示"为了……"；而 on 则表示"在……上面"。本句的意思是，为那些核电站的工作人员制定安全标准。因此，正确答案应该是选项 C）for。

12. **答案：D**

解析：词义辨析题。check over 表示"查看、检查"；check in 表示"在旅馆登记住宿"；check out 表示"结账并且离开旅馆"；而 check up on 则表示"调查、核对（数据、事实等）"。本句的意思是核对证据。因此，正确答案应该是选项 D）check up on。

13. **答案：B**

解析：词义辨析题。arouse 表示"引起、唤起"；release 表示"释放（人、能量等）"；flow 表示"（液体）流动"；而 discharge 则表示"放出（液体、气体、电流等）、排放（废气、废物）"。本句的意思是，辐射是物质微粒分裂时释放的能量。选项 A、C 和 D 均不符合题意。因此，正确答案应该是选项 B）released。

14. **答案：C**

解析：逻辑推理题。本题可以用排除法来做。although 表示"虽然……"；because 表示

"因为……"。这两个选项都是连词,用于从句结构,而本句只是简单句,不符合题意。so 表示"因此",也是连词。本句与上文并不存在因果关系,选项 D 也不符合题意。剩下选项 C) Ever since,表示"从那时起到现在"。根据句意,此处需要时间副词。因此,正确答案应该是选项 C) Ever since。

15. 答案:B

解析:词义辨析题。include 表示"包括、包含";contain 表示"包含",还表示"控制、遏制";possess 表示"拥有、占有";而 occupy 则表示"占用、占据"。本处的意思是,用科学来控制核辐射的巨大能量。因此,正确答案应该是选项 B) contain。

16. 答案:C

解析:词义辨析题。create 表示"创造";invent 表示"发明";find 表示"找到、发现",还表示"供应、提供";而 make 则表示"制造"。选项 A、B 和 D 均不符合题意。因此,正确答案应该是选项 C) found。

17. 答案:D

解析:词义辨析题。knock over 表示"撞倒、抢劫";knock down 表示"打倒";knock off 表示"减价、下班";而 knock out 则表示"击倒、使失去效能"。本句的意思是,射线可以用来摧毁病变部位。选项 A、B 和 C 都不符合题意。因此,正确答案应该是选项 D) knock out。

18. 答案:C

解析:词义辨析题。at 表示"在……、在……方面";on 表示"在……上面、关于……";inside 表示"在……里面";而 outside 则表示"在……外面"。根据句意,此处表示"体内"。因此,正确答案应该是选项 C) inside。

19. 答案:D

解析:上下文推理题。healthy 表示"健康的";feeble 表示"虚弱的";sick 表示"生病的";而 health 则表示"健康"。本题是用一个定语来修饰名词 workers,似乎前三个选项都能与 workers 搭配。但是,此处并不要说明 workers 的健康状况,而是要说明他们所从事的职业。因此,选项 A、B 和 C 均应排除。正确答案应该是选项 D) health,health workers 的意思是医疗机构的工作人员。

20. 答案:C

解析:结构搭配题。protection(保护)后的介词搭配是 from。因此,正确答案应该是选项 C) from。

Example ❹

Directions:

Read the following text. Choose the best word(s) for each numbered blank and mark A, B, C or D on the ANSWER SHEET 1. (10 points)

Americans today have different eating habits than in the past. They have a broader knowledge of ___1___, so they buy more fresh fruit and vegetables than ever before. Statistics show that the way people live ___2___ the way they eat. American changing life-styles are responsible for the

___3___ number of people who must rush meals or sometimes ___4___ them altogether. Many Americans have less time to eat. ___5___ as a result of this limited time, 60 percent of all American homes now have microwave ovens. ___6___, Americans eat out nearly four times a week on the ___7___. It is easy to study the amounts and kinds of food that people ___8___. The United States Department of Agriculture and the Food Industry ___9___ sales statistics and keep accurate records. This information tells us what people are eating and their changes ___10___ attitudes and tastes. For example, red meat is no longer an American favorite. ___11___, chicken, turkey, and fish have become more popular. This is probably a result of the ___12___ of the dangers of eating food which contains ___13___ levels of cholesterol, an obvious ___14___ to human health. According to a recent ___15___, Americans also change their eating ___16___ to meet the needs of different situations. They have certain ideas about which foods will make them ___17___ for business meetings, or put them in the mood for romance. Americans choose pasta, fruit, and vegetables, which supply them ___18___ carbohydrates, to give them strength for physical activities. For romantic dinners, ___19___, Americans choose shrimp and lobster. Americans' awareness of nutrition, along with their changing tastes and needs, leads them to consume a wide ___20___ of foods.

1. A) food
   B) diet
   C) nutrition
   D) hygiene
2. A) depends
   B) determines
   C) limits
   D) changes
3. A) growing
   B) decreasing
   C) broadening
   D) lessening
4. A) eat
   B) swallow
   C) skip
   D) digest
5. A) Completely
   B) Mainly
   C) Partly
   D) Basically
6. A) However
   B) Though
   C) Therefore
   D) Moreover
7. A) scale
   B) average
   C) majority
   D) whole
8. A) have
   B) waste
   C) consume
   D) purchase
9. A) gather
   B) collect
   C) compile
   D) accumulate
10. A) in
    B) on
    C) at
    D) for
11. A) Besides
    B) Instead
    C) Also
    D) Again
12. A) awareness
    B) clarity
    C) recognition
    D) consciousness
13. A) high
    B) large
    C) low
    D) little
14. A) harm
    B) threat
    C) fear
    D) damage
15. A) survey
    B) research
    C) study
    D) investigation
16. A) approaches
    B) patterns
    C) styles
    D) traditions
17. A) attentive
    B) shrewd
    C) acute
    D) alert
18. A) for
    B) to
    C) by
    D) with
19. A) however
    B) in addition
    C) meanwhile
    D) thus
20. A) sort
    B) variety
    C) kind
    D) variation

答案与解析

1. 答案：C

解析：上下文推理题。food 表示"食物"；diet 表示"日常饮食、日常食物"；nutrition 表示

"营养";而 hygiene 则表示"卫生、卫生学"。本文说的是美国人的饮食问题。选项 D 首先予以排除。众所周知,人们越来越关注自身的健康,出现在食谱中的不再是单一的肉类,而是加入了大量的蔬菜与水果。也就是说,人们更加注重营养问题。因此,正确答案应该是选项 C) nutrition。

2. 答案:B
   解析:词义辨析题。depend 通常与介词 on 搭配,depend on 表示"依靠、依赖";determine 表示"决定、使……下定决心";limit 表示"限制、限定";而 change 则表示"改变、变化"。本句的意思是,人们的生活方式决定了他们的饮食方式。因此,正确答案应该是选项 B) determines。

3. 答案:A
   解析:上下文推理题。grow 表示"增长、扩大";decrease 表示"减少";broaden 表示"加宽";而 lessen 则表示"减少、减轻"。下文提到,许多美国人吃饭的时间少。也就是许多美国人匆忙吃饭,而且他们的人数在增加。因此,正确答案应该是选项 A) growing。

4. 答案:C
   解析:上下文推理题。eat 表示"吃";swallow 表示"吞、咽";skip 表示"跳过、略过";而 digest 则表示"消化"。本句说的是,美国人不得不匆忙吃饭(rush meals)。有时候情况更糟,连匆忙吃饭的时间都没有,那就只能不吃饭了(skip meals)。因此,正确答案应该是选项 C) skip。

5. 答案:C
   解析:词义辨析题。completely 表示"完全地";mainly 表示"大体上、主要地";partly 表示"部分地、在一定程度上";而 basically 则表示"基本上、主要地"。选项 A、B 和 D 均不符合题意。因此,正确答案应该是选项 C) Partly。

6. 答案:D
   解析:逻辑推理题。however 表示"然而";though 表示"虽然";therefore 表示"因此";而 moreover 则表示"而且"。此处是很明显的递进关系。因此,正确答案应该是选项 D) Moreover。

7. 答案:B
   解析:词义辨析题。scale 表示"等级、规模",可以与介词 on 搭配,on a scale of…表示"处于……等级、处于……规模";average 表示"平均",与介词 on 搭配,构成词组 on the average,表示"平均起来、一般来说";majority 表示"多数",与介词 in 搭配,in the majority 表示"大多数";而 whole 则表示"全部、整体",与介词 on 搭配,on the whole 表示"总的看来、在大多数情况下"。这里,首先要排除选项 A 和 C,而选项 D 不符合句意,也予以排除。因此,正确答案应该是选项 B) average。

8. 答案:C
   解析:词义辨析题。have 表示"用、拥有";waste 表示"浪费、消耗";consume 表示"消费、消耗";而 purchase 则表示"买、购买"。本句的意思是,人们所吃食物的数量与种类。由此看来,选项 A、B 和 D 均不符合题意。因此,正确答案应该是选项 C) consume。

9. **答案**：D

   解析：近义词辨析题。这些动词的意思是：使聚集成为一组或一堆。gather 是最概括的说法，表示"聚集、收集"，指把分散的人或物聚集在一起；collect 表示"收集、集中"，通常可以与 gather 互换；compile 表示"编辑、汇编"，强调收集资料并编辑成书、表、报告等；而 accumulate 则表示"积累、聚积"，指相似或有联系的事物在一段较长时期内增长。compile 与句意不符，予以排除。在剩下的三个词中，accumulate 比 gather 和 collect 意思更为具体，因此，最佳答案应该是选项 D) accumulate。

10. **答案**：A

    解析：词义辨析题。本题表示"在态度和品位上的变化"，在这四个选项中，只有 in 合适。因此，正确答案应该是选项 A) in。

11. **答案**：B

    解析：逻辑推理题。besides 表示"此外"；instead 表示"代替"；also 表示"也、同样"；而 again 则表示"又、再次"。上文说，红色的肉不再是美国人的最爱了。本句说，人们更喜欢吃鸡、火鸡和鱼。可以看出，这里是转折关系。因此，正确答案应该是选项 B) Instead。

12. **答案**：A

    解析：词义辨析题。awareness 表示"知道、晓得"；clarity 表示"清晰、清楚"；recognition 表示"识别、承认"；而 consciousness 则表示"意识、知觉"。本句的意思是，人们意识到了食用高胆固醇食物的危害。因此，正确答案应该是选项 A) awareness。

13. **答案**：A

    解析：上下文推理题。high 表示"高的"；large 表示"大的"；low 表示"低的"；而 little 则表示"小的、少的"。本句有一个提示词 dangers，表示"危险、危害"。根据常识，胆固醇含量高的食物对人的健康不利。因此，正确答案应该是选项 A) high。

14. **答案**：B

    解析：词义辨析题。harm 表示"伤害、损害"；threat 表示"威胁、恐吓"；fear 表示"害怕、担心"；而 damage 则表示"损害、伤害"。本句的意思是，胆固醇含量高的食物对人的健康有影响，但也可能还没有造成伤害。选项 C 与句意不符，而选项 A 和 D 太绝对化，也不合适。因此，正确答案应该是选项 B) threat。

15. **答案**：A

    解析：近义词辨析题。survey 表示"调查、概论"，指调查某部分人的行为、意见等，通常以询问方式进行数据调查；research 表示"调查、研究"，指学术性或科学的调查或探究；study 表示"学习、研究"，目的是为了获取知识或理解某一课题；而 investigation 则表示"调查、研究"，指详细的查问或系统的检查，如犯罪调查。此处的意思是，对人们的饮食方式的调查。选项 B、C 和 D 均不合适。因此，正确答案应该是选项 A) survey。

16. **答案**：B

    解析：词义辨析题。approach 表示"步骤、方法"，指用于处理问题或完成工作的方法；pattern 表示"方式、形式"，指现实中事物存在、发展的形式；style 表示"风格、时尚",指说话、做事、表达及表演的一种方法、作风;而 tradition 则表示"传统、惯例",指被看作影响现在的一整套前代的风俗和习惯、某民族一代代人一直遵守的一种思想或行为方式、习惯或习俗。文中指的是,美国人的饮食结构,选项 A、C 和 D 均不合适。因此,正确答案应该是选项 B) patterns。

17. 答案:D
    解析:词义辨析题。attentive 表示"注意的、专心的";shrewd 表示"精明的、敏锐的";acute 表示"敏捷的、精明的";而 alert 则表示"提防的、警惕的"。本句是意思是,有些食物让人们在开商务会议时机警、敏捷。因此,正确答案应该是选项 D) alert。

18. 答案:D
    解析:结构搭配题。supply sb. with sth. 和 supply sth. for sb. 是固定搭配,表示"将某物提供给某人"。因此,正确答案应该是选项 D) with。

19. 答案:A
    解析:逻辑推理题。however 表示"然而";in addition 表示"另外";meanwhile 表示"同时";而 thus 则表示"因而"。此处谈论的是,在不同的场合人们吃不同的食物。这里上下文的逻辑关系是轻微的转折,表示事物的另一方面。因此,正确答案应该是选项 A) however。

20. 答案:B
    解析:词义辨析题。sort 表示"种类、别",词组 all sorts of 表示"各种各样";variety 表示"品种、多种多样",词组 a variety of 相当于 all kinds of,表示"各种各样";kind 表示"种类、别",词组 all kinds of 表示"各种各样";而 variation 则表示"变化、变更",指变化的动作、过程或结果。因此,正确答案应该是选项 B) variety。

Example ❺

Directions:

Read the following text. Choose the best word(s) for each numbered blank and mark A, B, C or D on the ANSWER SHEET 1. (10 points)

Scientists at Sussex University appear to be on the way to discovering how the mosquito homes in on its target. They have found that the best way to __1__ being bitten is: stop breathing, stop sweating, and keep down the temperature of your __2__ surroundings. Unfortunately the first suggestion is impossible and the others very __3__.

Scientists have found that there are three __4__ stages in a mosquito's assault. Stage one is __5__ fifty feet away, when the insect first __6__ a man or animal to bite. Stage two is thought to come into __7__ about 25 feet from the target, when the insect becomes __8__ by the carbon dioxide breathed out by the __9__ victim. Stage three is when the mosquito is only a matter of inches from its __10__, and the warmth and moisture given off by the victim is the final __11__. The researchers then examined how repellents interfere __12__ its three-stage attack. They found repellents act more __13__ than by just giving off a nasty smell. And they appear to __14__ mosquitoes first when they are following the carbon dioxide and second 15 the final approach. Air pervaded by one of the many chemical repellents stops the mosquito reacting 16 the target's carbon dioxide, and the repellent seems to affect the tiny hairs 17 which the insect senses moisture in the air. The sensors are blocked 18 the insect does not know when it is 19 through a moist current, or the sensors are made to send the wrong 20 .

1. A) stop   B) prevent   C) avoid   D) reject
2. A) instant   B) immediate   C) living   D) permanent
3. A) incredible   B) dubious   C) difficult   D) arduous
4. A) different   B) distinctive   C) discreet   D) distinct
5. A) off   B) in   C) at   D) of
6. A) tastes   B) smells   C) catches   D) stings
7. A) action   B) function   C) motion   D) operation
8. A) stunned   B) conducted   C) guided   D) fainted
9. A) intended   B) presumed   C) attracted   D) prepared
10. A) vulture   B) perch   C) animal   D) prey
11. A) plot   B) line   C) clue   D) target
12. A) with   B) away   C) to   D) off
13. A) subtly   B) foolishly   C) clearly   D) completely
14. A) surprise   B) confuse   C) attack   D) surround
15. A) at   B) of   C) under   D) during
16. A) on   B) into   C) to   D) in
17. A) of   B) by   C) at   D) with
18. A) as though   B) so that   C) in order that   D) even if
19. A) flying   B) working   C) behaving   D) moving
20. A) codes   B) signals   C) victims   D) models

答案与解析

1. 答案：C

   解析：词义辨析题。stop 表示"停止"，结构 stop doing sth. 表示"停止做某事"；prevent 表示"阻止"，结构 prevent sb. from doing sth. 表示"阻止某人做某事"；avoid 表示"避免"，结构 avoid doing sth. 表示"避免做某事"；而 reject 则表示"拒绝"，后加名词。本句的意思是，避免被蚊子叮咬。因此，正确答案应该是选项 C）avoid。

2. 答案：B

   解析：词义辨析题。instant 表示"立即的、紧迫的"；immediate 表示"立刻的、紧邻的"；living 表示"活着的、现存的"；而 permanent 则表示"永久的、持久的"。选项 C 和 D 与句意不符，先予以排除。instant 和 immediate 是近义词，instant 强调时间概念，而 immediate 可以用来修饰表示时间和空间的词汇。此处被修饰的词是表示空间概念的 surroundings（周围），因此，正确答案应该是选项 B）immediate。

3. 答案：C

解析：上下文推理题。incredible 表示"难以置信的"；dubious 表示"可疑的"；difficult 表示"困难的"；而 arduous 则表示"艰苦的"。上文说，有三种方法可以避免被蚊子叮咬：不呼吸，不流汗，控制周围的温度。根据常识，第一种方法根本不可能，而后两种方法理论上不是不可能，而是实际上很难做到。因此，正确答案应该是选项 C）difficult。

4. 答案：D

   解析：词义辨析题。different 表示"不同的"；distinctive 表示"与众不同的"；discreet 表示"慎重的"；而 distinct 则表示"明显的"。本题可以用排除法来做。本句的意思是，蚊子叮人有三个阶段。选项 B 和 C 搭配不合适，而选项 A 又是多余的。因此，剩下的选项 D）distinct 是应该正确答案。

5. 答案：C

   解析：词义辨析题。off 表示"距离……"，可以指时间和空间概念，后面接名词；in 表示"在……之内"；at 表示"在……"，指在某一点，既可以指时间，也可以指空间，后面接名词和数词；而 of 则表示"……的"。选项 B 和 D 不合适，而选项 A 用法不符合题意。因此，正确答案应该是选项 C）at。

6. 答案：B

   解析：词义辨析题。taste 表示"品尝"；smell 表示"闻到"；catch 表示"抓住"；而 sting 则表示"刺"。根据常识，蚊子凭嗅觉追踪猎物。因此，正确答案应该是选项 B）smells。

7. 答案：D

   解析：词义辨析题。action 表示"动作、行动"；function 表示"功能、作用"；motion 表示"运动、动作"；而 operation 则表示"操作、实施"。本句的意思是，第二阶段在离目标二十五英尺的地方开始进行。选项 A、B 和 C 都不符合题意，剩下选项 D，come into operation 在句中的意思是"实施、起作用"。因此，正确答案应该是选项 D）operation。

8. 答案：C

   解析：词义辨析题。stun 表示"使晕倒"；conduct 表示"带领、管理"；guide 表示"指导、指引"；而 faint 则表示"昏倒"。本句的意思是，受害者呼出的二氧化碳引导蚊子飞向目标。选项 A 和 D 与句意不符，予以排除。而选项 C 主要指导游领路，也不合适。因此，正确答案应该是选项 C）guided。

9. 答案：A

   解析：词义辨析题。intended 表示"预期的、未来的"；presumed 表示"假定的"；attracted 表示"被吸引的"；而 prepared 则表示"准备好的"。根据句意，蚊子攻击的目标将成为它的受害者，选项 B、C 和 D 均不合适。因此，正确答案应该是选项 A）intended。

10. 答案：D

    解析：词义辨析题。vulture 表示"秃鹫"；perch 表示"鸟类栖息的树枝"；animal 表示"动物"；而 prey 则表示"被捕食的动物、猎物"。上文中提到的攻击目标、受害者就是被捕食的动物、猎物。因此，正确答案应该是选项 D）prey。

11. 答案：C

解析：词义辨析题。plot 表示"情节、结构"；line 表示"线、线路"；clue 表示"线索、提示"；而 target 则表示"目标、对象"。本句的意思是，受害者散发出的体温与湿气是最后一个提示。因此，正确答案应该是选项 C）clue。

12. 答案：A

解析：结构搭配题。interfere with 是固定搭配，表示"干涉、妨碍"。因此，正确答案应该是选项 A）with。

13. 答案：A

解析：词义辨析题。subtly 表示"微妙地、细微地"；foolishly 表示"愚蠢地、愚笨地"；clearly 表示"明显地、清楚地"；而 completely 则表示"完全地、十分"。本句说的是驱虫剂的作用，选项 B、C 和 D 都不适合修饰 act。因此，正确答案应该是选项 A）subtly。

14. 答案：B

解析：词义辨析题。surprise 表示"使惊奇、使惊讶"；confuse 表示"使糊涂、使迷惑"；attack 表示"进攻、攻击"；而 surround 则表示"包围、围绕"。本句说的是驱虫剂对蚊子的行动有干扰作用。因此，选项 A、C 和 D 不符合题意，正确答案应该是选项 B）confuse。

15. 答案：D

解析：词义辨析题。at 表示"在……"，指时间点；of 表示"关于……的"；under 表示"在……下面"；而 during 则表示"在……期间"，指一段时间。此处是指时间段，因此，正确答案应该是选项 D）during。

16. 答案：C

解析：结构搭配题。react to 是固定的词组搭配，表示"对……做出反应"。因此，正确答案应该是选项 C）to。

17. 答案：D

解析：逻辑推理题。of 表示"关于……的"；by 表示"通过……"；at 表示"在……方面"；而 with 则表示"以……、用……"。此处是一个定语从句，先行词是 tiny hairs。本句的意思是，蚊子用它身上的绒毛来感应空气中的湿度。因此，正确答案应该是选项 D）with。

18. 答案：B

解析：逻辑推理题。as though 表示"好像、似乎"；so that 表示"以便、因此"；in order that 表示"为了"；而 even if 则表示"即使"。选项 A 和 D 在此不合适，予以排除。根据句意，此处是结果状语从句，而选项 C 引导目的状语从句。因此，正确答案应该是选项 B）so that。

19. 答案：A

解析：词义辨析题。fly 表示"飞"；work 表示"工作"；behave 表示"表现"；而 move 则表示"移动"。众所周知，蚊子是飞来飞去的。因此，正确答案应该是选项 A）flying。

20. 答案：B

解析：词义辨析题。code 表示"代码、密码"；signal 表示"信号、暗号"；victim 表示"受害者";而 model 则表示"样式、模型"。此处的意思是发信号。因此,正确答案应该是选项 B) signals。

Example ❻

Directions:

Read the following text. Choose the best word(s) for each numbered blank and mark A, B, C or D on the ANSWER SHEET 1. (10 points)

Today, most countries in the world have canals. Many countries have built canals near the coast, and parallel __1__ the coast. Even in the twentieth century, goods can be moved more cheaply by boat than by any other __2__ of transport. These __3__ make it possible for boats to travel __4__ ports along the coast without being __5__ to the dangers of the open. Some canals, such as the Suez of the Panama, save ships weeks of time by making their __6__ a thousand miles shorter. Other canals permit boats to reach cities that are not __7__ on the coast. Still other canals __8__ lands where there is too much water, help to __9__ fields where there is not enough water, and __10__ water power for factories and mills. The size of a canal __11__ on the kind of boats going through it. The canal must be wide enough to permit two of the largest boats using it to __12__ each other easily. It must be deep enough to __13__ about two feet of water beneath the keel of the largest boat using the canal.

When the planet Mars was first __14__ through a telescope, people saw that the round disk of the planet was crisscrossed by a(n) __15__ of strange blue-green lines. These were called "canals" __16__ they looked the same as canals on earth that are viewed from an airplane. __17__, scientists are now __18__ that the Martian phenomena are really not canals. The photographs __19__ from space-ships have helped us to __20__ the truth about the Martian "canals".

1. A) off   B) with   C) to   D) by
2. A) way   B) means   C) method   D) approach
3. A) waterways   B) waterfronts   C) channels   D) paths
4. A) among   B) between   C) in   D) to
5. A) revealed   B) exposed   C) opened   D) shown
6. A) trip   B) journey   C) voyage   D) travel
7. A) lain   B) stationed   C) set   D) located
8. A) escape   B) drain   C) dry   D) leak
9. A) water   B) wet   C) soak   D) irrigate
10. A) furnish   B) afford   C) offer   D) give
11. A) focuses   B) bases   C) depends   D) takes
12. A) cross   B) pass   C) move   D) advance
13. A) give   B) permit   C) leave   D) admit
14. A) studied   B) researched   C) surveyed   D) observed

15.	A）few	B）number	C）deal	D）amount
16.	A）although	B）because	C）so	D）if
17.	A）However	B）Though	C）Hence	D）Therefore
18.	A）exact	B）definite	C）certain	D）decisive
19.	A）held	B）taken	C）got	D）developed
20.	A）find	B）expose	C）uncover	D）discover

答案与解析

1. **答案：C**

   解析： 结构搭配题。be parallel to 是固定的词组搭配,表示"与……平行"。因此,正确答案显然是选项 C）to。

2. **答案：B**

   解析： 近义词辨析题。way 表示"路线、方式",指习惯的存在、生活或行为方式;means 表示"手段、方法";method 表示"方法、办法",指一个详细的、逻辑有序的计划;而 approach 则表示"步骤、途径",用于处理或完成的方法。本题是指交通工具,在这四个选项中,只有 means 符合题意。因此,正确答案应该是选项B）means。

3. **答案：A**

   解析： 词义辨析题。waterway 表示"水路、航道";waterfront 表示"水边码头区、滨水地区";channel 表示"海峡、沟渠";而 path 则表示"小路、路线"。本文说的是 canal（运河）,而运河是水道的一种。因此,正确答案应该是选项 A）waterways。

4. **答案：B**

   解析： 词义辨析题。among 表示"在……范围之内";between 表示"在……之间";in 表示"在……内";而 to 则表示"到……"。本句的意思是,船只穿梭于港口之间。因此,正确答案应该是选项 B）between。

5. **答案：B**

   解析： 词义辨析题。reveal 表示"揭示、显示";expose 表示"暴露";open 表示"打开、敞开";而 show 则表示"表示、展出"。本句的意思是,面临外界的危险、暴露在外界的危险之中。因此,正确答案应该是选项 B）exposed。

6. **答案：C**

   解析： 近义词辨析题。这四个单词都有"旅行"的意思。trip 表示"旅行、旅游",尤指短途旅行;journey 表示"旅行、旅程",通常指陆路旅行;voyage 表示"航海、航行";而 travel 则表示"旅行、旅程",主要指长途旅行。根据句意,此处是指航行。因此,正确答案应该是选项 C）voyage。

7. **答案：D**

   解析： 词义辨析题。lie 表示"躺、位于",没有被动语态;station 表示"派驻、驻扎";set 表示"放置";而 locate 则表示"位于、坐落于"。根据句意,此处表示的是位于海边。因此,正确答案应该是选项 D）located。

8. **答案：B**

   解析： 词义辨析题。escape 表示"逃脱、逃避";drain 表示"排水、流干";dry 表示"干燥、变干";而 leak 则表示"泄漏、渗漏"。根据句意,此处是指把过多的水排走。因此,正确答案应该是选项 B)drain。

9. 答案:D

解析:词义辨析题。water 表示"加水、注水";wet 表示"弄湿、使湿润";soak 表示"浸泡、浸透";而 irrigate 则表示"灌溉"。根据句意,此处是指灌溉水少的土地。因此,正确答案应该是选项 D)irrigate。

10. 答案:A

解析:近义词辨析题。这四个单词都可以表示"提供"的概念。furnish 表示"供应、提供",结构搭配是 furnish sth. for/to sb.;afford 表示"提供、给予",结构搭配是 afford sth. to sb.;offer 表示"提供、供给",结构搭配是 offer sth. to sb.;而 give 则表示"供给、给予",结构搭配是 give sth. to sb.。只有 furnish 能和介词 for 搭配。因此,正确答案应该是选项 A)furnish。

11. 答案:C

解析:词义辨析题。focus on 表示"集中注意力于……";base on 表示"以……为基础",depend on 表示"依靠……";而 take on 则表示"聘用、显现、奉行"。根据句意,运河的大小取决于船只的种类。因此,正确的选择应该是选项C)depends。

12. 答案:B

解析:词义辨析题。cross 表示"横穿、穿过";pass 表示"经过、路过";move 表示"移动、运行";而 advance 则表示"前进、向前移动"。根据句意,此处表达的意思是大型船只可以擦肩而过。因此,最佳答案应该是选项 B)pass。

13. 答案:C

解析:词义辨析题。give 表示"给予、供给";permit 表示"许可、允许";leave 表示"剩下、留出";而 admit 则表示"承认、接纳"。根据句意,此处是指留出一定的距离。因此,选项 C)leave 最符合题意。

14. 答案:D

解析:上下文推理题。study 表示"学习、研究";research 表示"研究、调查";survey 表示"调查、测量";而 observe 则表示"观察、观测"。本题有一个提示词,first(第一次)。人们可以观测火星,也可以对火星进行研究、调查。根据上下文,此处是指,用望远镜第一次观测到火星。因此,正确答案应该是选项 D)observed。

15. 答案:B

解析:词义辨析题。a few of 表示"少数",用于修饰可数名词;a number of 表示"一些",也用于修饰可数名词;而 a deal of 和 an amount of 表示"一些",用于修饰不可数名词。句中的 lines 是可数名词,不能选择 a deal of 或 an amount of。根据句意,此处是指,火星周围有一些蓝绿色的环绕带,数量并不是很少。因此,正确答案应该是选项 B)number。

16. 答案:B

解析:逻辑推理题。前一句说的是,这些色带被称作"运河"。下一句说,从飞机上看,这些色带和地球上的运河一样。前后句的逻辑关系很明显,前果后因,是因果关系。因此,正确答案应该是选项 B)because。

17. **答案**：A

　　解析：逻辑推理题。很明显，此处是一个转折关系。hence 和 therefore 表示结果"因此"，不符合题意。however 和 though 表示转折"然而"，但是，though 不能放在句首。因此，正确答案应该是选项 D) However。

18. **答案**：C

　　解析：词义辨析题。exact 表示"精确的、准确的"；definite 表示"明确的、一定的"；certain 表示"确定的、肯定的"；而 decisive 则表示"决定性的"。decisive 不符合题意，先被排除。在这四个形容词中，exact、definite 和 certain 意思比较接近。但是，exact 和 definite 用来修饰事物，而只有 certain 可以用来指人。因此，正确答案应该是选项 C) certain。

19. **答案**：B

　　解析：结构搭配题。表示"拍照"应该用 take photographs，其他三个动词都不能与 photograph 搭配。因此，答案很明确，是选项 B) taken。

20. **答案**：D

　　解析：近义词辨析题。本题的四个动词都有"揭露"的含义。reveal 表示"揭示、揭露"，指揭露被隐藏的事物；expose 表示"暴露、揭露"，是揭露出来供公众细察；uncover 表示"揭开、揭示"，指把覆盖物（如盖子）揭开；而 discover 则表示"发现、发觉"，指获得知识或明白以前所不知的事情。根据句意，人们以前不了解火星，而现在借助宇宙飞船，人们可以进一步研究火星。因此，最符合题意的答案应该是选项 D) discover。

Example ❼

Directions：

Read the following text. Choose the best word(s) for each numbered blank and mark A, B, C or D on the ANSWER SHEET 1. (10 points)

　　In my five years as a dietitian and nutrition counselor, I have seen a lot of people who feel miserable about their weight. In many ___1___ their struggles with food began in childhood.

　　Todd was a robust three-year-old whose parents came to me because he demanded ___2___ portions, plus second helpings, and had a temper tantrum if ___3___. Usually his parents ___4___, but even then Todd would ask for snacks right after a meal. The solution was not to put the child ___5___ a diet and promote undereating. It was to ___6___ Todd that he would not have to go hungry. When you give children enough food and ___7___ to eat, they relax and stop overeating. The object is to help your child ___8___, by himself, the amount he eats. Babies are born with the ___9___ to take in just the amount of food ___10___ for them. Each child has the genetic blueprint for his growth, and it's not only ___11___ but destructive to try to change it. I will help your child if you go easy ___12___ high-calorie foods like French fries and candy. ___13___ studies suggest that fat children are no more likely to eat excessive amounts of these foods ___14___ thin children; they pay more of a ___15___ because of their relative inability to ___16___ the excess calories. Don't ___17___ all high-calorie food, however. If you do, your child will want to sneak "sinful" foods. And don't be overzealous with low-calorie ___18___. I have had adult patients who couldn't look at a piece of broccoli because they had so much of it foisted ___19___ them ___20___ they were children.

1. A) places   B) states   C) cases   D) times
2. A) fewer   B) more   C) small   D) big
3. A) refused   B) disagreed   C) retorted   D) objected
4. A) gave up   B) gave in   C) gave out   D) gave away
5. A) through   B) at   C) in   D) on
6. A) insure   B) assure   C) reassure   D) ensure
7. A) admission   B) right   C) privilege   D) permission
8. A) regulate   B) manage   C) arrange   D) devise
9. A) gift   B) faculty   C) instinct   D) skill
10. A) eligible   B) right   C) balanced   D) appropriate
11. A) useless   B) futile   C) valueless   D) invalid
12. A) on   B) with   C) for   D) at
13. A) If   B) No matter   C) While   D) When
14. A) as   B) like   C) with   D) than
15. A) money   B) sum   C) price   D) cost
16. A) burn down   B) burn off   C) burn up   D) burn out
17. A) eliminate   B) abolish   C) suppress   D) omit
18. A) choices   B) alternatives C) selections   D) preferences
19. A) down   B) in   C) up   D) on
20. A) before   B) when   C) since   D) after

答案与解析

1. 答案: C
   解析: 词义辨析题。place 表示"地方、地点"; state 表示"情形、状态"; case 表示"状况、事例、病例"; 而 time 则表示"次数"。本文是一位营养学家谈论饮食问题, 此处是指事例。因此, 正确答案应该是选项 C) cases。

2. 答案: D
   解析: 上下文推理题。fewer 表示"更少的"; more 表示"更多的"; small 表示"小的"; 而 big 则表示"大的"。根据上下文, Todd 要吃很多东西。因此, 正确答案应该是选项 D) big。

3. 答案: A
   解析: 词义辨析题。refuse 表示"拒绝"; disagree 表示"不同意"; retort 表示"反驳"; 而 object 则表示"反对"。本句的意思是, 如果不给 Todd 吃东西, 他就会发脾气。因此, 正确答案应该是选项 A) refused。

4. 答案: B
   解析: 词义辨析题。give up 表示"放弃"; give in 表示"投降、让步"; give out 表示"分发、发出";而 give away 则表示"泄露"。根据句意,当 Todd 要吃东西时,他的父母总是做出让步。因此,正确答案应该是选项 B) gave in。

5. 答案：D

   解析：结构搭配题。on a diet 是固定搭配,表示"节食"。因此,正确答案应该是选项 D) on。

6. 答案：C

   解析：词义辨析题。insure 表示"给（某人）保险",指为防不测向保险公司付钱投保;assure 表示"保证",指向某人保证某事将要发生;reassure 表示"使安心、使放心",安慰忧郁不安的人;而 ensure 则表示"保证",确保某事发生。根据上文,Todd 要吃很多东西,不给他吃东西,他就发脾气。要想解决这一问题,就得安慰他,消除他的疑虑,让他知道他不会饿。因此,正确答案应该是选项 C) reassure。

7. 答案：D

   解析：词义辨析题。admission 表示"允许进入";right 表示"权利";privilege 表示"特权";而 permission 则表示"许可"。此处的意思,允许孩子吃东西。这与权利无关,选项 B 和 C 不符合题意。而选项 A 的意思是,允许某人进入某地、参加某组织,也不符合题意。因此,正确答案应该是选项 D) permission。

8. 答案：A

   解析：词义辨析题。regulate 表示"调节、调整";manage 表示"管理、操纵";arrange 表示"安排、整理";而 devise 则表示"设计、发明"。本句的意思是,让孩子自己控制、调节他吃的食物量。选项 B、C 和 D 与句意不符。因此,正确答案应该是选项 A) regulate。

9. 答案：C

   解析：近义词辨析题。gift 表示"天赋、才能";faculty 表示"才能、能力";instinct 表示"本能";而 skill 则表示"技能、技巧"。婴儿天生知道自己能吃多少东西,这不是能力,更不是技能,而是本能。因此,正确答案应该是选项 C) instinct。

10. 答案：D

    解析：词义辨析题。eligible 表示"具备必要条件的、有资格的";right 表示"正确的、合适的";balanced 表示"公平的、均衡的";而 appropriate 则表示"适当的、合适的"。根据句意,"合适的量",选项 A 和 C 意思不符合题意,予以排除。而 right 表示正确的、合适的意思时,通常用作定语修饰名词,在此也不合适。appropriate 通常与介词 for 搭配,be appropriate for。因此,正确答案应该是选项 D) appropriate。

11. 答案：B

    解析：近义词辨析题。useless 表示"无用的、无价值的",指东西没有用处;futile 表示"无效的、徒劳的",指无结果或不起作用;valueless 表示"没有价值的、毫无用处的",指东西没有价值;而 invalid 则表示"无效的、作废的",强调法律上是无效的、作废的。根据句意,改变孩子控制食物摄取量的这种想法或行为是不会有结果的,甚至是有害的。选项 A 和 C 用来修饰物,不合适,而这里并不涉及法律问题,选项 D 也不合适。因此,正确答案应该是选项B) futile。

12. 答案：A

解析：结构搭配题。go easy on 是固定搭配，表示"对……宽容、节省使用"，在句中的意思是，少吃高热量的食物。因此，正确答案应该是选项 A）on。

13. 答案：C

解析：逻辑推理题。if 表示"如果"；no matter 表示"不论"；while 表示"当……时候、虽然"；而 when 则表示"当……时候"。此处是让步状语从句，而不是时间状语从句。因此，正确答案应该是选项 C）While。

14. 答案：D

解析：结构搭配题。no more…than…是固定的结构搭配，表示"与……同样不……"。因此，正确答案应该是选项 D）than。

15. 答案：C

解析：近义词辨析题。这四个单词都和钱有关。money 表示"钱、货币"；sum 表示"金额、总数"；price 表示"价格、代价"；而 cost 则表示"成本、代价"。此处不是指钱，而是指代价，选项 A 和 B 不符合题意。而 cost 表示代价时，不与动词 pay 搭配，选项 D 也不合适。因此，正确答案应该是选项 C）price。

16. 答案：B

解析：词义辨析题。burn down 表示"全部焚毁"；burn off 表示"烧掉"；burn up 表示"烧起来"；而 burn out 则表示"燃尽后熄灭"。此处的意思是，消耗掉多余的热量。选项 A、C 和 D 意思均不合适，因此，正确答案应该是选项B）burn off。

17. 答案：A

解析：词义辨析题。eliminate 表示"排除、消除"；abolish 表示"废止、废除（法令、制度等）"；suppress 表示"镇压、压制"；而 omit 则表示"省略、遗漏"。本句的意思是，不应该排斥所有的高热量食物。因此，正确答案应该是选项A）eliminate。

18. 答案：B

解析：近义词辨析题。这四个单词都有"选择"的意思。choice 表示"选择"；alternative 表示"两者择一、可供选择的事物"；selection 表示"选择"；而 preference 则表示"偏爱、优先选择"。本句的意思是，人们在高热量食物和低热量食物中进行选择，即两者中选其一。因此，正确答案应该是选项B）alternatives。

19. 答案：D

解析：结构搭配题。foist on 是固定搭配，表示"把……强加于某人"。因此，正确答案应该是选项 D）on。

20. 答案：B

解析：逻辑推理题。before 表示"在……以前"；when 表示"当……时候"；since 表示"自从……以来"；而 after 则表示"在……以后"。本句是很简单的时间状语从句，表示当那些成年病人还是孩子时。因此，正确答案应该是选项B）when。

Example ⑧

Directions：

Read the following text. Choose the best word(s) for each numbered blank and mark A, B, C or D on the ANSWER SHEET 1. (10 points)

Auctions are public sales of goods, conducted by an officially approved auctioneer. He asks the crowd __1__ in the auction-room to make __2__, or "bids", for the various items __3__ sale. He encourages buyers to bid __4__ figures, and finally names the highest bidder __5__ the buyer of the goods. This is called "knocking down" the goods, __6__ the bidding ends when the auctioneer __7__ a small hammer on a table __8__ which he stands. This is often set on a __9__ platform called a rostrum.

The ancient Romans probably __10__ sales by auction and the English word __11__ from the Latin "auction", meaning "increase". The Romans usually sold in this way the spoils __12__ in war; these sales were called "sub hasta", meaning "under the spear", a spear being stuck in the ground as a __13__ for a crowd to gather.

In England in the eighteenth and nineteenth centuries goods were often sold "by the candle"; a short candle was lit by the auctioneer, and bids could be made while it stayed __14__. Practically all goods whose qualities __15__ are sold by auction. An auction is usually advertised beforehand with __16__ particulars of the articles to be sold and where and when they can be viewed by __17__ buyers. The auctioneer's services are paid __18__ in the form of a percentage of the price the goods are sold for. __19__, the auctioneer has a direct __20__ in pushing up the bidding as high as possible.

1. A) assembled   B) collected   C) associated   D) concentrated
2. A) proposals   B) offers   C) propositions   D) motions
3. A) in   B) at   C) by   D) on
4. A) bigger   B) more   C) higher   D) better
5. A) with   B) to   C) as   D) for
6. A) for   B) though   C) but   D) as
7. A) noises   B) voices   C) bangs   D) rings
8. A) on   B) at   C) by   D) for
9. A) increased   B) lifted   C) raised   D) risen
10. A) invented   B) made   C) created   D) worked
11. A) copies   B) takes   C) derives   D) borrows
12. A) taken   B) brought   C) held   D) gripped
13. A) signal   B) beacon   C) mark   D) symbol
14. A) light   B) lightish   C) alight   D) lighting
15. A) shift   B) vary   C) alter   D) change
16. A) complete   B) whole   C) all   D) full
17. A) possible   B) prospective   C) occasional   D) realizable
18. A) in   B) to   C) of   D) for
19. A) Therefore   B) However   C) Furthermore   D) But
20. A) benefit   B) profit   C) interest   D) advantage

答案与解析：

1. 答案：A

   解析：词义辨析题。assemble 表示"集合、聚集"；collect 表示"收集、搜集"；associate 表示"联合、结合"；而 concentrate 则表示"集中（思想、注意力等）"。此处是指人们聚集在一起，选项 B、C 和 D 均不合适。因此，正确答案应该是选项A）assembled。

2. 答案：B

   解析：上下文推理题。proposal 表示"建议、提议"；offer 表示"提供、出价"；proposition 表示"主张、建议"；而 motion 则表示"运动、动作"。本文谈论的是拍卖，make offers 和 make bids 表示"报价"。因此，正确答案应该是选项 B）offers。

3. 答案：D

   解析：结构搭配题。on sale 是固定搭配，表示"减价处理、降价"。因此，正确答案应该是选项 D）on。

4. 答案：C

   解析：结构搭配题。报价数额用高（high）或低（low）来形容，不用大 bigger、多 more 或好 better 来形容。另外，下文提到 the highest bidder（出价最高的投标人）。因此，正确答案应该是选项 C）higher。

5. 答案：C

   解析：词义辨析题。with 表示"和……"；to 表示"给……"；as 表示"作为……"；而 for 则表示"为了……"。此处的意思是，让出价最高的投标人成为该商品的持有人。选项 A、B 和 D 均不符合题意。因此，正确答案应该是选项 C）as。

6. 答案：A

   解析：逻辑推理题。for 表示"因为……"；though 表示"虽然……"；but 表示"但是……"；而 as 则表示"当……"。此处是原因状语从句。因此，正确答案应该是选项 A）for。

7. 答案：C

   解析：词义辨析题。noise 表示"谣传、传播"；voice 表示"表达、发出声音"；bang 表示"敲、重击"；而 ring 则表示"按铃、敲钟"。根据句意，用小锤敲桌子，正确答案应该是选项 C）bangs。

8. 答案：B

   解析：词义辨析题。on 表示"在……上面"；at 表示"在……附近"；by 表示"在……旁边"；而 for 则表示"为了……"。选项 C 和 D，可以组成两个固定词组搭配，stand by（旁观）和 stand for（代表），而这两个选项不符合题意。选项 A 也不合适，因为拍卖师不可能站在桌子上进行拍卖。拍卖师是站在桌子旁主持拍卖的。因此，正确答案应该是选项 B）at。

9. 答案：C

   解析：词义辨析题。这四个选项分别是动词 increase、lift、raise 和 rise 的过去分词结构。其中，increase、lift 和 raise 是及物动词，他们的过去分词可以用作形容词作定语修饰名词。increased 表示"增加的"；lifted 表示"被举起的"；raised 表示"高出来的、凸起的"。而 rise 是不及物动词，其过去分词 risen 不能用作定语修饰名词，选项

D 首先被排除。根据句意高台,选项 A 和 B 不合适,也被排除。因此,正确答案应该是选项 C) raised。

10. 答案:B
    解析:结构搭配题。make sales 为固定搭配,表示"做买卖"。因此,正确答案应该是选项 B) made。

11. 答案:C
    解析:结构搭配题。derive from 是固定词组,表示"起源于……"。因此,正确答案应该是选项 C) derives。

12. 答案:A
    解析:近义词辨析题。take 表示"拿、获得";bring 表示"拿来、带来";hold 表示"拿着、持有";而 grip 则表示"抓住、紧握"。本句的意思是,从战争中获得的战利品。因此,正确答案应该是选项 A) taken。

13. 答案:A
    解析:词义辨析题。signal 表示"信号";beacon 表示"灯塔";mark 表示"标志、记号";而 symbol 则表示"符号、代号"。此处的意思是,发信号让人们聚集在一起。因此,正确答案应该是选项 A) signal。

14. 答案:C
    解析:词义辨析题。light 表示"明亮的、有光线的";lightish 表示"略呈淡色的、略轻的";alight 表示"点着的、发亮的";而 lighting 则是动词 light 的现在分词,表示"变亮的"。此处的意思是,点着的蜡烛。因此,正确答案应该是选项 C) alight。

15. 答案:B
    解析:词义辨析题。shift 表示"转变";vary 表示"呈现不同";而 alter 和 change 则表示"改变"。选项 A、C 和 D 在此不符合题意,此处是指商品质量各不相同。因此,正确答案应该是选项 B) vary。

16. 答案:D
    解析:近义词辨析题。这四个单词都有"全部的、所有的"的意思。complete 表示"全部的、完全的",whole 表示"所有的、完整的",这两个单词用来修饰单数名词。all 表示"全部的、所有的",修饰复数名词,在复数名词前加定冠词或代词。而 full 则表示"充满的、完全的",既可以修饰单数名词,又可以修饰复数名词。因此,正确答案应该是选项 D) full。

17. 答案:B
    解析:词义辨析题。possible 表示"可能的";prospective 表示"预期的";occasional 表示"偶然的";而 realizable 则表示"可实现的"。选项 C 和 D 与句意不符合,予以排除。选项 A 通常用来表示事物的可能性,而选项 B 通常用来形容人,表示"可能成为……的人"。由此看来,正确答案应该是选项 B) prospective。

18. 答案:D
    解析:结构搭配题。pay for 是固定搭配,表示"支付"。因此,正确答案应该是选项 D) for。

19. 答案:A

解析：逻辑推理题。therefore 表示"因此"；however 表示"然而"；furthermore 表示"此外"；而 but 则表示"但是"。根据上下文，此处表示结果。因此，正确答案应该是选项 A）Therefore。

20. 答案：C

解析：近义词辨析题。benefit 表示"利益、好处"；profit 表示"利润、收益"；interest 表示"兴趣、利益"；而 advantage 则表示"优势、好处"。选项 A 和 B 指具体买卖所得的收益，选项 C 不仅表示兴趣，还可以表示利害关系，而选项 D 指有利条件。本句的意思是，拍卖师与拍卖价格的高低有直接的利害关系。因此，正确答案应该是选项 C）interest。

Example ❾

Directions：

Read the following text. Choose the best word(s) for each numbered blank and mark A, B, C or D on the ANSWER SHEET 1. (10 points)

Marco Polo was a Venetian traveler, whose descriptions of his journey from Venice to China and back, __1__ one of the greatest books of all time. He was the first to __2__ the West of the power of China and to give an intelligible __3__ of the ways there. Marco Polo was born on an island __4__ the Dalmatian coast. His father and his father's brother were members of a noble family __5__ Dalmatian origin. They were merchants and had commercial interests in the East, where they took Marco __6__ he was 17. Marco __7__ rapid progress in the Great Khan's __8__; he studied the Mongol language and was __9__ by the emperor with various missions to different parts of his __10__. As he became a __11__ man of business, Marco made careful __12__ of his itineraries, the state of the cities, the customs of the people, and the kinds of crops and other products. __13__ 17 years travelling in the service of the Khan, Marco, together with his father and uncle, __14__ leave to return to Venice. The journey __15__ them 3 years and they arrived in 1295. Marco could not remain __16__ and in 1298 he is reported __17__ commander of a Venetian warship. In battle against the Genoese, he was __18__ prisoner. His few months as prisoner of war were the __19__ for his book. While in prison, he met Rusticiano of Risa, __20__ whom he dictated the story of his adventures. He returned to Venice after a year and died there in January, 1324.

1. A) make	B) become	C) invent	D) create

2. A) assure	B) inform	C) remind	D) deprive

3. A) note	B) account	C) calculation	D) mention

4. A) in	B) on	C) at	D) off

5. A) with	B) to	C) of	D) in

6. A) because	B) when	C) now that	D) if

7. A) took	B) did	C) made	D) had

8. A) favor	B) finger	C) track	D) way

9. A）given	B）assigned	C）entrusted	D）put
10. A）realm	B）limit	C）range	D）scope
11. A）shrewd	B）clever	C）cunning	D）sly
12. A）signs	B）notes	C）marks	D）points
13. A）Since	B）With	C）In	D）After
14. A）maintained	B）obtained	C）acknowledged	D）enabled
15. A）cost	B）spent	C）took	D）paid
16. A）still	B）inactive	C）stationary	D）unmoved
17. A）to	B）as	C）of	D）in
18. A）made	B）put	C）thrown	D）taken
19. A）reason	B）cause	C）result	D）fruit
20. A）of	B）about	C）from	D）to

答案与解析

1. 答案：A

   解析：词义辨析题。make 表示"足以成为"；become 表示"变得、变成"；invent 表示"发明"；而 create 则表示"创造"。本句的意思是，马可·波罗关于他从维尼斯到中国再从中国返回维尼斯的旅行游记成为最畅销的书之一。选项 C 和 D 不符合题意，予以排除。选项 B 指变化，有一个转变的过程，在此也不符合题意。选项 A 指"可发展为……、适宜用作……"，强调具有某种性质，尤指好的方面。因此，正确答案应该是选项 A）make。

2. 答案：B

   解析：词义辨析题。assure 表示"保证"；inform 表示"告知"；remind 表示"提醒"；而 deprive 则表示"剥夺"。选项 A、C 和 D 与句意不符。因此，正确答案应该是选项 B）inform。

3. 答案：B

   解析：词义辨析题。note 表示"笔记、注释"；account 表示"记述、报告"；calculation 表示"计算、考虑"；而 mention 则表示"提及、说起"。根据句意，此处是指叙述，选项 A、C 和 D 不符合句意。因此，正确答案应该是选项 B）account。

4. 答案：D

   解析：词义辨析题。in 表示"在……里面"；on 表示"在……上面"；at 表示"在……附近"；而 off 则表示"距离……"。此处表示马可·波罗生于靠近达尔马提亚海岸的一个岛上。因此，正确答案应该是选项 D）off。

5. 答案：C

   解析：结构搭配题。of...origin 是固定搭配，表示"出身于……"。因此，正确答案应该是选项 C）of。

6. 答案：B

   解析：逻辑推理题。because 表示"因为……"；when 表示"当……时候"；now that 表示"既然……"；而 if 则表示"如果……"。根据上下文，此处是时间状语从句。因此,正确答案应该是选项 B）when。

7. 答案：C

   解析：结构搭配题。make progress 是固定搭配,表示"进步"。因此,正确答案应该是选项 C）made。

8. 答案：A

   解析：结构搭配题。in one's favor 是固定搭配,表示"对某人有利"。因此,正确答案应该是选项 A）favor。

9. 答案：C

   解析：结构搭配题。give 表示"给",其结构是 give sb. sth. 或 give sth. to sb. ;assign 表示"分配",其结构是 assign sb. sth. 或 assign sth. to sb. ;entrust 表示"委托",其结构是 entrust sb. with sth. ;而 put 则表示"提出",其结构是 put sth. to sb. 。句中用的是介词 with,选项 A、B 和 D 均不合适。因此,正确答案应该是选项 C）entrusted。

10. 答案：A

   解析：词义辨析题。realm 表示"王国、(活动、研究等的)领域";limit 表示"界限、限度";range 表示"(可度量的)变动范围、分布区域";而 scope 则表示"(问题、题目、活动等的)范围"。此处是指可汗所统治的王国。因此,正确答案应该是选项 A）realm。

11. 答案：A

   解析：词义辨析题。shrewd 表示"精明的";clever 表示"聪明的";cunning 表示"狡猾的";而 sly 则表示"狡诈的"。a shrewd businessman 是常见的搭配,表示精明的商人。因此,正确答案应该是选项 A）shrewd。

12. 答案：B

   解析：词义辨析题。sign 表示"符号、记号";note 表示"笔记、注释";mark 表示"标志、痕迹";而 point 则表示"点、尖端"。此处的意思是,记录,选项 A、C 和 D 都不合适。因此,正确答案应该是选项 B）notes。

13. 答案：D

   解析：逻辑推理题。since 表示"从……以来";with 表示"与……";in 表示"在……以内";而 after 则表示"在……之后"。本句的意思是,在为可汗奔波了十七年之后,马可·波罗和他的父亲及叔叔得到许可回到威尼斯。因此,正确答案应该是选项 D）After。

14. 答案：B

   解析：词义辨析题。maintain 表示"维持";obtain 表示"获得";acknowledge 表示"承认";而 enable 则表示"使能够"。本句的意思是,在为可汗奔波了十七年之后,马可·波罗和他的父亲及叔叔得到许可回到威尼斯。因此,选项 A、C 和 D 都不合适,正确答案应该是选项 B）obtained。

15. 答案：C

   解析：近义词辨析题。这四个单词都有"花费"的含义。cost 表示"花……钱",主语是物,常用结构是 It costs sb. some money to do sth. ; spend 表示"花……钱、花……时间",主语是人,常用结构是 sb. spend(s) some money on sth. 和 sb. spend(s) some time doing sth. ; take 表示"花……时间",主语是事,常用结构是 It takes sb. some time to do sth. ;而 pay 则表示"花……钱",主语是人,常用结构是 sb. pay(s) some money for sth. 。本句的意思是,这次旅行花了他们三年的时间。因此,正确答案应该是选项 C) took。

16. 答案:B
    解析:近义词辨析题。这四个单词都有"不动"的含义。still 表示"静止的、一动不动的";inactive 表示"不活跃的";stationary 表示"静止的、不动的";而 unmoved 则表示"无动于衷的、冷漠的"。根据句意,马可·波罗不可能静止不动,也不可能无动于衷,而是不活跃。因此,正确答案应该是选项 B) inactive。

17. 答案:B
    解析:词义辨析题。此处的意思是,1298 年,马可·波罗被宣布为威尼斯战船的指挥官。as 表示"作为……"。因此,正确答案应该是选项 B) as。

18. 答案:D
    解析:结构搭配题。take sb. prisoner 是固定搭配,表示"俘虏某人"。因此,正确答案应该是选项 D) taken。

19. 答案:A
    解析:词义辨析题。reason 后用介词 for,表示"原因";cause 后用介词 of,表示"起因";result 表示"结果";而 fruit 则表示"成果"。选项 C 和 D 不符合句意,予以排除。而选项 B 不和介词 for 搭配,也被排除。因此,正确答案应该是选项 A) reason。

20. 答案:D
    解析:词义辨析题。of 表示"……的";about 表示"关于……";from 表示"从……";而 to 则表示"向……、对……"。此处的意思是,向某人口述某事。因此,正确答案应该是选项 D) to。

Example 11

Directions:

Read the following text. Choose the best word(s) for each numbered blank and mark A, B, C or D on the ANSWER SHEET 1. (10 points)

Now for the bad news: hostility and anger can be fatal. They not only raise the ___1___ that you will develop coronary heart disease but may also increase your risk of ___2___ other life-threatening illnesses. ___3___ yours is a hostile heart, it is important that you learn to ___4___ your anger. The driving ___5___ behind hostility is a cynical mistrust of others. If we ___6___ others to mistreat us, we are seldom disappointed. This generates anger and ___7___ us to respond with aggression. The most characteristic ___8___ of a cynic is suspicion of the ___9___ of people he doesn't know. Imagine you are waiting for an elevator and it stops two floors above for longer than ___10___. You have no ___11___ of knowing what is causing the delay. Yet, in a few seconds, you have ___12___ hostile conclusions about unseen people. Your voice changes ___13___ a higher ___14___. The rate and depth of your breathing increase. Your heart is ___15___ faster and harder, and the muscles of your arms and legs ___16___. You feel "charged up", ready for ___17___. If you frequently experience these feelings, your anger quotient is too high, and you may be ___18___ increased risk of developing serious health problems. The cumulative ___19___ of the hormones released during these anger episodes can ___20___ to the risk of coronary and other diseases.

1. A）situation   B）occurrence   C）odds   D）matter
2. A）facing   B）taking   C）suffering   D）keeping
3. A）As   B）Unless   C）If   D）When
4. A）reduce   B）cut   C）decrease   D）alleviate
5. A）force   B）power   C）pressure   D）strength
6. A）think   B）let   C）expect   D）consider
7. A）makes   B）has   C）keeps   D）leads
8. A）treatment   B）attitude   C）behavior   D）movement
9. A）motif   B）motive   C）motivation   D）motivity
10. A）usual   B）natural   C）average   D）customary
11. A）means   B）method   C）approach   D）way
12. A）made   B）found   C）drawn   D）done
13. A）for   B）of   C）to   D）into
14. A）pitch   B）degree   C）height   D）point
15. A）jumping   B）beating   C）knocking   D）striking
16. A）tighten   B）strain   C）tense   D）pinch
17. A）move   B）start   C）action   D）operation
18. A）in   B）to   C）on   D）at
19. A）influence   B）effect   C）ability   D）effort
20. A）enrich   B）increase   C）add   D）raise

答案与解析

1. 答案：C
   解析：词义辨析题。situation 表示"情形"；occurrence 表示"出现"；odds 表示"可能性"；而 matter 则表示"事件"。此处是指增加……的可能性。即使不清楚 odds 的含义，也可以用排除法得出本题的答案。选项 A、B 和 D 都不能与动词 raise 搭配，因此，正确答案应该是选项 C）odds。

2. 答案：C
   解析：词义辨析题。face 表示"面对"；take 表示"拿"；suffer 表示"遭受"；而 keep 则表示"保持"。本题的意思是，有得病的危险。选项 A、B 和 D 都不符合句意。因此，正确答案应该是选项 C）suffering。

3. 答案：C
   解析：逻辑推理题。as 表示"……的同时"；unless 表示"除非……"；if 表示"如果……"；而 when 则表示"当……时候"。此处是一种假设，因此，正确答案应该是选项 C）If。

4. 答案：A

解析：近义词辨析题。这四个单词都有"减"的含义。reduce 表示"减少、降低"，指数量的减少或程度的下降；cut 表示"删减、削减"，指将某物删除并抛弃；decrease 表示"减少、下降"，指数量上的减少；而 alleviate 则表示"减轻、缓和"，指减轻痛苦。本句的意思是，怒气程度的下降。因此，正确答案应该是选项 A）reduce。

5. 答案：A

解析：近义词辨析题。这四个单词都可以表示"力"的概念。force 表示"力量、势力"，主要指力量或力气的使用；power 表示"力量、权力"，是做某事的能力，尤指产生效果的能力；pressure 表示"压力、压迫感"；而 strength 则表示"力气、力量"，尤指身体的、精神的或道德上的坚强力量或活力。此处是说敌意的推动力。首先可以排除选项 C，pressure 不能形容 hostility。选项 B 和 D 也不合适，hostility 不可能有做某事的能力（power），也不可能有力气（strength）做某事。因此，正确答案应该是选项 A）force。

6. 答案：C

解析：结构搭配题。think、let 和 consider 后不用动词不定式结构，只有 expect sb. to do sth.，表示"期待某人做某事、预期某人做某事"。因此，正确答案应该是选项 C）expect。

7. 答案：D

解析：结构搭配题。这四个单词的搭配分别是：make sb. do sth.，表示"促使某人做某事"；have sb. do sth.，表示"促使某人做某事"；keep doing sth.，表示"继续做某事"；而 lead sb. to do sth.，则表示"诱使某人做某事"。本句用的是不定式结构 to do sth.，因此，正确答案应该是选项 D）leads。

8. 答案：B

解析：上下文推理题。treatment 表示"对待、处理"；attitude 表示"态度、看法"；behavior 表示"举止、行为"；而 movement 则表示"运动、动作"。本句有一个提示词：suspicion（怀疑），suspicion 不是 treatment、behavior 或 movement，而是 attitude。因此，正确答案应该是选项 B）attitude。

9. 答案：B

解析：词义辨析题。这四个单词拼写相近，但意思不同。motif 表示"主题"；motive 表示"动机"；motivation 表示"动力"；而 motivity 则表示"原动力"。此处的意思是，人们的动机。因此，正确答案应该是选项 B）motive。

10. 答案：A

解析：词义辨析题。usual 表示"通常的"；natural 表示"自然的"；average 表示"平均的"；而 customary 则表示"习惯的"。选项 B 和 C 不符合句意，予以排除。而选项 D 指根据风俗习惯，也不合适。此处是指经常发生的，因此，正确答案应该是选项 A）usual。

11. 答案：D

解析：结构搭配题。本题的四个单词是近义词，都可以表示"方法"。但是，have no way of doing sth. 是固定搭配，表示"无法做某事"。因此，正确答案应该是选项 D）way。

12. 答案：C

解析：结构搭配题。draw a conclusion 是固定搭配,表示"得出结论"。因此,正确答案应该是选项 C) drawn。

13. 答案：C
    解析：词义辨析题。for 表示"为了……";of 表示"……的";to 表示"向……、到……";而 into 则表示"进入到……中"。本题的意思是,到达某一程度。因此,正确答案应该是选项 C) to。

14. 答案：A
    解析：词义辨析题。pitch 表示"音高、程度";degree 表示"度、程度";height 表示"高度、身高";而 point 则表示"点、尖端"。此处是指声音,因此,正确答案应该是选项 A) pitch。

15. 答案：B
    解析：词义辨析题。jump 表示"跳跃";beat 表示"(心脏)跳动";knock 表示"敲击";而 strike 则表示"撞击"。因此,正确答案应该是选项B) beating。

16. 答案：A
    解析：近义词辨析题。这四个单词都可以表示"紧"。tighten 表示"变紧、绷紧";strain 表示"拉紧、扭伤",尤指身体某部位因过度伸展或用力而损伤;tense 表示"紧张、拉紧",通常人作主语;而 pinch 则表示"捏、夹"。根据句意,肌肉绷紧,选项 B、C 和 D 都不合适。因此,正确答案应该是选项 A) tighten。

17. 答案：C
    解析：词义辨析题。move 表示"移动、步骤";start 表示"开始、动身";action 表示"动作、行动";而 operation 则表示"运转、军事行动"。此处的意思是,准备行动。选项 A 和 B 不符合题意,而选项 D 指军事作战行动,也不合适。因此,正确答案应该是选项 C) action。

18. 答案：D
    解析：结构搭配题。at the risk of…是固定的词组搭配,表示"冒……的危险"。因此,正确答案应该是选项 D) at。

19. 答案：B
    解析：词义辨析题。influence 表示"影响";effect 表示"结果、效果";ability 表示"能力";而 effort 则表示"努力"。根据句意,此处是指结果。因此,正确答案应该是选项 B) effect。

20. 答案：C
    解析：结构搭配题。add to 是固定搭配,表示"增加"。因此,正确答案应该是选项 C) add。

Section II Use of English

Exercises

Exercise ①

Directions:

Read the following text. Choose the best word(s) for each numbered blank and mark A, B, C or D on the ANSWER SHEET 1. (10 points)

Is language, like food, a basic human need without which a child at a critical period of life can be starved or damaged? Judging from the experiment of Frederick II in the 13th century it may be. Hoping to   1   what language a child would speak if he heard no mother tongue he told the nurses to keep   2   .

All the infants died before the first year. But clearly there was more than a mere problem of   3   language. What was missing was good mothering. Without good mothering,   4   in the first year of life, the capacity to survive is seriously affected.

Today no serious lacking   5   as that ordered by Frederick.   6   , some children are still backward in speaking. Most often the reason   7   this is that the mother is insensitive   8   the clues and signals of the infant, whose brain is programmed to   9   language rapidly. There are   10   times, it seems, when children learn more readily. If these sensitive   11   are neglected, the ideal time for acquiring skills   12   and they might never be learned so easily again.

Specialists suggest that speech milestones are reached in a fixed   13   and at a constant age, but there are   14   where speech has started   15   in a child who eventually   16   to be of high intelligence.

Recent evidence suggests that an infant is born with the   17   to speak. What is special about man's brain, compared with that of the monkey, is the   18   system which enables the child to   19   the sight and feel of an object with the   20   pattern that refers to the object.

1. A) expose   B) discover   C) uncover   D) reveal
2. A) silent   B) close   C) alert   D) busy
3. A) missing   B) abandoning   C) lacking   D) dropping
4. A) nearly   B) especially   C) comparatively D) partly
5. A) happens   B) appears   C) lasts   D) exists
6. A) Thus   B) So   C) And   D) Nevertheless
7. A) of   B) about   C) to   D) for
8. A) of   B) for   C) to   D) in
9. A) pick up   B) pick at   C) pick on   D) pick out
10. A) critical   B) difficult   C) reasonable   D) clear

11.	A) ages	B) conditions	C) periods	D) circumstances
12.	A) goes	B) leaves	C) passes	D) moves
13.	A) line	B) rule	C) procession	D) sequence
14.	A) cases	B) situations	C) conditions	D) circumstances
15.	A) early	B) last	C) late	D) finally
16.	A) turns in	B) turns on	C) turns out	D) turns over
17.	A) capability	B) capacity	C) opportunity	D) possibility
18.	A) basic	B) complex	C) different	D) varied
19.	A) connect	B) associate	C) communicate	D) relate
20.	A) sound	B) voice	C) noise	D) vibration

Exercise ❷

Directions:

Read the following text. Choose the best word(s) for each numbered blank and mark A, B, C or D on the ANSWER SHEET 1. (10 points)

Urbanization and industrialization demanded new directions in education. Public education, once a dream, now became a __1__. Education was forced to __2__ new social changes. American society was getting much more complex; __3__ became more __4__. Secondary education, which had been almost totally in the hands of __5__ individuals up to the time of the Civil War, __6__ became a public concern. By the early 1900s there were over 7,000 high schools, totaling in an enrollment of over 1 million. Technological changes __7__ more vocational training. Subjects such as bookkeeping, typing, agriculture, woodworking, and metalworking were __8__ into the curriculum. American education finally was becoming universal.

Teaching __9__ also were changing. John Dewey introduced a system of progressive education, which allowed children to be put into challenging environments and to react __10__ the best of their ability. __11__ learning by rote memorization and strict discipline came __12__ attack. Practical education or "learning by doing" __13__ vogue. Compulsory attendance laws became more popular, but enforcement of them was spotty. By 1907 only about one-third of students who entered elementary school ever graduated.

Higher education also responded to the __14__ for more and different education. The Morrill Act of 1862 established state land-grant colleges that taught agricultural methods and vocational subjects. __15__ curriculums included a large number of __16__ courses during the first two years of college, more elective subjects were __17__ during the last two years. In 1876 John Hopkins University instituted America's first graduate school for __18__ study. In general, American education began to respond to the complexities of the industrial __19__ and the need for a new __20__ in education.

1.	A) reality	B) truth	C) fact	D) actuality
2.	A) satisfy	B) meet	C) face	D) challenge

3. A) commerce	B) politics	C) culture	D) literacy
4. A) communities	B) individuals	C) groups	D) teams
5. A) completely	B) fortunately	C) gradually	D) necessarily
6. A) common	B) general	C) overall	D) gradually
7. A) demanded	B) offered	C) informed	D) claimed
8. A) provided	B) introduced	C) set	D) taken
9. A) patterns	B) approaches	C) methods	D) ways
10. A) on	B) with	C) to	D) at
11. A) Traditional	B) Basic	C) Original	D) Old
12. A) in	B) under	C) at	D) on
13. A) came to	B) came in	C) came out	D) came into
14. A) need	B) interest	C) investment	D) improvement
15. A) While	B) Although	C) Whereas	D) As
16. A) free	B) fixed	C) required	D) basic
17. A) lessons	B) classes	C) themes	D) subjects
18. A) higher	B) developed	C) improved	D) advanced
19. A) age	B) time	C) period	D) history
20. A) center	B) focus	C) concentration	D) emphasis

Exercise ❸

Directions:

Read the following text. Choose the best word(s) for each numbered blank and mark A, B, C or D on the ANSWER SHEET 1. (10 points)

Detroit has some of the most beautiful residential neighborhoods in the USA and at the same time some of the most shocking slums. In downtown Detroit there are some ___1___ skyscrapers and expensive restaurants and stores, and right on the ___2___ of the downtown area, facing Canada across the busy Detroit River, is the waterfront, and its civic center, with parks and a concert hall, ___3___ of the renowned Detroit Symphony Orchestra. This concert hall, called the Ford Auditorium, is a reminder that Detroit ___4___ its rapid growth and one-time ___5___ to the automobile, and above all to Henry Ford.

Henry Ford did not ___6___ the automobile, but he was the first man to mass-produce it, and thus make it ___7___ to the ordinary man. Many automobiles were being built by hand ___8___ the turn of the century and were much too expensive for all but the wealthy. In 1903 Henry Ford's first, mass-produced Model T cars ___9___ $850. By the early 1920s he was able to ___10___ the price to $350. Between 1903 and 1927 Ford manufactured 15 million Model T Fords and earned a(n) ___11___ of $700 million. In 1927 he produced his sedan Model A, which was much more ___12___ than the open, wind-swept Model T.

Ford's basic ___13___ of $5 a day caused not only a wages explosion in the city; it also caused a __14__ explosion. Blacks from the south __15__ into the city, __16__ there were almost as many blacks in Detroit as whites. Other industries connected with the automobile were __17__ to Detroit, and more and more factories __18__ in and around the city. Other automobile corporations also __19__ Detroit their headquarters. General Motors, an amalgamation of Chevrolet, Cadillac, Oldsmobile and Buick, built factories in Detroit as did Chrysler. In the 1960s, one __20__ three people who lived in Detroit worked in the Automobile industry.

1. A) tall   B) fine   C) high   D) lofty
2. A) line   B) border   C) edge   D) rim
3. A) home   B) place   C) spot   D) area
4. A) contributes   B) puts   C) owes   D) grants
5. A) fortune   B) wealth   C) explosion   D) prosperity
6. A) discover   B) design   C) organize   D) invent
7. A) acceptable   B) available   C) accessible   D) achievable
8. A) at   B) with   C) on   D) by
9. A) pay   B) take   C) cost   D) charge
10. A) lessen   B) decrease   C) drop   D) reduce
11. A) interest   B) profit   C) property   D) benefit
12. A) small   B) approximate   C) comfortable   D) complete
13. A) pay   B) wage   C) income   D) salary
14. A) people   B) persons   C) residents   D) population
15. A) poured   B) travelled   C) moved   D) came
16. A) until   B) before   C) when   D) while
17. A) persuaded   B) forced   C) attracted   D) introduced
18. A) went up   B) sprang up   C) came up   D) turned up
19. A) made   B) put   C) set   D) took
20. A) of   B) from   C) in   D) to

Exercise ❹

Directions:

Read the following text. Choose the best word(s) for each numbered blank and mark A, B, C or D on the ANSWER SHEET 1. (10 points)

With the support of tobacco industry representatives, the House passed a bill late last month that would set a three-year deadline for the development of a cigarette designed to reduce the __1__ of fire.

The __2__ directs the Consumer Product Safety Commission to develop a standard test method to __3__ the risks posed by __4__ cigarettes, says John Delano, a spokesman __5__ Pennsylvania Democrat Doug Walgren, chairman __6__ the House Energy and Commerce Subcommittee on Commerce, Consumer Protection and Competitiveness, which first __7__ the bill. "The __8__ line is, we're giving CPSC three years to __9__ the details for a fire-safe cigarette," Delano says, adding that fires caused by smoking __10__ "30 percent of all residential fire deaths and $295 million in property __11__" a year.

A safer cigarette has occupied Congress and industry researchers __12__ research in the mid-Eighties "concluded that the technology was there," Delano says. Thomas Lauria, from the Tobacco Institute, which backs the bill, says that __13__ congressional pressure, "you cannot order science to go __14__ than it can go." He says prototypes of loosely packed tobacco in less porous paper "don't act or __15__ like a cigarette. If you __16__ a cigarette much more loosely, it will __17__ after only a few puffs, which would __18__ theory be more fire-safe, but the __19__ is that smokers would have to draw on it __20__."

1. A) loss   B) burning   C) threat   D) possibility
2. A) way   B) method   C) approach   D) measure
3. A) take   B) incur   C) suffer   D) measure
4. A) dangerous   B) different   C) lit   D) packed
5. A) for   B) of   C) in   D) at
6. A) for   B) of   C) in   D) at
7. A) disapproved   B) approved   C) rejected   D) allowed
8. A) final   B) last   C) bottom   D) ultimate
9. A) come in   B) come out   C) come to   D) come up with
10. A) result in   B) contribute to   C) relate to   D) connect with
11. A) damage   B) harm   C) hurt   D) suffering
12. A) when   B) while   C) since   D) as
13. A) besides   B) with   C) under   D) despite
14. A) faster   B) further   C) sooner   D) farther
15. A) look   B) taste   C) feel   D) smell
16. A) wrap   B) pack   C) envelop   D) enfold
17. A) go by   B) go down   C) go out   D) go off
18. A) of   B) about   C) in   D) on
19. A) key   B) problem   C) core   D) center
20. A) harder   B) faster   C) more often   D) more frequently

Exercise ❺

Directions:

Read the following text. Choose the best word(s) for each numbered blank and mark A, B, C or D on the ANSWER SHEET 1. (10 points)

More and more residences, businesses, and even government agencies are using telephone answering machines to take messages or give information or instructions. Sometimes these machines give confusing instructions, or __1__ messages that are __2__ to understand. If you make telephone calls, you need to be ready to respond if you get a(n) __3__.

The most __4__ machine is the type used in __5__. If you call a home where there is a telephone answering machine in __6__ you will hear several __7__ and then a recorded message that __8__ says something like this, "Hello. We can't come to the phone right now. If you want us to call you back, please __9__ your name and number after the beep." Then you will hear a beep, which is a brief, high-pitched tone. After the beep, you can __10__ who you are, whom you want to speak __11__, and what number the person should call to reach you, or you can leave a message. Some telephone answering machines record __12__ only 20 or 30 seconds after the beep, so you must respond quickly.

Some large businesses and government agencies are using telephone answering machines to __13__ information __14__ topics about which they receive a large volume of inquires. Using these systems __15__ you to have a touch-tone phone(a phone with buttons rather than a rotary dial). The __16__ on the machine will tell you to push a certain button on your telephone if you want information about Topic A, another button __17__ Topic B, and so on. You listen __18__ you hear the topic you want to learn about, and then you push the __19__ button. __20__ making your selection, you will hear a recorded message on the topic.

1. A) have   B) leave   C) play   D) show
2. A) difficult   B) direct   C) different   D) definite
3. A) answer   B) message   C) problem   D) recording
4. A) confusing   B) satisfactory   C) common   D) general
5. A) agencies   B) residences   C) governments   D) companies
6. A) operation   B) fashion   C) usage   D) case
7. A) words   B) rings   C) sounds   D) voices
8. A) eventually   B) usually   C) frequently   D) quickly
9. A) leave   B) provide   C) tell   D) introduce
10. A) say   B) speak   C) tell   D) talk
11. A) of   B) on   C) to   D) about
12. A) in   B) within   C) for   D) at
13. A) present   B) produce   C) provide   D) promote
14. A) in   B) on   C) for   D) of
15. A) requires   B) forces   C) has   D) invites
16. A) voice   B) sound   C) sentence   D) information
17. A) of   B) on   C) with   D) for
18. A) as   B) when   C) while   D) until
19. A) certain   B) appropriate   C) exact   D) numbered
20. A) As   B) After   C) Before   D) Until

Exercise 6

Directions:

Read the following text. Choose the best word(s) for each numbered blank and mark A, B, C or D on the ANSWER SHEET 1. (10 points)

In most large cities stoves burn what is called "city gas". In country areas bottled gas is often used for stoves. Some people __1__ electric stoves even though they are __2__ to heat, because the heat is considered more even.

Most U. S. heating system today are oil burners __3__ by electric motors or else coal furnaces.

__4__ apartment buildings are nearly always __5__ with centrally operated air conditioning which can be __6__ by the occupants of each apartment. If you live in an older house, it is likely to have window air conditioners. If there are no window units and the need is great, one can rent air conditioners __7__ a monthly basis for the few hot months.

Normally __8__ for gas and electricity are not included in the monthly rent. Both bills will come from the electric company, but the gas bill will be itemized __9__.

Most of the country has 110—120 volt current, 60 cycles, A. C. A few older houses and areas are still wired for D. C. __10__ your own small appliances are geared for U. S. current or have been converted, you are well advised to __11__ them home. For small items, transformers can be a nuisance, __12__ they work well for major appliances such as refrigerators or stoves. However, you can buy all kinds of appliances here __13__ reasonable prices.

In most cities there is no __14__ for water, but outside city limits it may be metered, __15__ which case you pay either monthly or quarterly. Water rates are __16__.

You can drink water __17__ from taps anywhere in the U. S. DO NOT drink from brooks, wells, streams, or rivers, however. __18__ is, alas, widespread.

Tap water may taste __19__ because it contains a high __20__ of purifying chemicals. If you find this obnoxious, you can buy bottled water in the supermarket.

1. A) value   B) prefer   C) praise   D) appreciate
2. A) faster   B) easier   C) safer   D) slower
3. A) done   B) forced   C) operated   D) made
4. A) Recent   B) Present   C) Fashionable   D) Modern
5. A) armed   B) equipped   C) presented   D) provided
6. A) adjusted   B) operated   C) run   D) determined
7. A) under   B) on   C) over   D) in
8. A) fees   B) pay   C) rent   D) money
9. A) differently   B) individually   C) separately   D) specially
10. A) Although   B) When   C) Unless   D) If
11. A) bring   B) take   C) set   D) leave
12. A) although   B) unless   C) if   D) when

13.	A) on	B) at	C) of	D) by
14.	A) money	B) charge	C) rent	D) pay
15.	A) of	B) under	C) in	D) at
16.	A) few	B) small	C) little	D) low
17.	A) safely	B) immediately	C) quickly	D) conveniently
18.	A) Risk	B) Danger	C) Pollution	D) Hurt
19.	A) different	B) strange	C) strong	D) unpleasant
20.	A) amount	B) number	C) part	D) percentage

Exercise ❼

Directions：

Read the following text. Choose the best word(s) for each numbered blank and mark A, B, C or D on the ANSWER SHEET 1. (10 points)

The Los Angeles Marathon ran particularly smoothly this year, and part of the credit is going to a digital radio tag worn by the contestants. The device ___1___ and times each runner along the route to a(n) ___2___ of 0.1 second, making the determination of who finished when ___3___ than ever before.

Worn like a wristwatch, the tag contains a small transponder that ___4___ an identifying signal to a receiving station. As runners cross timing points, antennas along the route ___5___ their identification number signals.

The device is viewed ___6___ a major ___7___ over the method now widely used, ___8___ which each runner wears a numbered bib with a ___9___ strip, which is ___10___ as he crosses the finish line. At the same time, a person operating a counter is ___11___ to mark the time and ___12___ of each racer's finish.

Using the digital radio tag usually requires only two people to ___13___ runners' times as they are displayed, ___14___ many big races now employ as many as 60 or 70 people to tabulate results.

Errors are often made when thousands of contestants must be identified and accounted ___15___ manually as they cross the finish line, says John Morgan, president of American Sports Timing Systems Inc. of Topsfield, Mass., the maker of the device used in Los Angeles. "I can't say it happens ___16___ but I have seen it happen in some of the large marathon events," he says. "This device ___17___ changes and improves the ___18___ a race is timed."

This device and others like it are being used in triathlons, cycling and wind surfing ___19___, and companies as large as American Telephone & Telegraph Co. are also beginning to ___20___ their manufacture.

1.	A) monitors	B) tells	C) sees	D) identifies
2.	A) time	B) result	C) degree	D) accuracy
3.	A) easier	B) safer	C) clearer	D) wiser
4.	A) transits	B) transmits	C) translates	D) transforms

5. A) pick up   B) pick out   C) pick off   D) pick over

6. A) as   B) for   C) to   D) of

7. A) development   B) advancement   C) improvement   D) promotion

8. A) of   B) in   C) on   D) by

9. A) separate   B) single   C) detachable   D) different

10. A) pulled away   B) pulled off   C) pulled out   D) pulled down

11. A) put   B) pushed   C) supposed   D) set

12. A) sequence   B) time   C) role   D) order

13. A) see   B) monitor   C) control   D) decide

14. A) as   B) though   C) and   D) whereas

15. A) on   B) for   C) to   D) into

16. A) regularly   B) continuously   C) continually   D) steadily

17. A) importantly   B) significantly   C) essentially   D) meaningfully

18. A) approach   B) method   C) way   D) means

19. A) events   B) races   C) cases   D) occasions

20. A) study   B) research   C) do   D) explore

Exercise ❽

Directions:

Read the following text. Choose the best word(s) for each numbered blank and mark A, B, C or D on the ANSWER SHEET 1. (10 points)

The Constitution of the United States was written to insure liberty and justice for all Americans who owned property. It __1__ slaves, children and women. For the following years, a __2__ battle was waged against a male __3__ power structure in order to secure this __4__ right.

When the women's suffrage movement began, women were not allowed to control property, earnings, or __5__ free high schools. __6__, women organized the National Women Suffrage Association which gathered petitions, held rallies, and __7__ newspapers to persuade Congress to pass an amendment allowing women to vote.

The first __8__ came in 1870. __9__ it was not until 1920 that Congress finally passed the amendment granting suffrage __10__ all women of the land.

Southern Democrats were against granting women the vote. The liquor interests __11__ the measure. Political __12__ were afraid that women voters would be more moral and favor more reforms than men. Many business interests were afraid that women would try to __13__ their working conditions.

__14__ presenting petitions, staging demonstrations, and going to jail, women proved their __15__ to fight until their vote was __16__. One such demonstration __17__ the day before President Wilson was to be inaugurated. Five thousand women marched in their suffrage pageant.

Today, the new women's rights __18__ seeks to change attitudes __19__ traditional sex

__20__ and change economic conditions for women.

1. A) left off   B) left out   C) turned to   D) turned down
2. A) cruel   B) fierce   C) serious   D) violent
3. A) commanded   B) determined   C) dominated   D) supervised
4. A) civil   B) favorite   C) pleasant   D) political
5. A) achieve   B) attend   C) get   D) receive
6. A) However   B) Therefore   C) Though   D) Yet
7. A) delivered   B) made   C) produced   D) ran
8. A) chance   B) event   C) opportunity   D) victory
9. A) And   B) But   C) However   D) Then
10. A) for   B) into   C) to   D) with
11. A) declined   B) fought   C) objected   D) opposed
12. A) agents   B) departments   C) machines   D) interests
13. A) improve   B) develop   C) promote   D) advance
14. A) By   B) With   C) From   D) On
15. A) determination   B) decision   C) intent   D) purpose
16. A) passed   B) won   C) presented   D) received
17. A) appeared   B) happened   C) occurred   D) took place
18. A) action   B) activity   C) move   D) movement
19. A) about   B) of   C) on   D) to
20. A) conditions   B) situations   C) roles   D) parts

Exercise ❾

Directions:

Read the following text. Choose the best word(s) for each numbered blank and mark A, B, C or D on the ANSWER SHEET 1. (10 points)

A seeing-eye computer spots a telephone pole located 18 feet ahead at one o'clock. In about a second, it voices the word pole and indicates the direction and distance of the hazard by stimulating the __1__ of its blind user. This is just one of many new __2__ that have brought computers to the __3__ of the handicapped.

The brainchild of Carter Collins, of the Smith-Kettlewell Institute in San Francisco, the seeing-eye computer is __4__ being tested __5__ several blind people. A miniature TV camera propped over the ear sends pictures to a microcomputer that verbally identifies __6__ hazards within 20 feet. Stereophonic sound lets a user __7__ the direction of the objects; a tapping on the forehead __8__ the number of feet __9__. Collins believes it is __10__ to miniaturize the system; the camera would be __11__ in eyeglasses and the computer, now housed in a cart that is pushed by one of the Collins team, would be carried in a shoulder bag.

Physicist William Dobpelle of the Institute for Artificial Organism New York, and neurosurgeon

John Girvin, of the University of Western Ontario, have gone even   12   . They've implanted devices   13   as many as 64 electrodes on the visual cortices of a small number of   14   volunteers. A(n)   15   taken with a TV camera is translated by computer   16   electrical pulses, which cause the electrodes to   17   the brain. Patients have been able to see dots of light in patterns resembling the   18   image. The goal is to invent a miniature TV camera that could fit in a glass eye and be   19   ,   20   a computer in eye-glass frame, to as many as 512 electrodes in the brain.

1. A) face   B) skin   C) arm   D) hand
2. A) appliances   B) instruments   C) devices   D) tools
3. A) need   B) support   C) aid   D) convenience
4. A) currently   B) shortly   C) presently   D) temporarily
5. A) in   B) at   C) to   D) on
6. A) potential   B) obvious   C) serious   D) existing
7. A) situate   B) locate   C) settle   D) place
8. A) explains   B) exposes   C) indicates   D) reveals
9. A) away   B) ahead   C) before   D) forward
10. A) available   B) favorable   C) sensible   D) feasible
11. A) carried   B) prepared   C) supported   D) mounted
12. A) faster   B) further   C) sooner   D) nearer
13. A) retaining   B) containing   C) sustaining   D) obtaining
14. A) deaf   B) dumb   C) blind   D) disable
15. A) description B) representation C) symbol   D) image
16. A) into   B) in   C) on   D) at
17. A) call   B) stimulate   C) tell   D) influence
18. A) old   B) early   C) original   D) primary
19. A) linked   B) related   C) associated   D) connected
20. A) through   B) from   C) via   D) by

Exercise ⑪

Directions:

Read the following text. Choose the best word(s) for each numbered blank and mark A, B, C or D on the ANSWER SHEET 1. (10 points)

Man talks. He communicates. By speech he   1   to others his experience and thoughts, his hopes and fears by means of   2   sounds. As he does, men listen and   3   . This is true   4   all communities of men, from the most   5   to the most sophisticated.

There are, all in all, many ways of communication. Hand   6   , shrugs, nods, smoke signals and   7   on paper are a few of these. But the sounds made by man's vocal organs are basic; the   8   of sounds that form with them are the   9   materials of language. Each language community has a different ___10___ of rules, for stringing together sounds so that when one speaks, another one understands what is said. Among the more than 3,000 languages known to ___11___ in the world, only ___12___ a few have a ___13___ of the language. Those that have such a form have, ___14___, a grammatical system that is much less complex than our own. Some systems are ___15___ more complex. The fact that the language has such a form does not ___16___ mean its grammatical system is superior ___17___ the grammatical system of a language that has no such a form. If a language ___18___ the needs of those who used it, it is very ___19___ to judge it to be better or worse than a(n) ___20___ standard of our own.

1. A) transits   B) translates   C) transmits   D) transforms
2. A) spoken   B) oral   C) different   D) clear
3. A) analyze   B) feel   C) experience   D) comprehend
4. A) to   B) with   C) for   D) of
5. A) beginning   B) simple   C) primitive   D) early
6. A) signals   B) signatures   C) signs   D) signification
7. A) margins   B) spots   C) marks   D) points
8. A) methods   B) functions   C) uses   D) patterns
9. A) raw   B) different   C) various   D) original
10. A) kind   B) set   C) sort   D) group
11. A) grow   B) develop   C) exist   D) appear
12. A) considerately   B) comparably   C) comparatively   D) considerably
13. A) writing   B) rule   C) standard   D) form
14. A) yet   B) therefore   C) thus   D) nevertheless
15. A) almost   B) too   C) extremely   D) far
16. A) permanently   B) necessarily   C) nearly   D) truly
17. A) for   B) with   C) than   D) to
18. A) provides   B) asks   C) satisfies   D) solves
19. A) reasonable   B) considerable   C) unrealistic   D) meaningful
20. A) imagined   B) basic   C) known   D) common

IV. 参考答案
Exercise 1
1. B 2. A 3. C 4. B 5. D 6. D 7. D 8. C 9. A 10. A 11. C 12. C
13. D 14. A 15. C 16. C 17. B 18. B 19. A 20. A

Exercise 2
1. A 2. B 3. D 4. B 5. C 6. D 7. A 8. B 9. C 10. C 11. A 12. B
13. D 14. A 15. A 16. C 17. D 18. D 19. A 20. B

Exercise 3

1. B　2. C　3. A　4. C　5. D　6. D　7. B　8. A　9. C　10. D　11. B　12. C
13. B　14. D　15. A　16. A　17. C　18. B　19. A　20. C

Exercise 4

1. C　2. D　3. D　4. B　5. A　6. B　7. B　8. C　9. D　10. A　11. A　12. C
13. D　14. A　15. B　16. A　17. C　18. C　19. B　20. A

Exercise 5

1. C　2. A　3. D　4. C　5. B　6. A　7. B　8. B　9. A　10. A　11. C　12. C
13. C　14. B　15. A　16. A　17. D　18. D　19. B　20. B

Exercise 6

1. B　2. D　3. C　4. D　5. B　6. A　7. B　8. A　9. C　10. C　11. D　12. A
13. B　14. B　15. C　16. D　17. A　18. C　19. D　20. D

Exercise 7

1. D　2. D　3. A　4. B　5. A　6. A　7. C　8. B　9. C　10. B　11. C　12. D
13. B　14. D　15. B　16. A　17. B　18. C　19. A　20. D

Exercise 8

1. B　2. B　3. C　4. D　5. B　6. A　7. D　8. D　9. B　10. C　11. D　12. C
13. A　14. A　15. A　16. B　17. D　18. D　19. D　20. C

Exercise 9

1. B　2. C　3. C　4. A　5. D　6. A　7. B　8. C　9. A　10. D　11. D　12. B
13. B　14. C　15. D　16. A　17. B　18. C　19. A　20. C

Exercise 10

1. C　2. B　3. D　4. A　5. C　6. A　7. C　8. D　9. A　10. B　11. C　12. C
13. A　14. D　15. D　16. B　17. D　18. C　19. C　20. A

第四单元
阅读与理解

本单元分为三节（A、B、C），主要考察内容：要点、策略、精选和解析。也就是说，根据《大纲》的要求，指导学生阅读训练时要有一定的针对性。并且对阅读材料进行详细的解析，帮助学生掌握阅读的相关技巧，以便尽快地提高学生的阅读能力和应变能力。

I. 阅读与理解 A 节

1. 测试要点

《大纲》要求考生能读懂英美国家的各类书籍和报刊上的不同类型的文字材料和各种体裁的文章（短文），其中生词量不超过 3%。同时也要能读懂有关专业文章以及有关技术资料说明和产品介绍等方面的材料。具体要点如下：

1）读懂主旨要义和文章信息；

2）对文中的生词词义猜测和文章意思进行逻辑推理、判断和意义引申；

3）弄清上下文的语言结构关系；

4）弄懂作者的写作意图、目的、观点和态度；

5）弄清文中的论点和论据。

阅读是考试中的重要部分。主要考察考生对语篇意义的理解，而这又需通过词汇、短语、句型、习惯表达、语法结构、语用表达方式等语言知识技能的掌握，才能实现对语篇意义的理解。这就要求考生做到以下几点：

2. 扩大阅读量

尽量多阅读英语国家的政治、经济、科技、文化、历史、地理、社会生活等背景资料的文章，而这些文章涵盖着两个方面——自然科学和人文社会科学，反映当代的国际问题和社会问题，绝大多数是议论、评论、报导、分析和论证类的文章，概括性强，侧重抽象思维。考生根据上述提供的信息去进行阅读。

3. 扩大词汇量

首先要掌握基本词汇（《大纲》中规定的词汇）。使在阅读中尽量少出现生词，减少"拦路虎"。实际上在一篇文章中遇上几个生词，不一定会影响对文章的理解，考生可以根据上下文综观全文的意思以及利用构词法知识去进行判断、猜测。

4. 善于掌握阅读方法

解题前，考生可以掠读（skimming）全文。掠读时，不需要仔细地、透彻地去理解，只需要了解文章的大概内容,作者的立场、观点、态度以及文章的篇章结构,此时可以跳过细节或例子,为你的答题铺平道路,提高阅读效率。

另一种方法就是略读或查读(scanning)。考生在解题时,必须要去寻找特定的信息(如主题句、有关文章的细节、难句子等)。这种阅读方法是对材料已有所了解的情况下进行的,并且一定记住所需信息中最独特的词组、数字和符号(如生词、百分比、年代日期、货币代号等)。

5. 加快阅读速度

考生做阅读理解的参考时间为 60 分钟。在这个时间内,要阅读完几篇文章,理解好这几篇文章并且做好答题,这的确不是轻而易举就能完成的,需要提高阅读速度。除了全神贯注外,还要学会扩大视幅,就是要按照意义单位移动目光,而非一个词一个词去研读。一眼就可以扫视几个词汇,按意群成组视读,只要习惯了就不会影响理解词义。只要掌握文中的主要信息,关键性内容,就会提高阅读效率。

6. 解题技巧

实现把题型进行分类:1)事实/细节题;2)是非题/排除题;3)推理题;4)语义题。

事实/细节题:根据文章的某个具体事实或细节提出来的,用以考察学生理解书面材料中具体内容的能力。此题有两大特点:一是与文中某个事实直接相关。做题时可以采取"对号入座"的方式进行,即带着问题找句子。二是从字面上看,答案与原文差异较大。这就要求考生能准确地理解原文中与问题相关的某一段或某一句话。做题时要仔细地分析推敲此类事实和细节问题。

是非题/排除题:测试考生理解书面材料中具体内容的能力,并以文章的基本事实和文章中的有关细节为依据辨明是非的能力。

推理题:这类题做起来有一定难度。它的答案一般不能从原文中直接找到,而是要根据所提供的信息进行分析、推理、综合,然后作出合乎逻辑的推断。具体的做法是:① 推理文章的主题(three forms:topic sentence/questions, title questions, type questions),② 考生推理出作者的观点和态度。这个方面的内容可以从文章中的措词、文体风格和语言结构中发现。③ 考生推理文章上下文之间的逻辑关系。做此类题时,考生可以依据文章中的句型、语言结构、表达形式和内容,进行认真仔细地归纳、比较、分析研究,最后方可得出正确的答案。

语义题:要求考生能根据文章上下文所表达的意思,来分析、判断《大纲》外的某些词语或短语的含义,并能判断某个词或短语在句中的特定的含义。所要猜测的词可能是常用词或短语,也可能是较为偏僻的词或短语。这两种情况都需要考生认真仔细地读懂其前后的句子,然后判断它在上下文中的确切含义。

Part A

1) 例题及答案详解

Example ①

It is a wise father that knows his own child, but today a man can boost his paternal (fatherly) wisdom—or at least confirm that he's the kid's dad. All he needs to do is shell our $30 for paternity testing kit (PTK) at his local drugstore—and another $120 to get the results.

More than 60,000 people have purchased the PTKs since they first become available without prescriptions last year, according to Doug Fog, chief operating officer of Identigene, which makes the over-the-counter kits. More than two dozen companies sell DNA tests directly to the public, ranging in price from a few hundred dollars to more than $2,500.

Among the most popular: paternity and kinship testing, which adopted children can use to find their biological relatives and families can use to track down kids put up for adoption. DNA testing is also the latest rage a many passionate genealogists—and supports businesses that offer to search for a family's geographic roots.

Most tests require collecting cells by webbing saliva in the mouth and sending it to the company for testing. All tests require a potential candidate with whom to compare DNA.

But some observers are skeptical, "There is a kind of false precision being hawked by people claiming they are doing ancestry testing," says Trey Duster, a New York University sociologist. He notes that each individual has many ancestors—numbering in the hundreds just a few centuries back. Yet most ancestry testing only considers a single lineage, either the Y chromosome inherited through men in a father's line or mitochondrial DNA, which is passed down only from mothers. This DNA can reveal genetic information about only one or two ancestors, even though, for example, just three generations back people also have six other great-grandparents or, four generations back, 14 other great-great-grandparents.

Critics also argue that commercial genetic testing is only as good as the reference collections to which a sample is compared. Databases used by some companies don't rely on data collected systematically but rather lump together information from different research projects. This means that a DNA database may differ depending on the company that processes the results. In addition, the computer programs a company uses to estimate relationships may be patented and not subject to peer review or outside evaluation. （2009 真题）

1. In Paragraphs 1 and 2, the test shows PTK's _____.

    A. easy availability   B. flexibility in pricing

    C. successful promotion   D. popularity with households

2. PTK is used to _____.

    A. locate one's birth place   B. promote genetic research

    C. identify parent-child kinship   D. choose children for adoption

3. Skeptical observers believe that ancestry testing fails to _____.

    A. trace distant ancestors   B. rebuild reliable bloodlines

    C. fully use genetic information   D. achieve the claimed accuracy

4. In the last paragraph, a problem commercial genetic testing faces is _____.

    A. disorganized data collection   B. overlapping database building

    C. unreliable computer program   D. difficult sample selection

5. An appropriate title for the text is mostly likely to be _____.

A. Fors and againsts of DNA Testing	B. DNA testing and its problems
C. DNA testing outside the lab	D. Lies behind DNA testing

【答案与解析】

1. 推理题。问题是从第一二段文章表明什么。文中第一二段有多处体现,如首段最后一句话"只需花 30 美元在地方药房作亲子鉴定……"以及第二段第一句又谈到"自从去年不需要处方即可购买之后,已经超过 6 万人购买了 PTK",这都表明 PTK 很容易买到。B 项关于鉴定价格浮动只在第二段最后一句有所体现,C 选项项文中未提到,D 选项属过度推断,因此答案选 A。

2. 细节题。问题是 PTK 是用来做什么的。从文中第三段可以看到"被收养的孩子可以通过亲子鉴定找到他具有血缘关系的亲属"。A 选项比较具有迷惑性,根据第四段后半句"PTK 最近惹怒了很多谱系学家,他们支持用 PTK 来探寻一个家族的祖籍"可以看出 PTK 没有主要被用来寻找一个人的出生地,所以不选 A;而选项 B 和 D 文中并未提及,因此正确答案选 C。

3. 细节题。问题是持怀疑态度的观察者认为祖先鉴定没能做到什么。根据题干信息可以将答案定位到文中第五段第一句。由这一句可以看出:"那些正在做祖先鉴定的人们所宣扬的(祖先鉴定)精确度其实是错的"。这句话是对这一段的概括,ABC 三个选项都只是它的细节之一。因此,只有 D 选项正确。

4. 细节题。问题是最后一段中商业基因鉴定面临的一个问题是什么。从最后一段第二句可以看出"一些公司使用的数据库并不依赖于系统的数据收集而是把不同研究机构收集的信息结合在一起。这就意味着处理数据的公司不同,所用 DNA 数据库也会不同"。文中并未提及数据是否重合,所以 B 选项无根据,而选项 C 和 D 在文中没有体现,因此正确答案只有 A。

5. 主旨题。问题是本文最合适的题目是什么。由于从文中看不到作者有明显赞成 DNA 测试的倾向,因此不选 A;文中也没有特别强调实验室内外的问题,因此 C 选项也不对;作者只是客观地提出了 DNA 测试存在的不准确性问题,但并没有指明是哪些人的谎言,所以 D 选项也不能选,因此正确答案只有 B。

Example ❷

If you were to examine the birth certificates of every soccer player in 2006's World Cup tournament, you would most likely find a noteworthy quirk: elite soccer players are more likely to have been born in the earlier months of the year than in the later months. If you then examined the European national youth teams that feed the World Cup and professional ranks, you would find this strange phenomenon to be even more pronounced.

What might account for this strange phenomenon? Here are a few guesses: a) certain astrological signs confer superior soccer skills; b) winter-born babies tend to have higher oxygen capacity, which increases soccer stamina; c) soccer-mad parents are more likely to conceive children in springtime, at the annual peak of soccer mania; d) none of the above.

Anders Ericsson, a 58-year-old psychology professor at Florida State University, says he believes strongly in "none of the above". Ericsson grew up in Sweden, and studied nuclear engineering until he realized he would have more opportunity to conduct his own research if he switched to psychology. His first experiment, nearly 30 years ago, involved memory: training a person to hear and then repeat a random series of numbers. "With the first subject, after about 20 hours of training, his digit span had risen from 7 to 20," Ericsson recalls. "He kept improving, and after about 200 hours of training he had risen to over 80 numbers."

This success, coupled with later research showing that memory itself is not genetically determined, led Ericsson to conclude that the act of memorizing is more of a cognitive exercise than an intuitive one. In other words, whatever inborn differences two people may exhibit in their abilities to memorize, those differences are swamped by how well each person "encodes" the information. And the best way to learn how to encode information meaningfully, Ericsson determined, was a process known as deliberate practice. Deliberate practice entails more than simply repeating a task. Rather, it involves setting specific goals, obtaining immediate feedback and concentrating as much on technique as on outcome.

Ericsson and his colleagues have thus taken to studying expert performers in a wide range of pursuits, including soccer. They gather all the data they can, not just performance statistics and biographical details but also the results of their own laboratory experiments with high achievers. Their work makes a rather startling assertion: the trait we commonly call talent is highly overrated. Or, put another way, expert performers—whether in memory or surgery, ballet or computer programming—are nearly always made, not born. (2007 年真题)

1. The birthday phenomenon found among soccer players is mentioned to _____.
   A. stress the importance of professional training
   B. spotlight the soccer superstars at the World Cup
   C. introduce the topic of what makes expert performance
   D. explain why some soccer teams play better than others

2. The word "mania" (Line 4, Paragraph 2) most probably means _____.
   A. fun   B. craze   C. hysteria   D. excitement

3. According to Ericsson, good memory _____.
   A. depends on meaningful processing of information
   B. results from intuitive rather than cognitive exercises
   C. is determined by genetic rather than psychological factors
   D. requires immediate feedback and a high degree of concentration

4. Ericsson and his colleagues believe that _____.
   A. talent is a dominating factor for professional success
   B. biographical data provide the key to excellent performance
   C. the role of talent tends to be overlooked
   D. high achievers owe their success mostly to nurture

5. Which of the following proverbs is closest to the message the text tries to convey?
   A. "Faith will move mountains."   B. "One reaps what one sows."
   C. "Practice makes perfect."   D. "Like father, like son."

【答案与解析】

1. 推理题。根据题干中的定位信息"The birthday phenomenon found among soccer players"迅速找到文章的第一段。在此作者提到一个怪现象，即出色的足球运动员更可能出生在一年内的前几个月而不是后几个月，却并未在该段立刻对其做进一步解释说明，显然作者是想通过举例的方式引出文章主题，因此应该在下文中寻找答案。通过浏览后面的内容可知，Ericsson 和他的同事们致力于研究不同领域技艺精湛的从业者取得成就的原因，且作者在文章最后给出了答案，故 C 为正确答案。

2. 词汇题。首先找出"mania"出现第二段。本段对上一段提到的怪现象提出了四种推断性的解释，其中第三个解释中出现了"soccer-mad parents"一词，既然是足球疯狂的父母，那么他们选择在足球狂热的季节孕育孩子也不足为奇了，此处的"soccer mania"是"soccer mad"的同义词，因此正确答案选 B。

3. 细节题。在第三段 Ericsson 给出一个有关记忆的例子，然后在第四段对该题研究进行了说明。第四段第二句明确指出好的记忆力不是天生的，而是由个人解码信息能力的强弱决定的，这与 A 选项意思一致，故答案为 A。

4. 细节题。文章最后一句对 Ericsson 及其同事的研究结论进行了总结：那些技艺精湛的从业者，无论记忆力超群者，还是专家级外科医生，无论是卓越的芭蕾舞演员还是出色的计算机程序员，他们几乎都是后天练就的，而非天生。D 选项正是对该部分内容的归纳概括，而其他三个选项均与原文意思相反，故答案为 D。

5. 主旨题。本题是一道典型的主旨题，所特别的是，这里需要用一个常见成语对全文主旨进行归纳。本文开头由优秀的足球运动员出生月份这个话题引出 Ericsson 对成功是基于天生还是后天这个问题的研究；第三段用一个记忆数字的例子说明练习的重要性；全文最后得出结论：那些取得巨大成就的人都是后天练就的，并非天生的，由此可以推断出本文的主旨应该是只有依靠后天的勤奋，即不断地训练和练习，才能取得成功。选项 A 的意思是"信仰力能移山"；B 的意思是"种瓜得瓜，种豆得豆"或"自食其果"；D 的意思是"有其父必有其子"。C 选项的意思是"熟能生巧"，恰与作者所要传递的信息一致，故 C 为正确答案。

Example ❸

In spite of "endless talk of difference", American society is an amazing machine for homogenizing people. This is "the democratizing uniformity of dress and discourse, and the casualness and absence of consumption launched by the 19th-century department stores that offered vast arrays of goods in an elegant atmosphere, instead of intimate shops catering to a knowledgeable elite." These were stores "anyone could enter, regardless of class or background. This turned shopping into a public and democratic act." The mass media, advertising and sports are other forces for homogenization.

Immigrants are quickly fitting into this common culture, which may not be altogether elevating but is hardly poisonous. Writing for the National Immigration Forum, Gregory Rodriguez reports that today's immigration is neither at unprecedented level nor resistant to assimilation. In 1998 immigrants were 9.8 percent of population; in 1900, 13.6 percent. In the 10 years prior to 1990,

3.1 immigrants arrived for every 1,000 residents; in the 10 years prior to 1890, 9.2 for every 1,000. Now, consider three indices of assimilation—language, home ownership and intermarriage.

The 1990 Census revealed that "a majority of immigrants from each of the fifteen most common countries of origin spoke English 'well' or 'very well' after ten years of residence". The children of immigrants tend to be bilingual and proficient in English. "By the third generation, the original language is lost in the majority of immigrant families." Hence the description of America as a graveyard for language. By 1996 foreign-born immigrants who had arrived before 1970 had a home ownership rate of 75.6 percent, higher than the 69.8 percent rate among native-born Americans.

Foreign-born Asians and Hispanics "have higher rates of intermarriage than do U.S.-born whites and blacks". By the third generation, one third of Hispanic women are married to non-Hispanics, and 41 percent of Asian-American women are married to non-Asians.

Rodriguez notes that children in remote villages around world are fans of superstars like Amold Schwarzenegger and Garth Brooks, yet "some Americans fear that immigrant living within the United States remain somehow immune to the nation's assimilative power".

Are there divisive issues and pockets of seething in America? Indeed. It is big enough to have a bit of everything. But particularly when viewed against America's turbulent past, today's social induces suggest a dark and deteriorating social environment. (2006 年真题)

1. The word "homogenizing" (Line 2, Paragraph 1) most probably means _____.
   A. identifying   B. associating   C. assimilating   D. monopolizing

2. According to the author, the department stores of the 19th century _____.
   A. played a role in the spread of popular culture
   B. became intimate shops for common consumers
   C. satisfied the needs of a knowledgeable elite
   D. owed its emergence to the culture of consumption

3. The text suggests that immigrants now in the U.S. _____.
   A. are resistant to homogenization
   B. exert a great influence on American culture
   C. are hardly a threat to the common culture
   D. constitute the majority of the population

4. Why are Amold Schwarzenegger and Garth Brooks mentioned in Paragraph 5?
   A. To prove their popularity around the world
   B. To reveal the public's fear of immigrants
   C. To give examples of successful immigrants
   D. To show the powerful influence of American culture

5. In the author's opinion, the absorption of immigrants into American society is _____.
   A. rewarding   B. successful   C. fruitless   D. harmful

【答案与解析】

1. 词汇题。首先在原文中找到"homogenizing"所在的句子。这句话是以"in spite of"开头的一个让步状语从句,也就是说,"homogenizing"这个词应该和前文中提到的"difference"形成一种对比;而随后一句的解释中又出现了"uniformity",这必然是对"homogenizing"的同义替换,由此可以推断出"homogenizing"应该是同化、一致的意思。因此答案只有选 C。

2. 细节题。根据题干中的"19 世纪"找到第一段。选项 B 和 C 明显与原文意思相反,而 D 选项乍一看是文中表述过的,但仔细推敲后则不难发现它把因果关系颠倒了,因此正确的选择应该是 A。

3. 推理题。根据题干中明确的定位信息"immigrants now in the U. S.",快速找到第二段。选项 A 与此段第二句"nor resistant to assimilation"明显相悖;选项 B 与此段首句"not be altogether elevating"相悖;此外,文中只讲述了三个同化的标志"language, home ownership and intermarriage",而并未提及人口问题,因此选项 D 是一个文中未提及的信息,也不能选;而选项 C 是本段首句"but is hardly poisonous"的同义替换,因此答案只能是 C。

4. 细节题。根据"children in remote villages around world are fans of superstars"可知文化已经影响到了世界的每一个角落,因此选项 D 就是正确答案。A 选项没有出现文章的核心概念"文化",因此把它排除,而 B 和 C 选项明显与原文意思相左。

5. 态度题。根据最后一段的"but",可得知作者认为美国吸纳移民是不黑暗,没被恶化的,所以应该选择 B;不黑暗,没被恶化不能等同于有益的,因此排除 A 选项;C 和 D 选项明显与原文意思相反,当然也应该排除。

Example ❹

Of all the components of a good night's sleep, dreams seem to be least within our control. In dreams, a window opens into a world where logic is suspended and dead people speak. A century ago, Freud formulated his revolutionary theory that dreams were the disguised shadows of our unconscious desires and fears. By the late 1970s, neurologists had switched to thinking of them as just "mental noise"—the random byproducts of the neural-repair work that goes on during sleep. Now researchers suspect that dreams are part of the mind's emotional thermostat, regulating moods while the brain is "off-line". And one leading authority says that these intensely powerful mental events can be not only harnessed but actually brought under conscious control, to help us sleep and feel better. "It's your dream," says Rosalind Cartwright, chair of psychology at Chicago's Medical Center. "If you don't like it, change it."

Evidence from brain imaging supports this view. The brain is as active during REM (rapid eye movement) sleep—when most vivid dreams occur—as it is when fully awake, says Dr. Eric Nofzinger at the University of Pittsburgh. But not all parts of the brain are equally involved, the limbic system (the "emotional brain") is especially active, while the prefrontal cortex (the center of intellect and reasoning) is relatively quiet. "We wake up from dreams happy of depressed, and those feelings can stay with us all day." says Stanford sleep researcher Dr. William Dement.

The link between dreams and emotions shows up among the patients in Cartwright's clinic. Most people seem to have more bad dreams early in the night, progressing toward happier ones before awakening, suggesting that they are working through negative feelings generated during the day. Because our conscious mind is occupied with daily life we don't always think about the emotional significance of the day's events—until, it appears, we begin to dream.

And this process need not be left to the unconscious. Cartwright believes one can exercise conscious control over recurring bad dreams. As soon as you awaken, identify what is upsetting about the dream. Visualize how you would like it to end instead, the next time it occurs, try to wake up just enough to control its course. With much practice people can learn to, literally, do it in their sleep.

At the end of the day, there's probably little reason to pay attention to our dreams at all unless they keep us from sleeping of "we wake up in a panic," Cartwright says. Terrorism, economic uncertainties and general feelings of insecurity have increased people's anxiety. Those suffering from persistent nightmares should seek help from a therapist. For the rest of us, the brain has its ways of working through bad feelings. Sleep—or rather dream—on it and you'll feel better in the morning. (2005 年真题)

1. Researchers have come to believe that dreams _____.
   A. can be modified in their courses
   B. are susceptible to emotional changes
   C. reflect our innermost desires and fears
   D. are a random outcome of neural repairs

2. By referring to the limbic system, the author intends to show _____.
   A. its function in our dreams
   B. the mechanism of REM sleep
   C. the relation of dreams to emotions
   D. its difference from the prefrontal cortex

3. The negative feelings generated during the day tend to _____.
   A. aggravate in our unconscious mind
   B. develop into happy dreams
   C. persist till the time we fall asleep
   D. show up in dreams early at night

4. Cartwright seems to suggest that _____.
   A. waking up in time is essential to the ridding of bad dreams
   B. visualizing bad dreams helps bring them under control
   C. dreams should be left to their natural progression
   D. dreaming may not entirely belong to the unconscious

5. What advice might Cartwright give to those who sometimes have had dreams?
   A. Lead your life as usual.   B. Seek professional help.
   C. Exercise conscious control.   D. Avoid anxiety in the daytime.

【答案与解析】

1. 细节题。首先通过题干的主语"researchers"可以推断答案应该在文章的第一段中寻找。由于选项 B 和 C 是一个世纪以前弗洛伊德提出的理论,而选项 D 则是 20 世纪 70 年代之前神经学专家的看法,因此答案只可能选 A。

2. 推理题。作者引用"limbic system"是为了通过举例子来支持论点,即文章第二段的第一句话——"Evidence from brain imaging supports this view."因此这里的关键是了解指代词"this"所指代的对象是什么。根据上文可知,"this"所指代的应该是前一段的"Now researchers suspect that dreams are part of the mind's emotional thermostat…"。从而可知 C 选项——"梦和感情的关系"为正确答案。

3. 细节题。首先根据题干找到文章第五段:"在一天结束时,很少有理由会去注意我们的梦,除非它们使我们无法入睡,用卡特怀特的话说是:'我们在恐慌中保持清醒'",由此可以排除选项 B;选项 C 文章意思是从梦中醒来时的情感影响会持续一整天,而不是白天产生的消极情绪,所以不选;选项 A 文章中没有提到加剧,所以也不选;因此只有选项 D 和文章符合,所以选 D。

4. 细节题。本题 A 选项容易被误选,这里需要注意的是 A 只是作者建议练习的一部分,是要在梦中训练这种醒来赶走噩梦,不是真正的醒来,所以不选;B 选项原文不是想象噩梦,而是想象结束噩梦,题目偷换了概念,所以不选;C 选项和原文意思相反;根据文中第四段第一句——"这个过程并不需要留给潜意识",因此答案是 D。

5. 细节题。本题的关键在于注意题干中的"sometimes"一词。通过文章最后一段第一句可知这些有时做噩梦的人没有必要担心,从而 A 选项——"过正常的生活"为正确答案。根据文中最后一段倒数第三行的"persistent"可知,只有持续做不好梦的人才有必要找专家帮助,从而 B 选项——"找专家帮助"与题干不符;而 C 选项和 D 选项文章中并未提及。

Example ❺

Hunting for a job late last year, lawyer Gant Redmon stumbled across CareerBuilder, a job database on the Internet. He searched it with no success but was attracted by the site's "personal search agent". It's an interactive feature that lets visitors key in job criteria such as location, title, and salary, then E-mails them when a matching position is posted in the database. Redmon chose the keywords *legal*, *intellectual property*, and *Washington*, *D. C.* Three weeks later, he got his first notification of an opening. "I struck gold," says Redmon, who E-mailed his resume to the employer and won a position as in-house counsel for a company.

With thousands of career-related sites on the Internet, finding promising openings can be time-consuming and inefficient. Search agents reduce the need for repeated visits to the databases. But although a search agent worked for Redmon, career experts see drawbacks. Narrowing your criteria, for example, may work against you: "Every time you answer a question you eliminate a possibility," says one expert.

For any job search, you should start with a narrow concept—what you think you want to do—then broaden it. "None of these programs do that," says another expert. "There's no career counseling implicit in all of this." Instead, the best strategy is to use the agent as a kind of <u>tip service</u> to keep abreast of jobs in a particular database; when you get E-mail, consider it a reminder to check the database again. "I would not rely on agents for finding everything that is added to a database that might interest me," says the author of a job-searching guide.

Some sites design their agents to tempt job hunters to return. When CareerSite's agent sends out messages to those who have signed up for its service, for example, it includes only three potential jobs—those it considers the best matches. There may be more matches in the database; job hunters will have to visit the site again to find them—and they do. "On the day after we send our messages, we see a sharp increase in our traffic," says Seth Peets, vice president of marketing for CareerSite.

Even those who aren't hunting for jobs may find search agents worthwhile. Some use them to keep a close watch on the demand for their line of work or gather information on compensation to arm themselves when negotiating for a raise. Although happily employed, Redmon maintains his agent at CareerBuilder. "You always keep your eyes open," he says. Working with a personal search agent means having another set of eyes looking out for you. (2004 年真题)

1. How did Redmon find his job?
   A. By searching openings in a job database.
   B. By posting a matching position in a database.
   C. By using a special service of a database.
   D. By E-mailing his resume to a database.

2. Which of the following can be a disadvantage of search agents?
   A. Lack of counseling.   B. Limited number of visits.
   C. Lower efficiency.   D. Fewer successful matches.

3. The expression "tip service" (Line 3, Paragraph 3) most probably means _____.
   A. advisory   B. compensation
   C. interaction   D. reminder

4. Why does CareerSite's agent offer each job hunter only three job options?
   A. To focus on better job matches.
   B. To attract more returning visits.
   C. To reserve space for more messages.
   D. To increase the rate of success.

5. Which of the following is true according to the text?
   A. Personal search agents are indispensable to job-hunters.
   B. Some sites keep E-mailing job seekers to trace their demands.
   C. Personal search agents are also helpful to those already employed.
   D. Some agents stop sending information to people once they are employed.

【答案与解析】
1. 细节题。本题答案应在文章第一段中找。由于本文通篇都在讲 personal search agent 这项服务,因此答案应该选 C。A 选项"By searching openings in a job database"过于笼统;B 选项"By posting a matching position in a database"不是 Redmon 而是 database 或者 employer 所做的;而 D 选项"By E-mailing his resume to a database"又过于具体。

2. 细节题。根据第三段第一句"For any job search, you should start with a narrow concept——what you think you want to do——then broaden it"——在找工作时,一般是从较狭窄的意向开始,即你要干什么,然后再放宽一些,以及专业人士所说的:"None of these programs do that","There's no career counseling implicit in all of this."——没有一个程序是那样做的,所有这些程序都不包括职业咨询服务,可以判断出正确答案应该选 A。

3. 词汇题。此题只有 A 选项最具干扰性,因为 tip 有 advice 的意思,但这里的 tip service 不作 advisory service 讲,因为根据下文"consider it a reminder to check the database again"可知,这里的"it"指代的就是"tip service",因此答案选 D。

4. 细节题。根据上一题,既然"tip service"起到的是"reminder"的作用,那么 B"To attract more returning visits"便是唯一符合题目的答案,第四段"There may be more matches in the database; job hunters will have to visit the site again to find them——and they do",是对此进一步具体说明。

5. 细节题。本题可采用排除法。文中有提到并非所有人都依靠网络求职,所以 A 选项是不正确的表述;最后一段第二句说"Some use them to keep a close watch on the demand for their line of work…"——一些人用它们来密切关注自己的职业要求以作为升值时谈判的条件,因此 B 选项也是不正确的表述;D 选项在文中没有提及,由此可知答案选 C。

Example ❻

In recent years, railroads have been combining with each other, merging into super systems, causing heightened concerns about monopoly. As recently as 1995, the top four railroads accounted for under 70 percent of the total ton-miles moved by rails. Next year, after a series of mergers is completed, just four railroads will control well over 90 percent of all the freight moved by major rail carriers.

Supporters of the new super systems argue that these mergers will allow for substantial cost reductions and better coordinated service. Any threat of monopoly, they argue, is removed by fierce competition from trucks. But many shippers complain that for heavy bulk commodities traveling long distances, such as coal, chemicals, and grain, trucking is too costly and the railroads therefore have them by the throat.

The vast consolidation within the rail industry means that most shippers are served by only one rail company. Railroads typically charge such "captive" shippers 20 to 30 percent more than they do when another railroad is competing for the business. Shippers who feel they are being overcharged have the right to appeal to the federal government's *Surface Transportation Board* for rate relief, but the process is expensive, time consuming, and will work only in truly extreme cases.

Railroads justify rate discrimination against captive shippers on the grounds that in the long run it reduces everyone's cost. If railroads charged all customers the same average rate, they argue, shippers who have the option of switching to trucks or other forms of transportation would do so, leaving remaining customers to shoulder the cost of keeping up the line. It's theory to which many economists subscribe, but in practice it often leaves railroads in the position of determining which companies will flourish and which will fail. "Do we really want railroads to be the arbiters of who wins and who loses in the marketplace?" asks Martin Bercovici, a Washington lawyer who frequently represents shipper.

Many captive shippers also worry they will soon be his with a round of huge rate increases. The railroad industry as a whole, despite its brightening fortunes, still does not earn enough to cover the cost of the capital it must invest to keep up with its surging traffic. Yet railroads continue to borrow billions to acquire one another, with Wall Street cheering them on. Consider the $10.2 billion bid by Norfolk Southern and CSX to acquire Conrail this year. Conrail's net railway operating income in 1996 was just $427 million, less than half of the carrying costs of the transaction. Who's going to pay for the rest of the bill? Many captive shippers fear that they will, as Norfolk Southern and CSX increase their grip on the market. (2003 年真题)

1. According to those who support mergers, railway monopoly is unlikely because _____.

    A. cost reduction is based on competition

    B. services call for cross-trade coordination

    C. outside competitors will continue to exist

    D. shippers will have the railway by the throat

2. What is many captive shippers' attitude towards the consolidation in the rail industry?

    A. Indifferent.   B. Supportive.   C. Indignant.   D. Apprehensive.

3. It can be inferred from Paragraph 3 that _____.

    A. shippers will be charged less without a rival railroad

    B. there will soon be only one railroad company nationwide

    C. overcharged shippers are unlikely to appeal for rate relief

    D. a government board ensures fair play in railway business

4. The word "arbiters" (Line 6, Paragraph 4) most probably refers to those _____.

    A. who work as coordinators   B. who function as judges

    C. who supervise transactions   D. who determine the price

5. According to the text, the cost increase in the rail industry is mainly caused by _____.

    A. the continuing acquisition   B. the growing traffic

    C. the cheering Wall Street   D. the shrinking market

【答案与解析】

1. 细节题。问题问的是支持并购的人何以认为垄断不会发生。首先由题干中的"those who support merger"可知答案在文章第二段中找。这一段的前两句是支持兼并的观点。本题的答案在第二句话：他们说,任何垄断的威胁都将被卡车带来的激烈竞争消除掉。因为本文讲的是火车垄断,所以此处的卡车即与选项 C 中的"outside competitors"相对应,也就是说,因为还有别的竞争,所以铁路垄断不太可能,因此答案选 C。

2. 态度题。问题问的是被动发货商对铁路集团的出现持何种态度。选项中的四个形容词分别是 A：漠然的，不在乎的；B：支持的；C：愤怒的；D 担心的。本题最明显的线索在文中最后一段第一句话的开头部分，"Many captive shippers also worry…"。因此答案选 D。

3. 推理题。本题要求考生依据第三段推出一个结论。第三段的最后一句话告诉我们，虽然托运方可以向政府诉讼以获得费率补偿，但这个过程代价巨大、耗时太久，并且只适用于极端的情况，由此可以推断他们不大可能这样做，因此答案选 C。

4. 词汇题。本题可以利用上下文的重复来猜测词义。单词"arbiter"所在的短语"arbiters of who wins and who loses"对应于上一句中的 "…in the position of determining which companies will flourish and which will fail"，因此可以看出 "arbiters"可解释为"those who determine"，即引申为 judges，所以正确答案是 B。

5. 细节题。题干问的是铁路行业成本上升的主要原因是什么，这正是本文最后一段的主要内容，第二、三、四句合起来的意思是：铁路工业尽管前途一片光明，但目前仍入不敷出，仍然大量借贷进行亏本兼并。所以应选择 A，"acquisition"原意指获得，也有兼并之意。

Example ❼

If you intend using humor in your talk to make people smile, you must know how to identify shared experiences and problems. Your humor must be relevant to the audience and should help to show them that you are one of them or that you understand their situation and are in sympathy with their point of view. Depending on whom you are addressing, the problems will be different. If you are talking to a group of managers, you may refer to the disorganized methods of their secretaries; alternatively if you are addressing secretaries, you may want to comment on their disorganized bosses.

Here is an example, which I heard at a nurses' convention, of a story which works well because the audience all shared the same view of doctors. A man arrives in heaven and is being shown around by St. Peter. He sees wonderful accommodations, beautiful gardens, sunny weather, and so on. Everyone is very peaceful, polite and friendly until, waiting in a line for lunch, the new arrival is suddenly pushed aside by a man in a white coat, who rushes to the head of the line, grabs his food and stomps over to a table by himself. "Who is that?" the new arrival asked St. Peter. "Oh, that's God," came the reply, "but sometimes he thinks he's a doctor."

If you are part of the group which you are addressing, you will be in a position to know the experiences and problems which are common to all of you and it'll be appropriate for you to make a passing remark about the inedible canteen food or the chairman's notorious bad taste in ties. With other audiences you mustn't attempt to cut in with humor as they will resent an outsider making disparaging remarks about their canteen or their chairman. You will be on safer ground if you stick to scapegoats like the Post Office or the telephone system.

If you feel awkward being humorous, you must practice so that it becomes more natural. Include a few casual and apparently off-the-cuff remarks which you can deliver in a relaxed and unforced manner. Often it's the delivery which causes the audience to smile, so speak slowly and remember that a raised eyebrow or an unbelieving look may help to show that you are making a light-hearted remark.

Look for the humor. It often comes from the unexpected. A twist on a familiar quote "If at first you don't succeed, give up" or a play on words or on a situation. Search for exaggeration and under statements. Look at your talk and pick out a few words or sentences which you can turn about and inject with humor. (2002 年真题)

1. To make your humor work, you should _____.

   A. take advantage of different kinds of audience

   B. make fun of the disorganized people

   C. address different problems to different people

   D. show sympathy for your listeners.

2. The joke about doctors implies that, in the eyes of nurses, they are _____

   A. impolite to new arrivals   B. very conscious of their godlike role

   C. entitled to some privileges   D. very busy even during lunch hours

3. It can be inferred from the text that public services _____.

   A. have benefited many people

   B. are the focus of public attention

   C. are an inappropriate subject for humor

   D. have often been the laughing stock

4. To achieve the desired result, humorous stories should be delivered _____.

   A. in well-worded language   B. as awkwardly as possible

   C. in exaggerated statements   D. as casually as possible

5. The best title for the text may be _____.

   A. Use Humor Effectively   B. Various Kinds of Humor

   C. Add Humor to Speech   D. Different Humor Strategies

【答案与解析】

1. 推理题。本文的第一句指出"要想在讲话的时候使用幽默让他人发笑,你必须要知道如何辨明哪些是与听众共同的经历和问题。"第三句又指出"问题又因听众不同而不同"。综合这两句话的意思,即与 C 选项所表达的"与不同的人谈不同的问题"意思一致,因此答案选 C。

2. 推理题。文章第二段的最后两句为解本题提供了线索,表明了护士对医生的看法,即 B 选项所表达的"医生对他们上帝般的角色有清醒的认识",因此答案选 B。

3. 推理题。文章第三段的最后一句指出,"(与谈论食堂或主席相比),如果你谈论像邮政服务或电话系统之类的替罪羊会更安全。"由此可推断出公共服务部门经常成为大众的谈资或是笑料,所以答案是 D。

4. 推理题。本文第四段中的" natural, casual, off-the-cuff(临时的), relaxed, unforced manner"为解答本题提供了线索,因此 D 选项"尽可能地随意"为正确选项。

5. 推理题。本题是要为本文选择一个合适的题目,因此首先要弄清楚四个选项的意思: A:有效地使用幽默;B:各种各样的幽默;C:在言语中加进幽默;D:不同的幽默策略。

文章前两段讲的是要使幽默奏效应该有针对性,对不同的听众讲不同的话题;第三段讲的是怎样讲笑话才能取得最好的效果。纵览全文,作者给出的幽默策略只有一个,而不是几个不同的策略,所以排除了选项 B、C 和 D 后,只有选项 A 为正确答案。

Example ❽

Why do so many Americans distrust what they read in their newspapers? The American Society of Newspaper Editors is trying to answer this painful question. The organization is deep into a long self-analysis known as the journalism credibility project.

Sad to say, this project has turned out to be mostly low-level findings about factual errors and spelling and grammar mistakes, combined with lots of head-scratching puzzlement about what in the world those readers really want.

But the sources of distrust go way deeper. Most journalists learn to see the world through a set of standard templates (patterns) into which they plug each day's events. In other words, there is a conventional story line in the newsroom culture that provides a backbone and a ready-made narrative structure for otherwise confusing news.

There exists a social and cultural disconnect between journalists and their readers, which helps explain why the "standard templates" of the newsroom seem alien to many readers. In a recent survey, questionnaires were sent to reporters in five middle-size cities around the country, plus one large metropolitan area. Then residents in these communities were phoned at random and asked the same questions.

Replies show that compared with other Americans, journalists are more likely to live in upscale neighborhoods, have maids, own Mercedeses, and trade stocks, and they're less likely to go to church, do volunteer work, or put down roots in a community.

Reporters tend to be part of a broadly defined social and cultural elite, so their work tends to reflect the conventional values of this elite. The astonishing distrust of the news media isn't rooted in inaccuracy or poor reportorial skills but in the daily clash of world views between reporters and their readers.

This is an explosive situation for any industry, particularly a declining one. Here is a troubled business that keeps hiring employees whose attitudes vastly annoy the customers. Then it sponsors lots of symposiums and a credibility project dedicated to wondering why customers are annoyed and fleeing in large numbers. But it never seems to get around to noticing the cultural and class biases that so many former buyers are complaining about. If it did, it would open up its diversity program, now focused narrowly on race and gender, and look for reporters who differ broadly by outlook, values, education, and class. (2001 年真题)

1. What is the passage mainly about?

A. Needs of the readers all over the world.

B. Causes of the public disappointment about newspapers.

C. Origins of the declining newspaper industry.

D. Aims of a journalism credibility project.

2. The results of the journalism credibility project turned out to be _____.

    A. quite trustworthy   B. somewhat contradictory

    C. very illuminating   D. rather superficial

3. The basic problem of journalists as pointed out by the writer lies in their _____.

    A. working attitude   B. conventional lifestyle

    C. world outlook   D. educational background

4. Despite its efforts, the newspaper industry still cannot satisfy the readers owing to its _____.

    A. failure to realize its real problem

    B. tendency to hire annoying reporters

    C. likeliness to do inaccurate reporting

    D. prejudice in matters of race and gender

【答案与解析】

1. 主旨题。通读全文后不难发现,本文主要围绕文章第一段第一句"为什么这么多美国人不相信报刊上读到的东西?"这一问句展开,因此 B 选项"公众对新闻界感到失望的原因"为正确答案。A 选项"全世界读者的需求"过于宽泛;C 选项"美国报刊业日趋衰退的原因"显得答非所问;而 D 选项"新闻可信度调查项目的目的"在文章中未展开讨论。

2. 细节题。题干问的是新闻可信度调查项目的结果如何。根据文章第二段第一句"很遗憾,该项目在事实误差,拼写及语法错误,以及这些读者究竟需要什么等令人困惑的问题方面的调查结果大部分都是表面上的"。A 选项"相当可信"与内容不符;B 选项"有点矛盾"文章未提及;C 选项"非常有启发性"与事实相反;D 选项"相当肤浅"与此表述一致;因此答案选 D。

3. 细节题。该题问作者所指出的记者们存在的基本问题是什么。根据文章倒数第二段第二句"读者不相信新闻媒体不在于报导有误或报导技术差,而是在于记者与读者之间世界观方面的冲突",答案 C"世界观"为正确答案。答案 A"工作态度"在文中未提及;答案 B"传统生活方式"和答案 D"教育背景"都属于记者与读者不同的三个方面。

4. 推理题。问题问的是尽管新闻界付出了努力,仍然不能满足读者需要的原因是什么? 根据文章最后一段可推测出:新闻界的问题症结在于没能对症下药。因此,答案 A"没有认识到真正的问题所在"为正确答案;而答案 B"往往雇佣令人厌烦的记者",答案 C"可能做有误的报导"和答案 D"在种族和性别的问题方面有偏见"则都属于细节性问题,故答案选 A。

Example ❾

    Aimlessness has hardly been typical of the postwar Japan whose productivity and social harmony are the envy of the United States and Europe. But increasingly the Japanese are seeing a decline of the traditional work-moral values. Ten years ago young people were hardworking and saw their jobs as their primary reason for being, but now Japan has largely fulfilled its economic needs, and young people don't know where they should go next.

    The coming of age of the postwar baby boom and an entry of women into the male-dominated job market have limited the opportunities of teen-agers who are already questioning the heavy personal sacrifices involved in climbing Japan's rigid social ladder to good schools and jobs. In a recent survey, it was found that only 24.5 percent of Japanese students were fully satisfied with school life, compared with 67.2 percent of students in the United States. In addition, far more Japanese workers expressed dissatisfaction with their jobs than did their counterparts in the 10 other countries surveyed.

While often praised by foreigners for its emphasis on the basics, Japanese education tends to stress test taking and mechanical learning over creativity and self-expression. "Those things that do not show up in the test scores—personality, ability, courage or humanity—are completely ignored," says Toshiki Kaifu, chairman of the ruling Liberal Democratic Party's education committee. "Frustration against this kind of thing leads kids to drop out and run wild." Last year Japan experienced 2, 125 incidents of school violence, including 929 assaults on teachers. Amid the outcry, many conservative leaders are seeking a return to the prewar emphasis on moral education. Last year Mitsuo Setoyama, who was then education minister, raised eyebrows when he argued that liberal reforms introduced by the American occupation authorities after World War II had weakened the "Japanese morality of respect for parents".

But that may have more to do with Japanese life-styles. "In Japan," says educator Yoko Muro, "it's never a question of whether you enjoy your job and your life, but only how much you can endure." With economic growth has come centralization; fully 76 percent of Japan's 119 million citizens live in cities where community and the extended family have been abandoned in favor of isolated, two generation households. Urban Japanese have long endured lengthy commutes (travels to and from work) and crowded living conditions, but as the old group and family values weaken, the discomfort is beginning to tell. In the past decade, the Japanese divorce rate, while still well below that of the United States, has increased by more than 50 percent, and suicides have increased by nearly one-quarter. (2000 年真题)

1. In the Westerner's eyes, the postwar Japan was _____.
   A. under aimless development B. a positive example
   C. a rival to the West D. on the decline

2. According to the author, what may chiefly be responsible for the moral decline of Japanese society?
   A. Women's participation in social activities is limited.
   B. More workers are dissatisfied with their jobs.
   C. Excessive emphasis has been placed on the basics.
   D. The life-style has been influenced by Western values.

3. Which of the following is true according to the author?
   A. Japanese education is praised for helping the young climb the social ladder
   B. Japanese education is characterized by mechanical learning as well as creativity.
   C. More stress should be placed on the cultivation of creativity.
   D. Dropping out leads to frustration against test taking.

4. The change in Japanese Life-style is revealed in the fact that _____.

    A. the young are less tolerant of discomforts in life

    B. the divorce rate in Japan exceeds that in the U. S

    C. the Japanese endure more than ever before

    D. the Japanese appreciate their present life

【答案与解析】

1. 推理题。问题问的是在西方人眼里战后的日本是怎样的。文章的开头就谈到战后日本的生产能力和社会协调是美国和欧洲国家羡慕的对象,是一种称赞的语气,因此答案选 B "一个积极的榜样"。

2. 推理题。本题可以运用排除法。选项 A 与文章第二段的第一句不符;选项 B 与第二段的最后一句不符;而选项 C 则与本题的题意不符。文章第二段讲到二战后,与欧洲国家和美国相比日本工人对工作的不满意程度。第三段从教育方面做了解释,在段尾总结到美国职业权威人士介绍的自由改革削弱了日本人尊重父母的价值观,第四段的开头又明确点出:But that may have more to do with Japanese Life-style",所以生活方式的变化受到了西方价值观的影响,因此正确答案为 D。

3. 细节题。文章第三段第一句就指出日本教育在因为强调基础而受到赞扬的同时,也趋向于强调参加测试和机械的学习而不是其创造性和自我表现,这里作者想要表达的观点是教育的重点应该是培养创造性,这与选项 C 的表述一致,因此答案选 C。

4. 细节题。文章最后一段首先直接引用了一位日本教育家的话:"问题根本不是习惯工作和生活与否,而仅仅是能忍受多少",倒数第二句讲随着古老的家庭价值观念的削弱,不舒适也就变得越来越明显,然后作者又以离婚率和自杀人数的上升为例进一步说明了一个事实,那就是年轻人不如老年人能忍受,因此答案应该选 A。

Example *11*

    When a Scottish research team startled the world by revealing 3 months ago that it had cloned an adult sheep, President Clinton moved swiftly. Declaring that he was opposed to using this unusual animal husbandry technique to clone humans, he ordered that federal funds not be used for such an experiment—although no one had proposed to do so—and asked an independent panel of experts chaired by Princeton President Harold Shapiro to report back to the White House in 90 days with recommendations for a national policy on human cloning. That group—the National Bioethics Advisory Commission (NBAC)—has been working feverishly to put its wisdom on paper, and at a meeting on 17 May, members agreed on a near-final draft of their recommendations.

    NBAC will ask that Clinton's 90-day ban on federal funds for human cloning be extended indefinitely, and possibly that it be made law. But NBAC members are planning to word the recommendation narrowly to avoid new restrictions on research that involves the cloning of human DNA or cells—routine in molecular biology. The panel has not yet reached agreement on a crucial question, however, whether to recommend legislation that would make it a crime for private funding to be used for human cloning.

In a draft preface to the recommendations, discussed at the 17 May meeting, Shapiro suggested that the panel had found a broad consensus that it would be "morally unacceptable to attempt to create a human child by adult nuclear cloning". Shapiro explained during the meeting that the moral doubt stems mainly from fears about the risk to the health of the child. The panel then informally accepted several general conclusions, although some details have not been settled.

NBAC plans to call for a continued ban on federal government funding for any attempt to clone body cell nuclei to create a child. Because current federal law already forbids the use of federal funds to create embryos (the earliest stage of human offspring before birth) for research or to knowingly endanger an embryo's life, NBAC will remain silent on embryo research. NBAC members also indicated that they will appeal to privately funded researchers and clinics not to try to clone humans by body cell nuclear transfer. But they were divided on whether to go further by calling for a federal law that would impose a complete ban on human cloning. Shapiro and most members favored an appeal for such legislation, but in a phone interview, he said this issue was still "up in the air". (1999 年真题)

1. We can learn from the first paragraph that _____.

   A. federal funds have been used in a project to clone humans

   B. the White House responded strongly to the news of cloning

   C. NBAC was authorized to control the misuse of cloning technique

   D. the White House has got the panel's recommendations on cloning

2. The panel agreed on all of the following except that _____.

   A. the ban on federal funds for human cloning should be made a law

   B. the cloning of human DNA is not to be put under more control

   C. it is criminal to use private funding for human cloning

   D. it would be against ethical values to clone a human being

3. NBAC will leave the issue of embryo research undiscussed because _____.

   A. embryo research is just a current development of cloning

   B. the health of the child is not the main concern of embryo research

   C. an embryo's life will not be endangered in embryo research

   D. the issue is explicitly stated and settled in the law

4. It can be inferred from the last paragraph that _____.

   A. some NBAC members hesitate to ban human cloning completely

   B. a law banning human cloning is to be passed in no time

   C. privately funded researchers will respond positively to NBAC's appeal

   D. the issue of human cloning will soon be settled

【答案与解析】

1. 是非判断题。根据原文第一段前两句,可知克林顿得到有关克隆的消息后就立刻宣布他反对克隆人,因此答案选 B。

2. 是非判断题。根据第二段最后一句话"专家组在一个关键性问题上尚未达成一致意见，即是否建议立法规定，利用私人基金克隆人被视为犯罪行为"，选项 C 最符合此表述，因此答案选 C。

3. 细节题。问题问的是 NBAC 在胚胎研究问题上保持沉默的原因是什么。原文第四段第二句提到了原因，即法律已经对此作出了相关规定，因此正确答案为 D。

4. 推断题。根据原文最后一段第六行可知"他们在是否进一步要求联邦凭借法律完全禁止克隆人这一问题上存在分歧"，故答案为 A。

2）练习

Exercise ❶

Mapping the human genome opens a new era for medical science—and a new frontier for potential discrimination. New genetic research may make it possible to identify an individual's lifetime risk of cancer, heart attack and other diseases. Experts worry that this information could be used to discriminate in hiring, promotions, or insurance. Employers and insurers could save millions of dollars if they could use predictive genetics to identify in advance, and then reject, workers or policy applicants who are predisposed to develop chronic disease. Thus, genetic discrimination could join the list of other forms of discrimination: racial, ethnic, age and sexual.

Genetic discrimination is drawing attention this week because of the first publication of the complete human genome map and sequence. Two versions, virtually identical, were compiled separately by an international public consortium and by a private company. The journal *Nature* is publishing the work of the public consortium and the journal *Science* is publishing the sequence by Celera Genomics, a Rockville, Md., company.

Fear of such discrimination already is affecting how people view the medical revolution promised by mapping the human genome. A Time/CNN poll last summer found that 75 percent of 1,218 Americans surveyed did not want insurance companies to know their genetic code, and 84 percent wanted that information withheld from the government. "There has been widespread fear that an individual's genetic information will be used against them," said Sen. Bill Frist, R-Tenn. "If we truly wish to improve quality of health care, we must begin taking steps to eliminate patients' fears."

The Equal Employment Opportunity Commission filed its first lawsuit challenging genetic testing last week in U. S. District Court in the Northern District of Iowa. Burlington Northern Santa Fe Railroad was charged in the suit with conducting genetic testing on employees without their permission. At least one worker was threatened with dismissal unless he agreed to the test, the agency charges. The EEOC said the genetic tests were being run on employees who filed for worker's compensation as the result of carpal tunnel syndrome, a type of repetitive motion injury common to keyboard operators. Some studies have suggested that a mutation on chromosome 17 predisposes to the injury.

A survey of 2,133 employers this year by the American Management Association found that seven are using genetic testing for either job applicants or employees, according to the journal

Science. Many experts believe the only solution to potential genetic discrimination is a new federal law that specifically prohibits it. "Genetic testing has enormous potential for improving health care in America, but to fully utilize this new science, we must eliminate patients' fears and the potential for insurance discrimination," said Frist, the only physician in the Senate. Frist and Sen. Olympia Snowe, R-Maine, are introducing legislation that would prevent insurance companies from requiring genetic testing and ban the use of genetic information to deny coverage or to set rates.

Writing this week in the journal *Science*, Senators James M. Jeffords, R-Vt., and Tom Daschle, D-S. D., say they both favor legislation prohibiting genetic discrimination. "Without adequate safeguards, the genetic revolution could mean one step forward for science and two steps backward for civil rights," they write. "Misuse of genetic information could create a new underclass: the genetically less fortunate."

1. Which of the following statements is NOT true according to the text?

    A. As a result of research on the human genome, doctors will be able to make better decisions about their patients.

    B. Business could use genetic information to make decisions about employees.

    C. The Equal Employment Opportunity Commission supports widespread genetic testing as a way to improve the nations' economy.

    D. A mutation on a chromosome may be a cause of injured or sore wrists.

2. All of the following descriptions of "carpal tunnel syndrome" (Para. 4, Line 6) are true EXCEPT _____.

    A. an injury characterized by discomfort and weakness in the hands and fingers

    B. an injury often found in typists

    C. an injury probably caused by a sudden change on chromosome

    D. an injury caused by the heavy demand of one's work

3. Many experts believe that _____.

    A. genetic testing should be banned completely

    B. all the companies should conduct genetic testing on employees in hiring, promotions and insurance

    C. genetic tests should be run on employees who ask for worker's compensation as the result of carpal tunnel syndrome

    D. genetic tests cannot be fully utilized unless legislation is used to prevent potential genetic discrimination

4. What does "safeguard" in Paragraph 6, Line 3 refer to?

    A. EEOC   B. the press   C. federal law   D. the district court

5. Which of the following might be the best title of this text?

    A. Gene Mapping May Foster Discrimination

    B. Recent Discoveries on the Genome Map and Sequence

    C. Genetic Testing Used in Lawsuit

D. Genetic Therapy of Carpal Tunnel Syndrome

Exercise ❷

The earliest controversies about the relationship between photography and art centered on whether photograph's fidelity to appearances and dependence on a machine allowed it to be a fine art as distinct from merely a practical art. Throughout the nineteenth century, the defence of photography was identical with the struggle to establish it as a fine art. Against the charge that photography was a soulless, mechanical copying of reality, photographers asserted that it was instead a privileged way of seeing, a revolt against commonplace vision, and no less worthy an art than painting.

Ironically, now that photography is securely established as a fine art, many photographers find it pretentious or irrelevant to label it as such. Serious photographers variously claim to be finding, recording, impartially observing, witnessing events, exploring themselves—anything but making works of art. They are no longer willing to debate whether photography is or is not a fine art, except to proclaim that their own work is not involved with art. It shows the extent to which they simply take for granted the concept of art imposed by the triumph of Modernism: the better the art, the more subversive it is of the traditional aims of art.

Photographers' disclaimers of any interest in making art tell us more about the harried status of the contemporary notion of art than about whether photography is or is not art. For example, those photographers who suppose that, by taking pictures, they are getting away from the pretensions of art as exemplified by painting remind us of those Abstract Expressionist painters who imagined they were getting away from the intellectual austerity of classical Modernist painting by concentrating on the physical act of painting. Much of photography's prestige today derives from the convergence of its aims with those of recent art, particularly with the dismissal of abstract art implicit in the phenomenon of Pop painting during the 1960's. Appreciating photographs is a relief to sensibilities tired of the mental exertions demanded by abstract art. Classical Modernist painting—that is, abstract art as developed in different ways by Picasso, Kandinsky, and Matisse—presupposes highly developed skills of looking and a familiarity with other paintings and the history of art. Photography, like Pop painting, reassures viewers that art is not hard; photography seems to be more about its subjects than about art.

Photography, however, has developed all the anxieties and self-consciousness of a classic Modernist art. Many professionals privately have begun to worry that the promotion of photography as an activity subversive of the traditional pretensions of art has gone so far that the public will forget that photography is a distinctive and exalted activity—in short, an art.

1. According to the author, the nineteenth-century defenders of photography stressed that photography was _____.

   A. an art that would eventually replace the traditional arts

   B. a technologically advanced activity

   C. a device for observing the world impartially

D. an art comparable to painting

2. It can be inferred that the author most probably considers serious contemporary photography to be a _____ .

A. contemporary art that is struggling to be accepted as fine art

B. modern art that displays the Modernist tendency

C. craft requiring sensitivity but by no means an art

D. mechanical copying of reality

3. One adjective which best describes "the concept of art imposed by the triumph of Modernism" is _____ .

A. objective   B. superficial   C. dramatic   D. paradoxical

4. The author's attitude towards Abstract Expressionist painters is _____ .

A. objective   B. ambiguous   C. ambivalent   D. approving

5. In the passage, the author is primarily concerned with _____ .

A. defining the Modernist attitude towards art

B. explaining how photography emerged as a fine art

C. explaining the attitudes of serious contemporary photographers towards photography as art

D. defining various approaches serious contemporary photographers take towards their art

Exercise ❸

What accounts for the astounding popularity of Dr. Phil McGraw? Why have so many TV viewers and book buyers embraced this tough warrior of a psychologist who tells them to suck it up and deal with their own problems rather than complaining and blaming everyone else? Obviously, Oprah Winfrey has a lot to do with it. She made him famous with regular appearances on her show, and is co-producing the new *Dr. Phil* show that's likely to be the hottest new daytime offering this fall. But we decided to put Dr. Phil on the cover not just because he's a phenomenon. We think his success may reflect an interesting shift in the American spirit of time. Could it be that we're finally getting tired of the culture of victimology?

This is a tricky subject, because there are very sad real victims among us. Men still abuse women in alarming numbers. Racism and discrimination persist in subtle and not-so-subtle forms. But these days, almost anyone can find a therapist or lawyer to assure them that their professional relationship or health problems aren't their fault. As Marc Peyser tells us in his terrific profile of *Dr. Phil*, the TV suits were initially afraid audiences would be offended by his stern advice to "get real"! In fact, viewers thirsted for the tough talk. Privately, we all know we have to take responsibility for decisions we control. It may not be revolutionary advice (and may leave out important factors like unconscious impulses). But it's still an important message with clear echoing as, a year later, we contemplate the personal lessons of September 11.

Back at the ranch(livestock farm)—the one in Crawford, Texas-President Bush continued to issue mixed signals on Iraq. He finally promised to consult allies and Congress before going to war, and signaled an attack isn't coming right now ("I'm a patient man"). But so far there has been little consensus-building, even as the administration talks of "regime change" and positions troops in the gulf. Bush's team also ridiculed the press for giving so much coverage to the Iraq issue. Defense Secretary Rumsfeld called it a "frenzy", and Press Secretary Ari Fleischer dismissed it as "self-inflicted silliness". But as Michael Hirsh notes in our lead story, much of the debate has been inside the Republican Party, where important voices of experience argue Bush needs to prepare domestic and world opinion and think through the global consequences before moving forward. With so much at stake, the media shouldn't pay attention? Now who's being silly?

1. Faced with diversified issues of injustice, Dr. Phil McGraw advised that people should _____.
   A. strongly voice their condemnation of those responsible
   B. directly probe the root of their victimization
   C. carefully examine their own problems
   D. sincerely express their sympathy for the victims
2. One possible response, when the program *Dr. Phil* was first presented on TV, that people were afraid of was _____.
   A. suspicion   B. satisfaction   C. indifference   D. indignation
3. The word "tough" (Line 6, Paragraph 2) most probably means _____.
   A. piercing to the truth   B. using vulgar language
   C. mean and hostile   D. difficult to understand
4. The author advises the public to _____.
   A. leave out factors such as unconscious impulses
   B. draw lessons of their own from September 11
   C. respond decisively to September 11 tragedy
   D. accept decisions beyond our control
5. With a series of questions at the end of the text, the author _____.
   A. feels uncertain of what his own opinion is
   B. differentiates two conflicting views
   C. criticizes the Bush Administration
   D. argues for the US policy on Iraq

Exercise ❹

Social circumstances in Early Modern England mostly served to repress women's voices. Patriarchal culture and institutions constructed them as chaste, silent, obedient, and subordinate. At the beginning of the 17th century, the ideology of patriarchy, political absolutism, and gender hierarchy were reaffirmed powerfully by King James in The Trew Law of Free Monarchie and the Basilikon Doron; by that ideology the absolute power of God the supreme patriarch was seen to be imaged in the absolute monarch of the state and in the husband and father of a family. Accordingly, a woman's subjection, first to her father and then to her husband, imaged the subjection of English people to their monarch, and of all Christians to God. Also, the period saw an outpouring of repressive or overtly misogynist sermons, tracts, and plays, detailing women's physical and mental defects, spiritual evils, rebelliousness, shrewishness, and natural inferiority to men.

Yet some social and cultural conditions served to empower women. During the Elizabethan era(1558—1603) the culture was dominated by a powerful Queen, who provided an impressive female example though she left scant cultural space for other women. Elizabethan women writers began to produce original texts but were occupied chiefly with translation. In the 17th century, however, various circumstances enabled women to write original texts in some numbers. For one thing, some counterweight to patriarchy was provided by female communities—mothers and daughters, extended kinship networks, close female friends, the separate court of Queen Anne (King James' consort) and her often oppositional masques and political activities. For another, most of these women had a reasonably good education (modern languages, history, literature, religion, music, occasionally Latin) and some apparently found in romances and histories more expansive terms for imagining women's lives. Also, representation of vigorous and rebellious female characters in literature and especially on the stage no doubt helped to undermine any monolithic social construct of women's mature and role.

Most important, perhaps, was the radical potential inherent in the Protestant insistence on every Christian's immediate relationship with God and primary responsibility to follow his or her individual conscience. There is plenty of support in St Paul's epistles and elsewhere in the Bible for patriarchy and a wife's subjection to her husband, but some texts (notably Galatians 3: 28) inscribe a very different politics, promoting women's spiritual equality: "There is neither Jew nor Greek, there is neither bond nor free, there is neither male nor female: for ye are all one in Jesus Christ. " Such texts encouraged some women to claim the support of God the supreme patriarch against the various earthly patriarchs who claimed to stand toward them in his stead.

There is also the gap or slippage between ideology and common experience. English women throughout the 17th century exercised a good deal of accrual power: as managers of estates in their husbands' absences at court or on military and diplomatic missions; as members of guilds; as wives and mothers who apex during the English Civil War and Interregnum (1640—1660) as the execution of the King and the attendant disruption of social hierarchies led many women to seize new roles—as preachers, as prophetesses, as deputies for exiled royalist husbands, as writers of religious and political tracts.

1. All of the following are characteristics of Early Modern England EXCEPT _____.

    A. women's merits were extolled in publications

    B. women's opinions were not asked

    C. women were subject to their husbands

    D. women were often referred to

2. Elizabethan women writers began to write novel articles NOT because _____.

    A. there was struggle against women's subordination

    B. they were better educated

    C. they were materially independent

D. they were inspired by heroines in literary works

3. What did the religion do for the women?
   A. It did nothing.
   B. It appealed to the God.
   C. It supported women unconditionally.
   D. It asked women to be obedient except some texts.

4. It can be inferred from the last paragraph that in the 17th century, _____.
   A. women had a hard time in striving for their equal rights
   B. women made certain progress in their fight for equal rights
   C. women temporarily lost confidence in fighting for equal rights
   D. women triumphed over men in fighting for equal rights

5. What is the best title for this passage?
   A. Women's Position in the 17th Century
   B. Women's Subjection to Patriarchy
   C. Social Circumstances in the 17th Century
   D. Women's Rebellion in the 17th Century

Exercise ❺

Roger Rosenblatt's book *Black Fiction*, in attempting to apply literary rather than sociopolitical criteria to its subject, successfully alters the approach taken by most previous studies. As Rosenblatt notes, criticism of Black writing has often served as a pretext for expounding on Black history. Addison Gayle's recent work, for example, judges the value of Black fiction by overtly political standards, rating each work according to the notions of Black identity which it propounds.

Although fiction assuredly springs from political circumstances, its authors react to those circumstances in ways other than ideological, and talking about novels and stories primarily as instruments of ideology circumvents much of the fictional enterprise. Rosenblatt's literary analysis discloses affinities and connections among works of Black fiction which solely political studies have overlooked or ignored.

Writing acceptable criticism of Black fiction, however, presupposes giving satisfactory answers to a number of questions. First of all, is there a sufficient reason, other than the facial identity of the authors, to group together works by Black authors? Second, how does Black fiction make itself distinct from other modern fiction with which it is largely contemporaneous? Rosenblatt shows that Black fiction constitutes a distinct body of writing that has an identifiable, coherent literary tradition. Looking at novels written by Black over the last eighty years, he discovers recurring concerns and designs independent of chronology. These structures are thematic, and they spring, not surprisingly, from the central fact that the Black characters in these novels exist in a predominantly white culture, whether they try to conform to that culture or rebel against it.

Black Fiction does leave some aesthetic questions open. Rosenblatt's thematic analysis permits considerable objectivity; he even explicitly states that it is not his intention to judge the merit of the various works—yet his reluctance seems misplaced, especially since an attempt to appraise might have led to interesting results. For instance, some of the novels appear to be structurally diffuse. Is this a defect, or are the authors working out of, or trying to forge, a different kind of aesthetic? In addition, the style of some Black novels, like *Jean Toomer's Cane*, verges on expressionism or surrealism; does this technique provide a counterpoint to the prevalent theme that portrays the fate against which Black heroes are pitted, a theme usually conveyed by more naturalistic modes of expression?

In spite of such omissions, what Rosenblatt does include in his discussion makes for an astute and worthwhile study. *Black Fiction* surveys a wide variety of novels, bringing to our attention in the process some fascinating and little-known works like James Weldon Johnson's *Autobiography of an Ex-Colored Man*. Its argument is tightly constructed, and its forthright, lucid style exemplifies levelheaded and penetrating criticism.

1. The author of the text is primarily concerned with _____.

    A. evaluating the soundness of a work of criticism

    B. comparing various critical approaches to a subject

    C. discussing the limitations of a particular kind of criticism

    D. summarizing the major points made in a work of criticism

2. The author of the text believes that *Black Fiction* would have been improved had Rosenblatt _____.

    A. evaluated more carefully the ideological and historical aspects of Black fiction

    B. attempted to be more objective in his approach to novels and stories by Black authors

    C. explored in greater detail the recurrent thematic concerns of Black fiction throughout its history

    D. assessed the relative literary merit of the novels he analyzes thematically

3. The author's discussion of *Black Fiction* can be best described as _____.

    A. pedantic and contentious   B. critical but admiring

    C. ironic and deprecating   D. argumentative but unfocused

4. The author of the text employs all of the following in the discussion of Rosenblatt's book EXCEPT _____.

    A. rhetorical questions   B. specific examples

    C. comparison and contrast   D. definition of terms

5. The author of the text refers to James Weldon Johnson's *Autobiography of an Ex-Colored Man* most probably in order to _____.

    A. point out affinities between Rosenblatt's method of thematic analysis and earlier criticism

    B. clarify the point about expressionistic style made earlier in the passage

    C. qualify the assessment of Rosenblatt's book made in the first paragraph of the passage

    D. give a specific example of one of the accomplishments of Rosenblatt's work

Exercise 6

Almost exactly 30 years ago this week, *TIME* ran a cover story, *The Gun in America*, with a memorable image by the Pop artist Roy Lichtenstein that defined whole notion of in-your-face. That story appeared at a moment when the conduct of national affairs had collapsed into something armed and dangerous. It was 1968, just day after the murder of Robert Kennedy, and before him of Martin Luther King Jr., when the exit wound was becoming a standard problem in American politics. Though the bloodshed of those years emerged out of many causes, one of them was surely the long-standing American romance with guns—the mystique and abundance of firearms, and the ease with which they moved from one hand to another until they fell into the wrong ones. But that sequence of killings also produced a briefly effective national revulsion against gun violence. Before the year was out, Congress would pass the Gun Control Act of 1968, a milestone law that banned most interstate sales, licensed most gun dealers and barred felons, minors and the mentally ill from owning guns.

Now *TIME* returns again to the issue, prompted in part by the string of school shootings that began last year in Pearl, Miss. Gunfire has increasingly intruded into the possibilities of childhood, and the militant wing of adolescence has brought the possibility home. Recent statistics suggest that 1 in 12 high schoolers is threatened or injured with a weapon each year. And while juvenile crime as a whole is down—down even more dramatically than the already precipitous drop in adult crime—the number of youths murdered by firearms went up 153% 0 from 1985 to 1995.

In some ways the school-yard killings are aberrations. The percentage of households that own guns is actually declining, from a decades-long average of about 45% to something closer to 40%. All the same, there are still nearly as many firearms in the U. S. as people—more than 235 million by some estimates. At a time when crime rates are dropping, gun crime is dropping too. But gun murders in the U. S. are still far more common than they were 30 years ago, and more common than they are in any other western industrial nation. We've plateaued in no-man's-land.

Yet unlike in 1968, few people who watch the gun debate expect this moment to produce much in the way of gun-control legislation in congress. The first years of the Clinton Administration, when a Democratic president made deals with a Democratic Congress, saw the passage of the Brady Bill and the assault-gun ban. After the Republican sweep of congress in 1994, the assault-weapon ban was nearly overturned. What prevails in Washington now is a standoff in which only modest measures like the newly introduced proposal for gun safety locks, stand much chance of passage. On the state level, the most popular approach has been decontrol—laws that permit concealed weapons.

Millions in the U. S. believe passionately that their liberty, their safety or both are bound up with the widest possible availability of gun. So 30 years later, guns are still very much with us, murderous little fixtures of the cultural landscape. We live with them as we live with computers or household appliances, but with more difficult consequences—some of them paid in blood. Among the industrial nations, this cultural predicament is ours alone.

1. What is the topic of the article?

   A. The sequence of killings in 1968 produced an effective national revulsion against gun.

   B. Gun murders in the U. S. are still far more common than they were 30 years ago and more common than they are in any other western industrial nation

   C. The gun control in America seriously threatens social safety.

   D. The gun violence in America seriously threatens social safety.

2. The reason that *TIME* ran a cover story 30 years ago was about _____.

   A. the bloodshed caused by guns

   B. the assassination of political leaders such as Martin Luther King Jr. and Robert Kennedy

   C. the frequent interstate gun sales

   D. the mystique and abundance of firearms

3. What is the reason that *TIME* returns to the gun issue?

   A. The string of school shootings happened in Pearl, Miss.

   B. Gunfire threatens the safety of children.

   C. A large number of firearms in the hands of American people.

   D. All of the above.

4. What is the attitude of Americans towards guns?

   A. There is a traditional romantic love for guns in America.

   B. After the Gun Control Act of 1968 people began to give up their fantasy for guns.

   C. American people believe strongly that their liberty, their safety or both will be protected by gun-control legislation.

   D. Millions in the U. S. has realized that they cannot live with guns as they live with computers or household appliances.

5. The author thinks that _____.

   A. the Gun Control Act of 1968 effectively cut down the numbers of gun murders

   B. the legislation today does not produce much to control firearms

   C. the Republican congress in 1994 took active measures to control assault-guns

   D. the modest measures will contribute much to gun-control

Exercise ❼

Telecommuting—substituting the commuter for the trip to the job—has been hailed as a solution to all kinds of problems related to office work. For workers it promises freedom from the office, less time wasted in traffic, and help with child-care conflicts. For management, telecommuting helps keep high performers on board, minimizes tardiness and absenteeism by eliminating commutes, allows periods of solitude for high concentration tasks, and provides scheduling flexibility. In some areas, such as Southern California and Seattle, local governments are encouraging companies to start telecommuting programs in order to reduce rush-hour congestion and improve air quality.

But these benefits do not come easily. Making a telecommuting program work requires careful planning and an understanding of the differences between telecommuting realities and popular images. Many workers are seduced by rosy illusions of life as a telecommuter. A computer programmer from New York City moves to the tranquil Adirondack Mountains and stays in contact with her office via computer. A manager comes into his office three days a week and works at home the other two. An accountant stays home to care for her sick child: she hooks up her telephone modern connections and does office work between calls to the doctor.

These are powerful images, but they are a limited reflection of reality. Telecommuting workers soon learn that it is almost impossible to concentrate on work and care for a young child at the same time. Before a certain age, young children cannot recognize, much less respect, the necessary boundaries between work and family. Additional child support is necessary if the parent is to get any work done.

Management, too, must separate the myth from reality. Although the media has paid a great deal of attention to telecommuting, in most cases it is the employees' situation, not the availability of technology, that precipitates a telecommuting arrangement.

That is partly why, despite the widespread press coverage, the number of companies with work-at-home programs or policy guidelines remains small.

1. Which of the following is not mentioned as a problem related to office work?
   A. Wasting time in traffic.
   B. The conflict between child-care and work.
   C. The inflexible schedule.
   D. The high expense on office equipment.

2. According to the passage, how does telecommuting benefit management?
   A. It enables workers to work intensively without being disturbed by colleagues.
   B. It can reduce the rush-hour congestion.
   C. It can free workers from office.
   D. It can stabilize the staff since they can better take care of the family.

3. What subject does the passage mainly talk about?
   A. Business management strategies.
   B. The use of computer.
   C. The life style of telecommuters.
   D. Extending the workplace by means of computers.

4. According to the passage, the idea of telecommuting is not very realistic because _____.
   A. it's difficult to take care of small children and concentrate on work at the same time
   B. computer technology is not advanced enough
   C. electrical malfunctions can destroy a project
   D. the workers do not always have all the needed resources at home

5. Which of the following is an example of telecommuting as described in the passage?
   A. A scientist in a laboratory developing plans for a space station.
   B. A technical writer sending via computer documents created at home.

C. A computer technician repairing an office computer network.

D. A teacher directing computer assisted learning in a private school.

Exercise ❽

As a young bond trader, Buttonwood was given two pieces of advice, trading rules of thumb, if you will: that bad economic news is good news for bond markets and that every utterance dropping from the lips of Paul Volcker, the then chairman of the Federal Reserve, and the man who restored the central bank's credibility by stomping on runaway inflation, should be respected than Pope's orders. Today's traders are, of course, a more sophisticated bunch. But the advice still seems good, apart from two slight drawbacks. The first is that the well-chosen utterances from the present chairman of the Federal Reserve, Alan Greenspan, is of more than passing difficulty. The second is that, of late, good news for the economy has not seemed to upset bond investors all that much. For all the cheer that has crackled down the wires, the yield on ten-year bonds—which you would expect to rise on good economic news—is now, at 4.2%, only two-fifths of a percentage point higher than it was at the start of the year. Pretty much unmoved, in other words.

Yet the news from the economic front has been better by far than anyone could have expected. On Tuesday November 25th, revised numbers showed that America's economy grew by an annual 8.2% in the third quarter, a full percentage point more than originally thought, driven by the ever-spendthrift American consumer and, for once, corporate investment. Just about every other piece of information coming out from special sources shows the same strength. New houses are still being built at a fair clip. Exports are rising, for all the protectionist crying. Even employment, in what had been mocked as a jobless recovery, increased by 125,000 or thereabouts in September and October. Rising corporate profits, low credit spreads and the biggest-ever rally in the junk-bond market do not, on the face of it, suggest anything other than a deep and long-lasting recovery. Yet Treasury-bond yields have fallen.

If the rosy economic backdrop makes this odd, making it doubly odd is an apparent absence of foreign demand. Foreign buyers of Treasuries, especially Asian central banks, who had been swallowing American government debt like there was no tomorrow, seem to have had second thoughts lately. In September, according to the latest available figures, foreigners bought only $56 billion of Treasuries, compared with $25.1 billion the previous month and an average of $38.7 billion in the preceding four months. In an effort to keep a lid on the yen's rise, the Japanese central bank is still busy buying dollars and parking the money in government debt. Just about everybody else seems to have been selling.

1. The advice for Buttonwood suggests that _____.

   A. Paul Volcker enjoyed making comments on controlling inflation

   B. the Federal Reserve has an all-capable power over inflation control

   C. economy has the greatest influence upon the daily life of ordinary people

   D. the economic sphere and bond markets are indicative of each other

2. The word "passing" (Line 7, Paragraph 1) most probably means _____.

A. instant   B. trivial   C. simple   D. negligible

3. Which of the following is responsible for the rapid economic growth in the U. S. ?

    A. Domestic consumers.   B. Foreign investments.

    C. Real estate market.   D. Recovering bond market.

4. According to the last paragraph, most Asian central banks are becoming _____.

    A. rather regretful   B. less ambitious

    C. more cautious   D. speculative

5. The phrase "keep a lid on" (Line 6, Paragraph 3) most probably means _____.

    A. put an end to   B. set a limit on

    C. tighten the control over   D. reduce the speed of

Exercise ❾

Psychologist Yueh-Ting Lee received an electronic mail message several years ago that included some barbed observations about the quality of life in several countries. "Heaven is a place with an American house, Chinese food, British police, a German car, and French art. " Lee's correspondent wrote, "Hell is a place with a Japanese House, British food, German art, and a French car. " While these national stereotypes fall short of absolute truths, asserts Lee of Westfield (Mass.) State College, they are accurate enough to give the aphorism its humorous punch. Houses in the United States indeed boast more space, on average than Japanese dwellings. A Chinese inn probably holds greater culinary potential than a British pub.

In this respect, stereotypes, rather than representing unjustified prejudices, typically function as thought-efficient starting points for understanding other cultures and social groups, as well as the individuals who belong to them, Lee holds. "Stereotypes are probabilistic beliefs we use to categorize people, objects, and events," Lee proposes. "We have to have stereotypes to deal with so much information in a world with which we are often uncertain and unfamiliar. " Many psychologists find this opinion about as welcome as a cut in their research grants. They view stereotyping as a breeding ground for errant generalizations about others that easily lead to racism, sexism, and other forms of bigotry.

In the realm of stereotypes, intelligence gives way to misjudgment, maintains Charles Stangor of the University of Maryland at College Park. People employ stereotypes mainly to simplify how they think about others and to enhance their views of themselves and the groups to which they belong, Stangor holds. In the hands of politically powerful folks, stereotypes abet efforts to stigmatize and exploit selected groups, he adds. Stangor's argument fails to give stereotypes their due as often helpful, if not absolutely precise, probes of the social world, Lee responds. He contends that a growing body of research suggests that in many real-life situations, stereotypes accurately capture cultural or group differences.

For more than 60 years, scientists have treated stereotypes as by definition erroneous, illogical, and inflexible. This view was voiced in journalist Walter Lippman's 1922 book *Public Opinion*, in which he argued that stereotypes of social groups invariably prove incomplete and biased. In the 1950s, psychologist Gordon W. Allport characterized stereotypes as invalid beliefs about all members of a group. Allport treated the opinion "all Germans are efficient" as a stereotype, but not "Germans, on average, are more efficient than people in other countries". Debate arose at that time over whether some stereotypes encase a "kernel of truth".

Lippman's fear that stereotypes cause social harm gained particular favor after 1970, as psychologists rushed to expose errors and biases in social judgments. Recently, however, psychologists have shown more interest in delineating the extent to which decision making proves accurate in specific contexts.

Lee's approach to stereotypes falls squarely within the focus on accuracy of judgment. His interest in how people comprehend ethnic and cultural differences intensified after he emigrated from China to the United States in 1986 to attend graduate school. At that point, he began to suspect that a keener scientific understanding of stereotypes might have valuable applications. For instance, Lee asserts, efforts at conflict resolution between ethnic groups or nations may work best if both sides receive help in confronting real cultural differences that trigger mutual animosities. "Group differences, not prejudice, are the root cause of tension and contact between various cultural and racial groups," he contends. "The most effective way to improve intergroup relation, is to admit and to discuss frankly the existing differences at the same time explaining that there is nothing wrong with being different."

Bridge-building efforts of the kind counteract the natural tendency to emphasize negative features in stereotypes, argues Reuben M. Baron of the University of Connecticut in Storrs. Humans evolved in groups that negotiated a dangerous world, he states. Our ancestors must have relied on stereotypes to marshal quick responses to potential threats, such as distinguishing predators from prey, friends from enemies and fellow group members from outsiders. Baron asserts. The ability to categorize individuals into types may also have been crucial for communicating with others as group, grew in size and complexity, Baron proposes. In large communities, stereotypes capitalized on people's propensity to fill social roles that match their own personal qualities. Warriors in an ancient society, for instance, might reasonably have been stereotyped as aggressive and unemotional, while story-tellers and musicians were accurately tagged as, expressive and friendly. Despite their handiness, even accurate stereotypes can result in mistaken beliefs about others, according to Baron.

Consider the misunderstandings over punctuality that develop between Mexican and U. S. businesspeople. Lee says that north of the border, Mexicans get stereotyped as "the manana people" because of their tendency to show up for meetings considerably after prearranged times and to miss deadlines for completing assigned tasks. U. S. officials may see this trait as unforgivable deal breaking, whereas their Mexican counterparts—who do not dispute their own tardiness—deride Americans as "robots" who rigidly reach conclusions by specified dates before gathering all relevant data and fully grasping tile issues. Businesspeople from each culture perceptively categorize the behavior of those in the other group but misunderstand the cultural roots of their different time perspectives, Lee says.

Such subtleties of stereotyping have gone largely unexplored, remarks David C. Funder, a psychologist at the University of California, Riverside. Most research of the past 25 years has tried to catalog the ways in which expectations about social categories distort a person's judgment, usually by placing the individual in laboratory situations intended to elicit racial or sexual stereotypes. This approach neglects to ask whether people in a wide array of real-life situations incorporate accurate information into their stereotypes, Funder holds. "We desperately need to know which of the judgments we make of each other and of ourselves are right, which are wrong, and when," Funder contends.

1. The word "stereotype" most probably means _____?
   A. category   B. conflict   C. prejudice   D. truth

2. According to the passage, which of the following statements is true?
   A. According to Yueh-Ting Lee, national stereotypes represent unjustified prejudices.
   B. Charles Stangor believes that stereotypes accurately reflect cultural or group differences.
   C. Lee believes that understanding stereotypes can be helpful in understanding others.
   D. Reuben M. Baron sees no danger in stereotypes.

3. Which of the following researchers and writers cited in the passage presents a positive opinion of stereotypes?
   A. Yueh-Ting Lee   B. Charles Stangor
   C. Walter Lippman   D. Gordon W. Allport

4. The passage tends to agree with all of the following statements except _____.
   A. We can use stereotypes to help with conflict resolution
   B. Understanding stereotypes may help us survive in a complex and dangerous world
   C. A further research into stereotypes is highly necessary
   D. Stereotypes are invalid so that we do not need them at all

5. Which one of the following might be the best title for this passage?
   A. The Inflexibility of Stereotypes   B. The Stereotype of Stereotypes
   C. The Malfunction of Stereotypes   D. The Illogicality of Stereotypes

Exercise 11

Tourism has seriously damaged fragile ecosystems like the Alps—the winter skiing playground of Europe—and the trekking areas of the Himalayas. Worldwide, it poses a serious threat to coastal habitats like dunes, mangrove forests and coral reefs. It fuels a booming and usually illegal trade in the products of threatened wildlife, from tortoiseshell and coral to ivory. Its "consumers" inevitably bring their habits and expectations with them—whether it's hot showers and flush toilets or well-watered greens for golfers. In the Himalayas, showers for trekkers often mean firewood, which means deforestation. In Hawaii and Barbados, it was found that each tourist used between six and ten times as much water and electricity as a local. In Goa, villagers forced to walk to wells for their water had to watch as a pipeline to a mew luxury hotel was built through their land. Over the past decade golf, because of its appetite for land, water and herbicides, has emerged as one of the biggest culprits, so much so that "golf wars" have broken out in parts of Southeast Asia; campaigners in Japan, one of the chief exponents of golf tourism, have launched an annual World No Golf Day.

This is not to say tourism can't do some good—but the cost-benefit equation is complex. Historic monuments, houses and gardens thrive on visitors. Throughout much of the world, but notably in southern and eastern Africa, tourism underpins the survival of wildlife. Why else would small farmers put up with elephants trampling their crops? Whale watching is now a bigger business than whaling. In the uplands of Rwanda, known to millions through the film *Gorillas in the Mist*, the mountain gorilla's salvation lies partly in the income and interest generated by tourists visiting in small groups. In Kenya a lion's worth is estimated at $7,000 a year in tourist income—for an elephant herd the figure is $610,000. And if large animals, with large ranges, are protected, then so are their habitats—the national parks.

Yet none of these gains is unqualified. To get to see your whales and your gorillas, for example, you have to travel, by car, coach or plane. Each time you do so you're effectively setting fire to a small reservoir of gasoline—and releasing several roomfuls of carbon dioxide into the atmosphere. Transport is the world's fastest growing source of carbon dioxide emissions: leisure travel accounts for half of all transport. The cumulative result of such activity is one of the biggest disruptions in the Earth's history—global warming, climate change and rising seas.

Some observers now argue that tourism can strengthen local cultures by encouraging an awareness of tradition and the ceremonies and festivals that go with it. But what's the value of tradition if it's kept alive self-consciously, for profit, and bears little relation to real life—which, today, across the world, grows ever more uniform? The pressures of tourism breed a phenomenon often referred to as "Densification", in which culture and history are transformed, the authentic giving way to Disney-like replicas. What's undeniable is that tourism, in one way or another, changes tradition.

In truth, there are no easy answers to the dilemmas posed by mass tourism. Awareness, certainly, is a step forward—the knowledge of what it means to be a tourist. With that comes the ability to make better choices, where and how and even whether to travel. An increasing number of nonprofit organizations offer working holidays, in which the economic and social asymmetries that lie at the heart of the holiday industry are somewhat redressed: The tourist takes but also gives. Among the best-known is the research organization Earthwatch.

Such initiatives are undoubtedly one of the ways forward for tourism. The world, clearly, is not going to stop taking holidays—but equally clearly we can no longer afford to ignore the consequences. And if one of the major culprits has been the industrialization of travel, a genuinely postindustrial tourism, with the emphasis on people and places rather than product and profits, could turn out to be significantly more planet-friendly.

1. Which of the following places is cited to illustrate the positive part of tourism?

   A. Rwanda.　　　B. Hawaii.　　　C. Goa.　　　D. the Alps.

2. What does "culprit" in Para. 1 Line 11 most probably mean?

A. Entertainment.   B. Crime.

C. Punishment.   D. Competition.

3. What can we infer from the passage?

   A. Leisure travel is the world's largest source of carbon dioxide emissions.

   B. Since tourism may bring a large sum of revenue annually, the government should spare no effort to develop local tourism.

   C. A tourist should have a serious consideration before he decides to travel.

   D. Some observers contend that traditions and the ceremonies and festivals that go with local cultures are weakened due to the quick spread of tourism.

4. Earthwatch is an organization which _____.

   A. is money-oriented

   B. studies the asymmetries between economy and society

   C. urges people to give up their holiday plans

   D. offers people some tasks to do during their trips

5. What is the author's attitude towards tourism?

   A. Tourism must be highly industrialized.

   B. Something must be done urgently to assure the sustained development of tourism.

   C. The more money we make from tourism, the better world it will be.

   D. The problems generated by mass tourism can be tackled in a walk.

参考答案

Exercise 1

1. C 2. D 3. D 4. C 5. A

Exercise 2

1. D 2. B 3. D 4. A 5. C

Exercise 3

1. C 2. D 3. A 4. B 5. C

Exercise 4

1. A 2. C 3. D 4. B 5. A

Exercise 5

1. A 2. D 3. B 4. D 5. D

Exercise 6

1. C 2. B 3. D 4. A 5. B

Exercise 7

1. D　2. A　3. D　4. A　5. B

Exercise 8

1. D　2. D　3. A　4. C　5. B

Exercise 9

1. C　2. C　3. A　4. D　5. B

Exercise 10

1. A　2. B　3. C　4. D　5. B

参考文献

1. Bruce Bower,"The Stereotype of Stereotypes", *Science News*, June 29, 1996.

2. David Nicholson-Lord,"The Politics of Travel", *The Nation*, October 6, 1997.

3. Paul Recer, "Gene Mapping May Foster Discrimination", *Ann Arbor News*, February 12, 2001.

4. Sandra Silberstein, Barbara K. Dobson and Mark A. Clarke,"Reader's Choice"(4th ed.), Beijing World Publishing Corporation, 2002.

5. Aaron Scharf, "Art and Photography", Penguin, 1983.

6. 《历年考研真题集—英语》,http://edu.sina.com.cn/focus/kaoyzt/index.html.

7. 《2009 年硕士研究生入学考试英语真题》,http://cet.hjenglish.com/detail_63512.htm.

8. 《2008 年教育部考试中心考研英语模拟试题—阅读理解部分汇编》,http://bbs.freekaoyan.com/thread-219164-1-1.html.

Ⅱ. 阅读与理解 B 节

　　B 节共有三种备选题型:提供文章的部分框架,测试其余部分。考生根据已给部分结构或内容方面的信息对其进行"部分还原"。这种题型是打乱文章的顺序,要求考生将其"完整还原"。这就要求考生要善于捕捉和把握文章的整体语言结构和各选项结构或内容之间的关系。

1. 备选题 1 和备选题 2

　　备选题型 1 和备选题型 2 测试的目的:文章的整体结构和各个部分之间在逻辑结构和语言功能等方面的关系。

　　这类文章的语言体现的特点有"显性的"和"隐性的"。前者是文章语言框架结构和各个部分之间衔接关系有明显的词语特征,如:举例(for example, for instance, as is shown in 等),因果(for, because, thus, as a result 等),转折(however, but, yet 等),递进(in addition, moreover, furthermore 等),对比(by contrast, whereas, meanwhile 等),强调(in fact, as a matter of fact, indeed, as it were 等)。后者没有明显的语言结构特征,所以有些文章只靠内

容的逻辑关系来构成文章的结构框架,并衔接文章的各个部分。这就要求考生去读懂文章的内容,抓住要义,把握文章结构,认清文章结构发展的顺序,培养自己的推理、判断的能力。

2. 备选题 3

备选题 3 测试重点放在"文章的局部",这就要求考生深刻地理解和熟练地把握文章各个部分的内容逻辑关系。具体地说,考点可能是小节标题、观点或论点,也可能是部分内容的综合,还有可能是支撑论点或观点的例证。

Part B

1) 试题特点及应对策略

Text 1

Directions: In the following text, some sentences have been removed. For Questions (1—5), choose the most suitable one from the list A-G to fit into each of the numbered blank. There are two extra choices, which do not fit in any of the blanks.

In the last 18 months many immigrants are leaving United Stated willingly or unwillingly. And countless others are deciding not to come. The reasons: a slowing U. S. economy and impressive growth in developing countries, where many immigrants hail from.

The slowing economy means less work for immigrants, and for the people who make a living providing services to them. Julio Duarte, a Honduran who was among a group of 50 day laborers outside a Home Depot in Hempstead, N. Y. , recently, has lived in America for three years, and he's found it tough going lately. "For four months I haven't been able to work," he says. __1__. Alam Espinoza, 53, who cuts hair at the Ely Ella Salon in central Phoenix, has seen her daily business drop from \$500 to \$100 since last year. "If this goes on," Espinoza says, "the salon won't stay open. "

Most immigrants seek work that enables them to support families back home. But in the first quarter of 2008, Mexico's central bank said remittances from the United States fell 2. 9 percent. __2__. About one third of those surveyed—and 49 percent of those who have been in the United States fewer than five years—said they were thinking about going home.

__3__. Brazil's chronically weak currency, the real, has gained strength against the dollar. Travel agents in areas with large Brazilian communities report that thousands of Brazilian clients have purchased one-way plane tickets in recent months. Workers from South American countries like Ecuador and Bolivia are increasingly seeking their fortune in Spain, __4__.

Strength in emerging economies is also exerting a gravitational pull on potential migrants. Today, about 84 percent of the graduates of the prestigious Indian Institutes of Technology decide to pursue careers at home, compared with only 65 percent seven years ago. __5__. "The lure of immigration to the U. S. is still pretty strong, though its intensity is declining," says Shubha Singh, a writer on the Indian diaspora. The American Dream still holds of a powerful strong appeal for around the world. But the choice of whether to immigrate to the United States requires a careful weighing of the costs and benefits, the risks and rewards. Given the climate—at home and abroad—people like Salvador Luna in Mexico City are thinking more than twice about embarking on the journey.

[A] The weak dollar, which reduces the amount of money people can send home, is a contributing factor.

[B] Nationwide, deportations of illegal immigrants rose from 178,657 in fiscal 2005 to 282,548 in fiscal 2007 up 58 percent.

[C] In the Southwest, commercial districts of cities that were once thronged with construction workers now resemble ghost towns.

[D] And a survey released by the Inter-American Development Bank in April found that 3 million fewer Latino immigrants are sending money home from the United States this year compared with two years ago.

[E] The government has also been going after employers who hire undocumented workers. The combined number of arrests of employers and illegal workers has increased greatly.

[F] where language, lenient immigration policies and the strong euro make the environment more congenial.

[G] Rising living standards and the spread of Western-style capitalism are responsible.

分析:

本文是一篇有关移民的文章.

第一段是开头段落,介绍了过去十八个月里许多移民离开美国,而原本准备移民美国的人也放弃了去美国的打算.

第二段主要介绍了美国经济衰退造成了工作岗位的减少,使得一些移民开始离开美国.

第三段讲的还是美国经济放缓,造成现在从美国汇回墨西哥养家的汇款有所下降.

第四段主要讲的是美元走低,使得南美的一些人寻求去欧洲发展.

第五段讲了其他国家的经济发展挽留了很多的本国人才,使得移民美国的诱惑开始下降.

试题解析:

我们先大体浏览一下各个选项的内容.

选项 A 主要介绍了美元贬值是造成移民汇款数量下降的原因。第三段作者具体介绍了"Brazil's chronically weak currency, the real, has gained strength against the dollar."由此引出很多南美人去西班牙淘金。可以看出美元贬值是一个直接诱因。所以第 3 题应该是 A 选项。

选项 B 的大体意思是:全美国移送非法移民的人数上升了 58 倍。通过阅读我们发现文章里并没有讨论移送非法移民。

选项 C 的意思是在美国的西南部曾经的建筑工人聚集地,现在好似一座城市的废墟。通读文章我们在第二段里发现造成这种现象主要是由于美国经济放缓,许多工人找不到工作,被迫离开那里。例子之一就是连"Ely Ella Salon"的"daily business"也从 $500 下降到 $100,所以 C 选项应该是第 1 题。

选项 D 讲的是"the Inter-American Development Bank"的调查表明"Latino immigrants"从美国汇回家的钱要比两年前少。暗示了美国经济不景气,移民的工作受了很大的影响。正因为如此,才有了后面的句子"About one third of those surveyed—and 49 percent of those who have been in the United States fewer than five years—said they were thinking about going home."所以第 2 题的答案是 D。

选项 E 说,美国政府正在追查雇佣非法移民的雇主。受到逮捕的雇主和非法移民的人数有了很大地增长。通读文章,我们不难发现在开头段落里,解释美国移民减少的原因时,作者给出文章的关键句是"a slowing U. S. economy and impressive growth in developing countries",并没有涉及政府追查雇佣非法移民这一说。

选项 F 我们可以看到这里考的是一个句子结构。"where language, lenient immigration policies and the strong euro make the environment more congenial."是一个定语从句,修饰前面的"西班牙"。意思是由于语言相通、宽松的移民政策和欧元强劲使得西班牙成了一个移民的最佳地点。作者用这个定语从句进一步说为什么有很多的南美人去欧洲发展。所以第 4 题的答案是 F。

选项 G 的意思是"主要的原因是生活水平的提高和西方模式的资本主义在全球的传播"。一些发展中国家的经济发展挽留了很多的本国人才,使得移民美国的诱惑开始下降。"Indian Institutes of Technology"的例子说明,七年前只有 65% 的人在国内求职,而现在有 84% 的人愿意在国内发展。其原因正是 G 选项。所以第 5 题的答案是 G。

Text 2

Directions: In the following text, some sentences have been removed. For Questions (1—5), choose the most suitable one from the list A-G to fit into each of the numbered blank. There are two extra choices, which do not fit in any of the blanks.

A fatal night of excessive drinking at a Louisiana university stirs up the debate over the drinking culture in American colleges. __1__ . By early morning Wynne was found dead after downing the equivalent of about 24 drinks, had a blood-alcohol level six times the amount at which the state considers a person intoxicated. His death sent a tremor and set off a round of back-to-school soul searching about binge drinking on campuses all over the U. S. __2__ .

The fact that many college students, like Wynne, are under the legal drinking age is rarely an obstacle. Many drink at private parties off campus, which an older student buying the alcohol. __3__ . In fact, raising the legal drinking age from 18 to 21, may actually have made the binging problem worse. Instead of drinking in well-monitored settings, the young often experiment in private homes and bars, where there are few checks in place to deter dangerous practices.

Now American colleges today are among the nation's most alcohol-drenched institutions. American's 12 million undergraduates drink 4 billion cans of beer a year and spend $446 on alcoholic beverages—more than they spend on soft drink and textbooks combined. Excessive drinking among college students has been blamed for at least six deaths in the past years. __4__ . Several schools, including the University of Colorado, the University of Iowa and Ohio State, have recently been the site of "beer riots", some set off by toughened alcohol policies.

Many colleges have been getting tougher on the issue. Schools are still handing out literature and holding workshops, but they know that education is not enough to solve the problem. Administrators have become quicker to penalize campus groups that sponsor reckless parties. __5__. "The most important area for schools to focus on now is working with the larger community to ensure that students cannot abuse alcohol at private homes and bars. And those of legal drinking age are encouraged to drink responsibly on campus." says William DeJong, a professor of the Harvard School of Public Health.

[A] Benjamin Wynne, 20, received a pledge pin from the fraternity that voted him into the brotherhood, and he got rip-roaring drunk to celebrate.

[B] The incident illustrates that although the drinking age is now 21 everywhere in America, making almost college students, underage, alcohol remains widely available—and highly promoted—to students of all ages.

[C] Fraternity parties are famous for drinking games that make a sport of quick and excessive consumption. Bars in college neighborhoods pull in students with all-you-can-drink policies—$6.50 for as much beer as a customer can hold.

[D] Bar's enforcement of the drinking age can be lax, false IDs are common, and legal-age friends are often willing to buy the drinks and bring them back to the table.

[E] Studies show that excessive drinking affects not only the bingers but also fellow students, who are more likely to report lost sleep, interrupted studies and sexual assaults on campuses with high binge-drinking rates.

[F] And more than 50 colleges now permit students to avoid temptation and rowdy behavior by living in alcohol-free dorms. But banning alcohol on campus does nothing about the dangers that lurk just outside.

[G] Social life is still synonymous with alcohol-lubricated gatherings at fraternities and sororities, as well as the tailgate-party and hip-flask scene that accompanies athletic events,

分析：

本文是一篇有关当前美国大学酗酒问题的文章。

第一段是开头段落，介绍了"Louisiana university"发生一件因为酗酒而造成的死亡事件，此事件在美国大学里引起了轰动。

第二段主要介绍了美国大学不到合法喝酒年龄的学生可以通过各种渠道弄到酒，而对他们的监控基本上处于失控状态。

第三段进一步介绍了大学是美国酒的最大消费市场之一，1,200万大学生一年要喝掉40亿听啤酒，人均消费额为446美元。而所造成的后果是校园暴力、性攻击等事件。

第四段主要讲的是虽然学校当局认真地对待校园酗酒，但他们也知道光是使用教育手段解决问题是不够的。还要严惩举办酗酒聚会的发起人，还要和一些大型的社团一起来解决问题。

试题解析：

我们先大体浏览一下各个选项的内容。

选项 A 主要是拓展文章的第一句"A fatal night of excessive drinking at a Louisiana university stirs up the debate over the drinking culture in American colleges."说明"Louisiana university"的一个夜晚发生一件致命事件。通过后面一句"By early morning Wynne was found dead…"，我们可以确定第 1 题应该是 A 选项。

选项 B 的大体意思是这起事件表明虽然美国喝酒的法定年龄是二十一岁，但是不到法定年龄的大学生照样可以得到酒精，暗指了 Wynne 的死因。这句是第一段的结尾句，但同时又起到了承上启下的作用，所以第 2 题应该是 B 选项。

选项 C 的意思是兄弟会以玩酗酒游戏而著称，大学地区的酒吧也会推出活动，只要付 6.5 美元就可以尽情地喝啤酒。此选项不符合任何一题。

选项 D 讲的是酒吧对喝酒年龄限制也不是很严，人们可以使用假身份证，到达法定年龄的朋友在酒吧里得到酒精。这一句实际上是这一段主题句"The fact that many college students, like Wynne, are under the legal drinking age is rarely an obstacle."的第二个拓展句，所以第 3 题的答案是 D。

选项 E 是说，研究表明大学生酗酒影响的不仅是他们自己，还影响其他的同学，甚至造成校园暴力、性攻击等事件。从文章结构上来说这一选项是拓展"Now American colleges today are among the nation's most alcohol-drenched institutions."作者在量化了大学生酗酒之后（1,200 万大学生一年要喝掉 40 亿听啤酒，人均消费额为 446 美元），用研究结果来表明酗酒的后果。所以第 4 题应该是 E 选项。

选项 F 的大意是，现在尽管有超过 50 所的学校让学生住在"alcohol-free dorms"里，但是校园里禁酒令对于来自于校外的危险仍然无所作为。这一选项除了是拓展句外，还有承上起下的作用。一是强调了学校禁止校园酗酒的措施，还引出了学校应该和一些大型的社团联手起来解决大学生酗酒的问题。所以第 5 题的答案是 F。

选项 G 的意思是社交依然是聚会灌酒男女生联谊的聚会，足球赛前停车场相聚都会猛喝一通，观看体育比赛也会掏出随身带来的小酒加以助兴。通读全篇，我们会发现此选项不符合任何一题。

Text 3

Directions：In the following text, some sentences have been removed. For Questions（1—5），choose the most suitable one from the list A-G to fit into each of the numbered blank. There are two extra choices, which do not fit in any of the blanks.

As questions about the effectiveness of mass marketing have grown, advertising has been assailed by other doubts, too. Where once it was thought that commercials sold goods, it is now acknowledged that many of them do no such thing：most people never actually buy the majority of products they see advertised on television.

Apart from the special case of new product launches, it seems that advertising's main role is not to get people to switch from one brand to another, but to reinforce the loyalty of people already predisposed towards a particular brand. "Most advertising is not trying to sell. It's just maintaining your position in a competitive market," says Andrew Ehrenberg, professor of marketing at London's South Bank University. __1__.

But if mass-market advertising does not sell products, what will? For some companies, the answer lies in direct marketing. This means talking to customers one-to-one by telephone, mail or, increasingly, the Internet. A decade ago, this option was less attractive. For a given amount of money, a television commercial would reach about 50 times as many people as one of the crudely written junk mail—shots of the period, and achieve a better response. __2__.

This change has been reflected in the growth of new direct marketing techniques. __3__. On the Internet, companies collect information on customers electronically and send them e-mails about new products.

__4__. In February, WPP, the world's second biggest advertising group, reported that its revenues from marketing and Internet advertising overtook those from traditional advertising for the first time last year. That could turn out to be a sign of the times as companies explore the new marketing opportunities that technology is opening up. Nicholas Negroponte, director of the media lab at Massachusetts Institute of Technology, predicts an "enormous decline" in network television advertising over the next few years. __5__.

[A] Many companies now use loyalty programs to collect information about their customers, then use it as a marketing tool. Telephone call centers have mushroomed, using databases and market segmentation techniques to target consumers for telemarketing campaigns.

[B] But in the last few years, the quality of direct marketing has improved. The falling cost and rising power of information technology have increased the ability of companies to collect, sort and refine data on potential customers. This allows them to target consumers more effectively.

[C] As spending on direct marketing has risen, the big advertising agencies have added to their traditional advertising operations by buying marketing and Internet companies.

[D] He says it will be replaced in the emerging digital world by tailored advertising "so timely and so personal we will say thank you when we see it".

[E] Every company has put resources and energy into improving manufacturing efficiency, into reducing overhead, into optimizing the supply chain and generally re-engineering their businesses.

[F] Today, rising prosperity in developed countries and a vast increase in the range of goods an services have encouraged much greater individualism. People conform less to stereotypes based on age, gender, class or occupation.

[G] It's about reminding people and keeping brands salient to people, so that they go on asking for Coke rather than Pepsi, or Bingo rather Bango.

分析：

本文是一篇有关美国广告的文章。

第一段是开头段落,主要讲的是尽管很多商品在大做广告,但是实际上大多数人从来没有购买过在电视广告上看到的商品。

第二段主要介绍了除了特殊情况,新产品的推出,似乎其广告的主要作用不是让人们从一个品牌切换到另一个,而是要强化人们对于某一特定品牌也已存在的喜爱。

第三段介绍了商家所采取的营销手段是直接营销。这意味着商家需要和客户之间进行电子邮件或越来越多的互联网的联系,达到一对一通话。在过去几年中,直接营销质量有所改善。成本的下降和日益强大的信息技术增强了公司的能力,增加了公司的收集、分类和优化潜在客户的信息。这使他们能够更有效地锁定消费者。

第四段主要讲的是许多公司现在使用忠诚度计划,收集有关顾客的信息,然后用它作为营销工具。

第五段主要讲的是由于在直销上的支出有所增长,大型广告代理商已经加入到他们的传统广告业务的销售和购买的互联网公司。比如这一措施使 WPP 集团,这个世界上第二大广告集团公司收入第一次超过了传统广告模式的收入。而美国麻省理工学院媒体研究室主任 Nicholas Negroponte 认为,在新兴的数字化世界里,电视网广告将被具有针对性的广告取代,这种广告"非常及时,非常适应个人需要"。

试题解析:

我们先大体浏览一下各个选项的内容。

选项 A 的意思是:许多公司现在使用忠诚度计划,收集有关顾客的信息,然后用它作为营销工具。电话呼叫中心如雨后春笋般,利用数据库和市场分割技术,目标是针对消费者的促销活动。A 选项是对这一段第一句"This change has been reflected in the growth of new direct marketing techniques."的拓展。解释了新的直销方法是什么。由此我们可以确定第 3 题应该是 A 选项。

选项 B 的意思是,但在过去几年中,直接营销质量有所改善。成本的下降和日益强大的信息技术的能力,增加了公司收集、分类和优化潜在客户信息的能力,这使他们能够更有效地锁定消费者。

作者用了一个问题开始了第三段——如果大众市场的广告不销售产品,将如何?但是,对于一些公司来说,答案就在于直接营销。B 选项是对这一部分的进一步拓展。所以第 2 题应该是 B 选项。

选项 C 的意思是,由于在直销上的支出有所增长,大型广告代理商已经加入到他们的传统广告业务的销售和购买的互联网公司。这一措施使 WPP 集团,这个世界上第二大广告集团公司收入第一次超过了传统广告模式的收入。我们通过阅读第五段"WPP"的案例会发现,正因为 C 选项,这个世界上第二大广告集团公司收入第一次超过了传统广告模式的收入。所以第 4 题应该是 C 选项

选项 D 讲的是美国麻省理工学院媒体研究室主任 Nicholas Negroponte 认为在新兴的数字化世界里,电视网广告将被具有针对性的广告取代,这种广告"非常及时,非常适应个人需要,我们看过后会说声谢谢"。Nicholas Negroponte 预言了电视网广告在来的几年里将会急剧衰退。D 选项是对这一预言的进一步说明。所以第 5 题的答案定位到选项 D。

选项 E 是说,每家公司都投入财力和精力,提高生产效率,缩减管理费用,改善供货体系,调整企业整体结构。通读全篇,我们会发现此选项不符合任何一题。

选项 F 的大意是,今天,发达国家日益繁荣,商品和服务的种类大幅增加,这使得消费者

有可能在更大程度上表现自己的个性。人们不像以前那样追随以年龄、性别、阶层或职业为基础的模式。通读全篇,我们会发现此选项不符合任何一题。

选项 G 的意思是广告就是提醒人们,保持他们对品牌的注意,这样,他们会继续买可口可乐,而不买百事可乐。作者用了"Andrew Ehrenberg, professor of marketing at London's South Bank University"所说的两句话来作为这一段的拓展句,G 选项是他所说的第二句话。所以第 1 题的选项是 G。

Text 4

Directions: **In the following text, some sentences have been removed. For Questions (1—5), choose the most suitable one from the list A-G to fit into each of the numbered blank. There are two extra choices, which do not fit in any of the blanks.**

A U. S. News analysis shows that towns with casinos have experienced an upsurge of crime at the same time it was dropping for the nation as a whole. ___1___. (The crime rate in small cities and towns, with populations similar to those that have embraced casinos, rose by 1 percent in the same period.).

The gambling industry argues that crime often drops when casinos move in, saying that the rates should account for the upsurge of visitors to gambling locales. By adjusting for visitors—e. g., since 5 million people visited Shreveport, La. 's casinos, add 5 million to the city's population—gambling backers can show crime rates dropping. ___2___.

For a nation that gets its popular history of gambling from movies like *The Godfather* and *Casinos*, however, there is one myth that dies slowly: that legalized gambling is controlled by organized crime. Today's casino executives are more likely to have Harvard M. B. A. 's than mob ties, thanks to corporation ownership and tight casino regulation.

Still big money attracts opportunistic criminals. Some Los Angeles street gang members have relocated to Las Vegas. And organized crime groups have managed to infiltrate many ancillary businesses such as maintaining the machines or providing other services, says a senior FBI official who specializes in mob matters. ___3___. In New Orleans, FBI agents bugged an Italian restaurant to eavesdrop on the video-poker-machine-skimming plans of organized crimes bosses with nicknames like Noogie and Fat Frank. The result was 24 convictions against members of the Marcello, Gambino and Genovese crime families. ___4___.

Although corruption of public figures remains rare, gambling interests have become adept players in legal political influence—through lavish campaign contributions. ___5___. The $ 3. 1 million in contributions to candidates and parties in 2000 ranked just below those of a long-powerful lobby, the National Rifle Association.

[A] The commander of the growing backlash against the multibillion-dollar gambling industry has no office, no staff, no regular salary.

[B] They recorded a 5. 8 percent jump in crime rates in 2000, while crime around the country fell 2 percent. The 31 places that got new casinos just the year before saw their crime jump the most: 7.7 percent.

[C] But even crime-troubled tourist destinations like New York and Washington, D. C., don't adjust their crime statistics. The FBI calls such studies "self-serving".

[D] Young workers see a fast-track future in working for the casinos rather than in retrenching factories like Caterpillar.

[E] He also says they often use labor unions to do so. Other criminals get involved in places where regulations are weak.

[F] The FBI is also investigating allegations that Louisiana state legislators took multimillion-dollar payoffs to approve an expansion of video poker.

[G] The U. S. News computer analysis found that gambling companies have cracked the top five among interest group givers.

分析：

本文是一篇有关美国赌博之风的文章。

第一段大意是：美国新闻分析表明，有赌场的城镇就会有犯罪高潮。2000 年记录表明犯罪率上升了 5.8%，而全国各地的犯罪下降 2%。新开了赌场的 31 个的地方，犯罪率上升了 7.7%。

第二段大意是：博彩业人士的观点正相反，他们认为开赌场降低了犯罪。

第三段大意是：赌博合法化是有组织的犯罪活动。而今天的赌场管理人员更可能有哈佛大学工商管理硕士学位，非暴徒。

第四段大意是：赚大钱的机会吸引了犯罪分子。有组织的犯罪团伙已经渗透到许多辅助性业务，如维护机器，或提供其他服务。

第五段大意是：尽管公众人物的腐败仍然是罕见的，但赌博集团却通过大量的捐款来施加政治影响。

试题解析：

我们先大体浏览一下各个选项的内容。

选项 A 意思是：美国赌博业营业额多达数 10 亿美元，反赌博力量日益增长，但这支力量的领导人没有办公地点，没有一套工作班子，也没有固定收入。A 选项不符合任何一题。

选项 B 的大体意思是：2000 年记录表明犯罪率上升了 5.8%，而全国各地的犯罪下降 2%。新开了赌场的 31 个的地方，犯罪率上升了 7.7%。B 选项是主题句"A U. S. News analysis shows that towns with casinos have experienced an upsurge of crime at the same time it was dropping for the nation as a whole"拓展句，交代了犯罪率上升的具体的百分比。所以第 1 题应该是 B 选项。

选项 C 的意思是，即使像深陷犯罪的纽约和华盛顿特区那样的旅游目的地也没有调整自己的犯罪统计数据。联邦调查局称此为"损人利己"。C 选项拓展了主题句"博彩业人士的观点正相反，他们认为开赌场降低了犯罪。"所以即使像纽约和华盛顿特区那样的旅游目的地，为了维护自身的利益也没有调整自己的犯罪统计数据。所以第 2 题应该是 C 选项。

选项 D 讲的是年轻工人觉得在赌馆工作比在凯特皮勒履带拖拉机公司这类削减开支的工厂干活更有发展前途。D 选项不符合任何一题。

选项 E 是说，他说他们经常利用工会来从事犯罪活动，其他的罪犯则会渗透到一些法纪法规比较薄弱的地方。在第四段里我们看到"FBI"的一个高级官员说，有组织的犯罪团伙已经渗透到许多辅助性业务，如维护机器，或提供其他服务。以"He also says…"这一句来判断第 3 题的选项，关键词是"also"，所以第 3 题应该是 E 选项。

选项 F 的大意是：FBI 同时通过调查声称路易斯安那州官员收受数百万美元的回扣，从而批准扩大赌博机数量。所以根据 4 前面的内容——FBI 在一家意大利餐厅安装窃听器，偷听犯罪分子瞒报电子赌博机的策划情况，我们可以看出 F 选项实际上是 FBI 的又一个调查结果。所以第 4 题的答案是 F。

选项 G 的意思是：根据美国新闻网站计算机的分析指出，那些赌博公司已经跻身于前五位的利益集团支持者。我们根据其拓展句，"The $3.1 million in contributions to candidates and parties in 2000 ranked just below those of a long-powerful lobby, the National Rifle Association."便可得知第 5 题的答案是 G。

Text 5

Directions: In the following text, some sentences have been removed. For Questions (1—5), choose the most suitable one from the list A-G to fit into each of the numbered blank. There are two extra choices, which do not fit in any of the blanks.

Decades-old theories about how the economy performs and the statistics used to track it are being challenged by business and labor leaders as well as by congressmen and even an increasingly vocal minority of corporate and regional economist. ___1___ .

But the debate is about more than interest rates. ___2___ . For example, traditional economic theory holds that if capacity utilization—the rate at which factories are operating—is too high, then inflation is sure to result. Typically the figure that's seen as triggering inflation is about 85 percent, and Fed Chairman Alan Greenspan has said he is watching this statistic with particular interest. But it covers just a quarter of GDP.

___3___ . For example, the application of new software from German company SAP that links manufacturing, inventory, and other functions is dramatically increasing efficiency. For years, experts have wrung their hands over the "productive paradox", or why billions of dollars have been spent on technology without much impact. But now, "management practices are beginning to catch up with the installed technology base," says Donald F. Smith Jr., executive director of the Center for Economic Development at Carnegie Mellon University.

Above all, the new economy calls into question two related but different economic concepts: namely, how fast the economy can grow, and how many people can hold a job, without triggering inflation. Economists believe that if the U.S. economy expands faster than 2.5 percent, productive resources will be strained beyond what they can bear, thereby causing prices to rise. ___4___ .

What these concerns don't take into account, however, is the decidedly uneven impact the new economy has had on different layers of the work force. Each tier has its own dynamics. At the top of the pyramid, ___5___ . The technology sector is growing at an overall annual clip of 40 percent, and the Information Technology Association of America estimates that high-tech companies need 190,000 new workers and can't immediately find them. But the vast majority of high-tech firm, both hardware and software, operate under the iron assumption that final prices for their goods will continue to fall. One reason is that computer power keeps increasing as the cost of computation plummets—simply put, this allows workers to get more productive while the technology costs less.

[A] Likewise, unemployment that is too low—below 5 percent—has been assumed to overstrain the labor market, in turn raising wages.

[B] where 20 percent to 30 percent of Americans work in the technology-and service-oriented economy, the salaries are strong and there are not enough people to fill some specialized jobs such as software programming.

[C] The government-induced breakup of AT&T and deregulation of telecommunications have help turn the telephone into an important source of growth, allowing Sioux Falls, S. D. , and Omaha to become major centers of credit-card processing and telemarketing.

[D] However brutal that may be for workers who are displaced or paid less well, that flexibility means old theories about the labor force moving in lockstep are antiquated.

[E] Even in the manufacturing sector, long-held assumptions are being exploded.

[F] It's about the fundamental nature of the economy and how it behaves. The tools the government uses to understand the economy—its dashboard indicators—are increasing under attack as dated and faulty.

[G] One reason this debate is so important is that the Federal Reserve Board has started raising interest rates to slow the economy and, in a kind of pro-emptive strike, to stop inflation from re-emerging.

分析：

本文是一篇有关美国新经济的文章。

第一段的大意是：企业主、劳工领袖和国会议员，甚至少数越来越直言不讳的企业和地方经济专家，对盛行几十年的经济运作理论和记录经济运作情况的统计数字提出质疑。这种争论非常重要，原因之一是：联邦储备委员会已经开始提高利率，以便减缓经济发展速度，并且预防通货膨胀重新出现。

第二段主要介绍了争论不仅是有关利率的，而且是有关经济基本性质以及其是如何运作的。政府用来了解经济情况的手段——经济的仪表指针——越来越受到指责，有人认为，它们陈旧过时，充满错误。

第三段进一步介绍了即使是在制造业领域，人们长期持有的看法证明是错误的。许多年来，专家们对于"生产率矛盾"感到焦虑不安、束手无策，他们不明白，为什么技术上数十亿美元的投入未能取得很大的成效。

第四段大意是：新经济所质疑的是两个相关但又不同的经济概念，即在不触发通货膨胀的前提下，经济如何快速增长，以及有多少人能拥有一份工作。

第五段大意是：而所没有放在考虑之列的显然是新经济活动对不同层次劳动力所产生的不均衡的影响，而最高层面大约只有20%－30%的美国人在工作，报酬丰厚。

试题解析：

选项 A 大意是：同样，人们认为失业率太低——低于百分之五——就会造成劳动力市场过度受压，反过来就要给雇员提高工资。4 选项是这一段中经济学家的看法之一。另外一个是"Economists believe that if the U. S. economy expands faster than 2.5 percent, productive resources will be strained beyond what they can bear, thereby causing prices to rise."。由此我们可以确定第 4 题应该是 A 选项。

选项 B 的大体意思是：有百分之二十到三十的美国人是在以工作的技术和服务为导向的经济领域里工作，报酬丰厚，而且像软件一类的特殊工作却没有足够的人来做。而没有放在考虑之列的显然是新经济活动对不同层次劳动力所产生的不均衡的影响。B 选项实际上是一个定语从句，修饰"At the top of the pyramid"。所以第 5 题应该是 B 选项。

选项 C 的大意是政府促成美国电话电报公司的解体，取消对电信业的限制。这促使电话业务成为经济增长的重要因素，使苏瀑布城和奥马哈市成为信用卡和电话销售的主要中心。此选项不符合任何一题。

选项 D 讲的是，这种薪金调整的灵活性对于被解雇或减薪的人不管是怎样无情，它却意味着以前那种认为劳工薪金调整步调一致的理论已经陈腐过时了。通读全篇，我们会发现此选项不符合任何一题。

选项 E 从文章结构上来说是第三段的主题句。"Even in the manufacturing sector, long-held assumptions are being exploded."意思是：既使在制造业领域，人们长期持有的看法证明是错误的。这一段是通过后面举例来拓展的。根据例子我们可以判断，F 选项是这一段的主题句。所以第 3 题应该是 E 选项。

选项 F 的大意是：争论是有关经济基本性质以及其是如何运作的。政府用来了解经济情况的手段—经济的指针—越来越受到指责，有人认为，它们陈旧过时，充满错误。选择 F 选项主要根据第二段的第一句"But the debate is about more than interest rates."，关键词是"more than"。而其后的举例说明则更好地说明第 2 题的答案是 F。

选项 G 的意思是这种争论非常重要，原因之一是联邦储备委员会已经开始提高利率，以便减缓经济发展速度，并且预防通货膨胀重新出现。G 选项实际上是对第一段第一句的进一步解释。所以 G 选项应该是第 1 题。

2）试题精选与解析

Text 6

Directions：In the following text, some sentences have been removed. For Questions 1—5, choose the most suitable one from the list A-G to fit into each of the numbered blanks. There are two extra choices which do not fit in any of the gaps.

In future trade the key development to watch is the relationship between the industrialized and the developing nation. Third World countries export their mineral deposits and tropical agricultural products, which bring them desired foreign exchange. Tourism has also been greatly responsible for the rapid development of some developing nations. Many third World nations with high unemployment and low wages have seen an emigration of workers to the developed nations. Western Europe has received millions of such workers from Mediterranean countries. The developing nations profit when Western nations establish manufacturing in their countries to take advantage of cheap labor.

As economies mature, economic growth rates lend to level off. The rate of population growth is leveling off today in Western nations. This leveling-off eventually leads to static non-growth markets. A point of saturation sets in—technology and innovation have seemed to achieve the impossible, but then how much further can it go? Herman Kahn, in his book The Next 200 Years', says that a shift in priorities will have to occur for industrialized nations. No longer is the creation of money and jobs essential; it is rather the improvement of the quality of life that must be our concern. Today pollution is of major concern for industrialized nations. Environmentalists are worried about the relationship between industrial objectives and preserving the environment. In developing nations, however, the problem of pollution is ignored for the sake of development.

The Western World will eventually move to a period of relatively low economic growth, coupled with a high rate of unemployment. A so-called welfare society will emerge. The unemployed in the new welfare society will be taken care of by the employed through generous contributions to the social welfare system.

Political questions remain as to the world's future. We can only speculate as to whether organized markets such as the Common Market and COMECON could eventually merge. In the present political climate, this would seem impossible, although some cooperation agreements are already in effect. Obviously a merger between the Western and Eastern European markets would greatly enhance world trade.

International monetary cooperation will have a significant impact on future trade. If the IMF countries are not able to agree upon a new international monetary order in the years to come, international trade may become too risky for some companies to get involved in. if the IMF is unable to create sufficient international liquidity reserves in the future, there may not be enough liquidity to sustain growth in trade.

However, growing international consultation and cooperation in economic, monetary, and political matters will certainly contribute to the flourishing of world trade for years to come.

[A] The industrialized nations are much concerned for the improvement of the environment for raising their quality of life, and on the contrary, the developing nations neglect preserving the environmental protection for the development of their nations.

[B] The Third World countries export their mineral deposits and tropical agricultural products, develop the tourism and the workers move into the developed countries, which profits the people of the developing nations to get employments.

[C] At present, the organized markets could not eventually come out, and the whole European economic merger will be helpful for promoting the would trade.

[D] A high-rate of unemployment will make those western nations slow down in the economic growth.

[E] International monetary cooperation keeps a new international monetary order and IMF creates sufficient international liquidity reserves in the future so as to avoid risking in trade, and sustain growth and the flourishing of the world trade.

[F] From now to future, the economy of the developing countries will develop by depending on themselves and is not related to the developed countries.

[G] Due to the economic globalization, international monetary cooperation and EMF will have a slight influence on future trade.

试题解析

本文主要讲的是在未来的国际贸易中,发展中国家和发达国家之间所存在的问题,即旅游、人口流动、失业现象、环保等将对世界经济的发展带来一些影响,尤其是国际货币合作。制定国际货币新秩序,创造足够的国际流动资金储备等一系列问题将会对经济、贸易的发展产生重大的影响。

1. [B] 文章第一段主要讲发展中国家和发达国家之间的经济关系。发展中国家利用出口矿床和农产品赚取外汇,发展旅游业推动经济发展。低收入高失业人群流入发达国家,发达国家利用廉价劳动在他们国家发展制造业,这样也使得发展中国家受益。根据内容,本题答案应该选[B]。

2. [A] 第二段讲述的是随着经济的成熟、增长以及人口增长率的逐渐趋于平衡,今后对工业化国家来说,优势转化问题一定会发生,它们关注的重点是保护环境,改善人们生活质量;而在发展中国家,环保问题往往会被忽略。因此本题答案应该是[A]。

3. [D] 第三段主要叙述的是由于高失业率的成倍增长,西方国家会出现一段时期的经济低迷,一个所谓的福利型的社会将会出现,尽管对社会福利体系付出很多,但是失业问题还是倍受关注。此题答案应该是[D]。

4. [C] 第四段是叙述政治问题会影响贸易和市场。当前虽然一些合作协议已经生效,像共同市场和经互会这类的有组织的市场暂时还不会出现。显然东西欧市场的融合会大大地促进世界贸易。故本题答案为[C]。

5. [E] 本文第五段是讲国际货币合作对未来的贸易有着重大影响,如果国际货币基金组织不能选定一个国际货币新秩序,不能营造充足的国际流动储备金,会将给有些公司带来贸易风险,也无法维持贸易增长。第六段主要是讲日益增加的经济、货币以及政治问题的国际磋商和合作对未来的世贸繁荣将有积极的贡献。所以答案是[E]。

Text 7

Directions: In the following text, some sentences have been removed. For Questions 1—5, choose the most suitable one from the list A-G to fit into each of the numbered blanks. There are two extra choices which do not fit in any of the gaps.

Every year, more people face poverty and hunger and more of the earth's resources are ruined. The problems are enormous, but many experts believe that the situation is not hopeless. The solution will require big changes in how we think about agriculture, food, and our plant.

First of all, farmers everywhere need to develop methods that are less destructive to the environment. The changes from single crop farming to a mixed crop system would be one important step. The planting of various crops improves the soil and helps prevent erosion. Erosion could further be prevented by planting trees to protect the fields from the wind. Another way farmers could improve their soil is to stop deep plowing. In fact, only a light plowing is necessary, or sometimes no plowing at all.

If the soil were treated better, farmers would not need to use chemical fertilizers. They could use natural animal and vegetable products instead. With mixed crops, farmers would also not need as much or any chemical insecticides. They could use other biological methods of controlling insects and disease.

Farmers could also help save some of the earth's precious supplies of water and petroleum. To save water, they could plant less "thirsty" crops, instead of the standard types of wheat or corn. They could also use watering systems that are much less wasteful. To save petroleum, farmers could make use of bio-gas generators for energy. These generators could be fueled by the vegetable and animal wastes of the farms. In less-developed countries, bio-gas generators could reduce the need for firewood and so help save forests, as well.

In less-developed countries, the small farmers need help. They need to learn more about crops that are better suited to the local conditions. They need to learn how to limit erosion and make the best use of their resources. But these farmers will never be successful without land for themselves and economic aid. This should be the aim of government and international agencies. The present policies of encouraging industry and cash crops are only making the situation worse.

The industrialized countries could use their economic resources to help bring about these changes. They also could make some changes in their own policies. At present, much food is wasted in these countries for political reasons. In Europe alone mountains of fruit and dairy products are thrown away every year. Eating habits, too, could be changed in these countries. For example, people often eat foods from distant places instead of local foods. The transportation of the imported foods adds to the global pollution problem. People in the industrialized countries also eat a lot of meat, especially beef. In fact, a large percentage of the grain grown in these countries is used for feeding cattle. If people in these countries ate less meat, there would be more grain to feed the hungry people of the would.

[A] The government of less-developed countries and international agencies need to help small farmers.

[B] Although there are some big changes in how farmers think of agriculture, food and their plant, it is no much help to the environmental destruction.

[C] Now, in those industrialized countries, much food is wasted for some reasons, and eating habits could be greatly changed as well.

[D] Mixed crops farming can reduce the need of the chemical insecticides, so it is useful to farming.

[E] The experts recognize how farmers can change the way food is produced worldwide.

[F] Water and energy are very precious on the earth, specially for farming, farmers should take more measures to save water and energy.

[G] In less developed countries, the small farmers need to learn more about crops which are better suited to the local conditions, but they don't need any aid of the government or the international agencies.

试题解析:

本文是讲每年地球上有更多的人面临贫困、饥饿和更多的地球资源被毁坏,问题严重。在我们考虑农业、粮食种植的时候,应该首先考虑到对他们进行很大的改变。

1. [E] 文中第一段和第二段讲述的是,每年有更多的人面临饥饿和贫困,问题严重。解决问题的答案就是要改变农业、粮食和我们的种植模式。同时减少环境污染,防止土壤贫瘠化和深耕,最重要的是最大范围地改变粮食生产方式。所以答案是[E]。

2. [D] 第三段主要讲利用好土壤可以不用化肥,种多种农作物就可以不必使用那么多的化学杀虫剂,可以运用生物方式来控制病虫害。所以答案应该是[D]。

3. [F] 本文第四段主要讲水资源和能源的珍贵。农民们应该多种抗旱作物和建立水系来节约用水,可以用其他原料或废物作为燃料以便节省油料。所以选[F]。

4. [A] 本文第五段主要讲述欠发达国家的小农需要本国政府和国际机构的帮助。他们需要学习关于适合于本地条件种植的庄稼,需要防止土壤贫瘠化并要更好地利用他们的资源。没有上述这些,他们决不能有所作为的。任何鼓励发展工业和经济作物都将使情况越来越糟。由此可以判断本题答案为[A]。

5. [C] 本文第六段讲的是在工业化的国家里由于某些原因,导致了粮食食品浪费和饮食习惯的改变。所以答案应是[C]。

Text 8

Directions: In the following text, some sentences have been removed. For Questions 1—5, choose the most suitable one from the list A-G to fit into each of the numbered blanks. There are two extra choices which do not fit in any of the gaps.

Cars also contribute enormously to pollution. In major cities in America now, legislation is being passed which will require pollution from automobile to be drastically reduced. Many cities are restricting access by automobile to cars with two or more passengers or make other regulations which encourage "car pooling", persuading commuters to share driving and riding to cut down on the numbers of cars on the highways. Government regulations now prevent the burning of fuels with lead in them.

If we also thin just purely in terms of how our resources are used to accommodate the automobile, we find some other interesting facts. The space requited for roads and parking lots in America right now is equal to the entire area of the six New England states. This is land on which nothing can grow, no one can play or build, or which has any other use whatsoever than the movement or storing of automobiles. All the same, as anyone knows who has been in city traffic at rush hour, still more land and more highways are needed to accommodate our cars. It has been sad that if everyone tried to drive his or her car at the same time no one could go anywhere!

The amount of junk from automobiles-whether the bodies of old cars, or used tires and batteries-has also caused serious problems for many of our communities. A fire in a dump of used tires in New Hampshire(新罕布什尔州) caused massive smoke pollution and required the resources of several fire companies before it was brought under control. Environmentalists have noted that one of the favorite breeding grounds of mosquitoes now is in the water that collects in junk automobile tires. And in many communities land that otherwise might be turned to productive uses has been declared poisoned by gasoline and oil that was improperly disposed of. These poisons eventually find their way, of course,, into the water supply.

Another dubious consequence of the automobile culture is to isolate people from the communities in which they work. American cities, for example, are surrounded by what are commonly called "bedroom communities", where people go mainly to sleep after working in the city. Their taxes do not support the city they work in: the commuters do not vote in the cities, either; and the money they earn, of course, leaves with them. This phenomenon has been blamed in part for creating serious economic divisions between city and suburb, with the poor left to try to run a city without resources, and the middle class and the wealthy off to the more affluent suburbs. It may seem quite a stretch of logic(并非无稽之谈) to say that automobile culture has contributed to inequality in educational opportunities, but in this analysis there is indeed a connection. Suburban schools are comparatively better financed; urban schools, with many exceptions, comparatively struggle along. But automobile culture creates a system which, for the past fifty years at least, has encouraged a division between city and town and between the poorest of our citizens and the middle class.

Finally, consider how automobile culture has shaped our relations with the rest of the would. We now use the word "petrodollars" to describe that significant portion of our money which is used to buy oil and oil-related products—petroleum is indeed money. Furthermore, a culture and an economy which is dependent on oil and oil resources, is also at the mercy of those who have these resources. I think it's obvious that automobile culture goes hand in hand with automobile economics and automobile politics. I'm not saying that this is an "evil" thing, or a bad consequence of driving a car: I'm simply saying that a country which wants to enter the automotive world full-scale is going to enter also the world of petro-politics. Personally, I indeed think there are better options: superb public transportation systems; ecological alternatives to burning petroleum; and even-yes-bicycles!

[A] If we use our resources to accommodate the automobiles, we will strangely find that there are such many problems as roads and parking lots in America which occupy a bigger land area in which there is no space to be used.

[B] The automobile culture brings about an isolation of people from the communities in which they work, creating an inequality in educational opportunities, causing many divisions in cities.

[C] There are a great number of the junk from the old cars, used tires and batteries which have caused serious pollution problems for numberless households in communities and land poisoned by gasoline and oil, these poisons entering water supply.

[D] There are many cars in many cities in America now, so the government has made many regulations to restrict cars or bicycle which move into cities and encourages commuters or bicycle to go to work.

[E] The automobile culture has formed our relations with the rest of the world by buying oil or oil-related products. So the automobile culture goes hand in hand with automobile economics and automobile politics.

[F] In major cities in America, there are many cars which bring about much pollution in cities, but there no any regulations to restrict cars entering cities.

[G] American automobile culture has formed a relations with the rest of the world, at the same time it has not influenced on any equality relations among Americans.

试题解析：

本文讲述美国汽车泛滥,带来了许多社会问题。如道路堵塞,停车场占用土地太多,使得土地问题越来越严重。同时汽车本身也产生许多废物,造成严重的社会环境污染。政府采取调控措施,限制汽车流量,鼓励人们乘坐公交车或骑自行车上下班。同时汽车文化也影响到社区教育不平等。但是对贸易往来也有促进作用。

1. [D] 第一段主要讲述在美国许多城市里,汽车给城市造成严重污染,于是政府采取调控措施对汽车入城加以限制,并鼓励市民乘公交车或自行车上下班。目的是要减少城市城市污染和交通拥堵。所以答案应选[D]。

2. [A] 本文第二段叙述美国要是顺应汽车业的发展的话,就会发现道路问题,停车场就要占掉六个新英格兰州的总面积,而且在这片土地上无任何利用空间,上班高峰时仍然拥堵不堪,需要更多的土地和高速路来解决汽车问题。所以答案应该是[A]。

3. [C] 本文第三段叙述了废旧的汽车,用过的轮胎和电池引起了严重的社会污染问题,燃烧的废轮胎导致浓烟污染,社区土地被汽油和油污所中毒,并无法处理,最后流入供水之中。所以答案是[C]。

4. [B] 本文第四段主要讲述汽车文化导致的另一个可疑的结果就是使市民与他们工作的社区隔开,下班后主要就是睡觉,无其他活动空间。同时还造成市3与郊区分割,穷人逃离城市,中产阶级和富人离开市区去较富裕的郊区。汽车文化还导致了教育机会的不平等,城市与乡镇、城市贫民与中产阶级的分离。由此推断答案应该是[B]。

5. [E] 本文第五段讲述汽车文化是通过买石油或其他石油产品与外界建立了关系,所以汽车文化与汽车经济和汽车工业是紧密相连的。可以推断答案是[E]。

Text 9

Directions: In the following text, some sentences have been removed. For Questions 1—5, choose the most suitable one from the list A-G to fit into each of the numbered blanks. There are two extra choices which do not fit in any of the gaps.

When I got out of graduate school, I wanted to be successful like most others who got M. B. A. 's. I was convinced I wanted to be a C. E. O. and thought I could. I was a cashier of a small bank at first, and finally I got the opportunity. In 1992, I became C. E. O. of Tesoro, even though the company almost bankrupted. The debt was 84 percent and the company hadn't made money for years. I took the position because I was ready to start moving on. I threw myself into the process of recapitalizing this company. It took me two years to reconstruct the balance sheet, and in 1995 the board gave me the opportunity to reconstruct the operation.

I have a strong belief in taking risks. I saw this with my father. He had an oil business, drilling oil and gas wells in the late 60s. At one point, business got bad. I know we can't imagine it now, but crude was $4 or $5 a barrel. He went back to school, sold the business and became a hospital administrator. He was in his early 40s.

During the Vietnam War, I was working at Ford in the management program, but in 1969 they had run to the bottom of the recruits, so I was drafted into the army. I went through induction and basic training and I got my orders to go to the next base. I thought, given my background in finance, they were sending me to Fort Polk, La. , as an accountant. When I got there, the sergeant said be was going to make me a combat clerk. That meant there was a good chance I was going to be sent to Vietnam. I went right out and found the finance office and went in and said I wanted to see the person who ran it. It was a captain. I told him, "I have an M. B. A. and an accounting background. "I ended up working in the finance office.

Another great influence on me, next to being married and having a great life companion, was the two years I lived in London. I was in my early 30s, and here I was, a small-town boy from Kansas making the leap and moving to a large city. It was the early 1970s, and the Chicago bank I was working for sent me there. The first time I ever left the United States was when I went to London.

Looking back, what was so meaningful for me was dealing with another culture, learning how to listen to people and be observant. I really tried, not quite to become English, but tried to blend in by not being the typical ugly American with tennis shoes and a camera wrapped around my neck. I was trying to learn the customs and trying to understand the people and the culture.

[A] After a period of time, I worked at Ford, and then I became a soldier in the army and sent to Vietnam as a combat clerk.

[B] I dare to take risks in my cause because of my father's influence on me.

[C] After graduation from school, I took a position in the company which gave me an opportunity to start an undertaking under the situation of the company almost bankrupted.

[D] I was doing my best to make a command of another customs and culture so as to get to the bottom of other people.

[E] Later on, I changed the place which I lived in and also changed my work.

[F] After graduation, I took a position as a clerk in a company, I paid off all the debt which the company owed in a period of time.

[G] After I was married, I was living in the United States without leaving the country and didn't learn the customs and culture from another country.

试题解析：

本文叙述我大学毕业以后曾做过银行职员和一家公司职员。公司不景气以至于破产，我试图重新振兴公司，再创利润。我的坚强信心是受了父亲的影响。后来中越战争爆发，我投军入伍，当上了一名战地记账员。若干年后，我从一个小镇步入大城市，从而改变了生活环境和工作。从此开始学习异国文化，了解别国的风土人情，融入当地社会。

1．[C] 本文第一段叙述我大学毕业后，先在一家银行当职员，后来又去一家公司工作，该公司经营不景气，濒临破产。我准备投身于重新调整公司的结构，再创利润。根据意思本题答案应该是[C]。

2．[B] 我有敢于冒险的坚强信念，从我父亲身上看到了这种精神。父亲原有一个石油公司，后来生意不好，他卖掉了公司，他又回到了学校，成为医院里的管理者。

3．[A] 在中越战争爆发之后，先是在福特工厂工作，后来经过培训参军入伍，因为我有财务知识，当上一名战地记账员。根据意思答案应该是[A]。

4．[E] 对我影响很大的还是在伦敦生活的那两年，从一个小镇跳到一个大城市，改变了环境，更换了工作。本题的答案应该是[E]。

5．[D] 我回想起来，了解另一种文化是非常有意义的事，学会听取别人的意见，顺从别人，想融入英国文化，了解他们的人民和风俗习惯。根据意思，本题答案是[D]。

3）练习

Exercise ❶

Directions：In the following text，some sentences have been removed. For Questions（1—5），choose the most suitable one from the list A-G to fit into each of the numbered blank. There are two extra choices，which do not fit in any of the blanks.

When Paul Halpern petitioned for visitation rights, the California courts denied his request in what has become an often-cited legal landmark. Because he was a stepparent during the marriage, the divorce made him nothing more than a "nonparent" in the eyes of the court. The judge dismissed Paul and his claims with this terse comment：__1__.

The Halpern case took place nearly two decades ago, but it has remained a symbol in the legal profession of the gross disregard and lack of protective laws that puzzle stepparents and step-families. Sadly, the shaky status of stepparents is just as much a fact of life today as it was in the Halperns' time. __2__. The critics are using the scientific theory as ammunition to lobby for stronger "pro-family" social policies. If stepfamilies are so unnatural from a genetic point of view that they imperil children's welfare, the argument goes, then anything that can be done to prevent divorce and preserve traditional families ought to be. __3__.

Biological determinists represent a minority viewpoint in family-policy debates. Other social critics contend that if there is a genetic predisposition that favors biological children over stepchildren, it's just that—a predisposition—and predisposition is not destiny. Creating social policies that keep unhappy families trapped in the same house, these critics argue, would be wrongheaded and far more risky psychologically than life in a stepfamily. __4__.

Changes in their legal status are one possibility. Like domestic partners, step-parents currently have almost no legal standing in most states, which means that even when they assume responsibility for their stepchildren—supporting them emotionally and financially, for example—they have no corresponding rights. __5__. Existing family law has been challenged in various ways in different localities, but the resulting legal rulings have been inconsistent. In a case now pending before the Supreme Court, a child's grandparents are suing for visitation rights but some legal experts believe that a ruling for the grandparents could be interpreted as an affirmation of stepparents' right as well.

[A] "He absolutely has no relationship to the child bloodwise or otherwise, and I can't accept I should burden all of the parties in this matter, including Mr. Halpern, with conflicts, struggles, and disruptions for years to come because of Mr. Halpern's present emotional state in connection with the child. "

[B] The theory is that giving the stepparent enhanced status will legitimate his or her role, both in the family and in society, and that the very process of asking for rights and responsibilities will support the stepparent-stepchild bond.

[C] Indeed, it is now under fresh assault: Conservative critics have recently embraced the sweeping biological charge of stepfamilies proposed by evolutionary psychologists, who contend that parents have evolved over years to care only about the welfare of their genetic offspring.

[D] Through the effort of the Step-family Association of America and other advocates, schools around the country have begun changing their policies to acknowledge the increasingly important role of stepparents.

[E] This includes a number of ideas proposed by the nascent "marriage movement"—from pro-marriage tax policies to the so-called covenant marriages that are intended to make divorce (and thus remarriage) more difficult.

[F] What's needed, these critics argue, is not more stigmatizing of stepfamilies, but rather policies that strengthen stepfamilies and reduce any risks that might exist.

[G] If the marriage ends, the stepparent has no legal standing to ask for custody or visitation. Similarly, stepchildren rarely have rights—to life insurance benefits, for example—or, if the marriage ends, to continued support or inheritance.

Exercise ❷

Directions: In the following text, some sentences have been removed. For Questions (1—5), choose the most suitable one from the list A-G to fit into each of the numbered blank. There are two extra choices, which do not fit in any of the blanks.

There are many theories about the beginning of drama in ancient Greece. __1__. In the beginning, human beings viewed the natural forces of the world—even the seasonal changes—as unpredictable, and they sought through various means to control these unknown and feared powers. Those measures which appeared to bring the desired results were then retained and repeated until they hardened into fixed rituals. Eventually stories arose which explained or veiled the mysteries of the rites. __2__ .

Those who believe that drama evolved out of ritual also argue that those rites contained the seed of theater because music, dance, masks, and costumes were almost always used. __3__ . In addition, there were performers, and since considerable importance was attached to avoiding mistakes in the enactment of rites, religious leaders usually assumed that task. __4__ . Eventually such dramatic representations were separated from religious activities.

Another theory traces the theater's origin from the human interest in storytelling. According to this view, tales (about the hunt, war, or other feats) are gradually elaborated, at first through the use of impersonation, action, and dialogue by a narrator and then through the assumption of each of the roles by a different person. __5__ .

[A] A closely related theory traces theater to those dances that are primarily rhythmical and gymnastic or that are imitations of animal movements and sounds.

[B] They also developed passion to perform dramas which depicted the life of Christ. Beginning in the 13th century these began to be performed outside of churches as part of festivals or by travelling companies.

[C] The one most widely accepted today is based on the assumption that drama evolved from ritual. The argument for this view goes as follows.

[D] Wearing masks and costumes, they often impersonated other people, animals, or supernatural beings, and mimed the desired effect-success in hunt or battle, the coming rain, the revival of the Sun—as an actor might.

[E] Some of the middle Ages in the form of music for the drama have laid the foundation. First of all, the end of the century religious drama, then the religious mystery play by play (Mystery) and miracle plays (Miracles) to replace, the prevalence of 14-16 in the century; followed by the pastoral drama genre with this music, poetry, drama performance of the means of villages *The Scenes of Life*, it has been popular in the 16th century to become a major origin of one of the opera.

[F] Furthermore, a suitable site had to be provided for performances, and when the entire community did not participate, a clear division was usually made between the "acting area" and the "auditorium".

[G] As time passed some rituals were abandoned, but the stories, later called myths, persisted and provided material for art and drama.

Exercise ❸

Directions: In the following text, some sentences have been removed. For Questions (1—5), choose the most suitable one from the list A-G to fit into each of the numbered blank. There are two extra choices, which do not fit in any of the blanks.

Pizza Hut was started in 1958, by two brothers in Wichita, Kansas. Frank and Dan Carney had the idea to open a pizza parlor. In 1986, Pizza Hut introduced delivery service, something no other restaurant was doing. By the 1990's Pizza Hut sales had reached $4 billion worldwide. In 1998, Pizza Hut celebrated their 40th anniversary, and launched their famous campaign "The Best Pizzas Under One Roof". In 1996, Pizza Hut sales in the United States were over $5 million.   1 . Home delivery was a driving force for success, especially for Pizza Hut and Domino's.

In the past, Pizza Hut has always had the first mover advantage. Their marketing strategy in the past has always been to be first. One of their main strategies that they still follow today is the diversification of the products they offer.   2 . For example, chicken is now a common topping found on pizzas. Pizza Hut is always adding something new to their menu, trying to reach new markets.   3 .

Another opportunity that Pizza Hut has is their new ordering online system.   4 .

Lastly, Pizza Hut has always valued customer service and satisfaction.   5 .

[A] Another strategy they used in the past and are still using is the diversification of their pizzas. Pizza Hut is always trying to come up with some innovative way to make a pizza into something slightly different—different enough that customers will think it is a whole new product.

[B] In 1995, Pizza Hut began two customer satisfaction programs: a 1—800 number customer hotline, and a customer call-back program. These were implemented to make sure their customers were happy, and always wanted to return.

[C] The current trend in pizza chains today is the same. They all try to come up with some newer, bigger, better, pizza for a low price. Offering special promotions and new pizza variations are popular today as well.

[D] For example, in 1992 the famous buffet was launched in Pizza Hut restaurants worldwide. They were trying to offer many different food items for customers who didn't necessarily want pizza.

[E] Out of all the existing pizza chains, Pizza Hut had the largest market share, 46.4%. However, Pizza Hut's market share has slowly eroded because of intense competition from their rivals Domino's, Little Caesar's and newcomer Papa John's.

[F] Anyone with Internet access can order whatever they wish and get it delivered to their house without even speaking to someone. This program has just been started, so we do not have any numbers to support whether or not it will be a success.

[G] However, this forced competitors to look for new methods of increasing their customer bases. Many pizza chains decided to diversify and offer new non-pizza items such as Buffalo wings, and Italian cheese bread.

Exercise ❹

Directions: In the following text, some sentences have been removed. For Questions (1— 5), choose the most suitable one from the list A-G to fit into each of the numbered blank.

There are two extra choices, which do not fit in any of the blanks.

A European study has revealed that 100 percent fruit and vegetable juices are as effective as their whole fruit/vegetable counterparts in reducing risk factors related to certain diseases. __1__.

Juices are comparable in their ability to reduce risk compared to their whole fruit/vegetable counterparts, according to several researchers in the United Kingdom who conducted the literature review. The researchers analyzed a variety of studies that looked at risk reduction attributed to the effects of both fiber and antioxidants. __2__. "When considering cancer and coronary heart diseases prevention, there is no evidence that pure fruit and vegetable juices are less beneficial than whole fruit and vegetables," the researchers said. The researchers added that the positioning of juices as being nutritionally inferior to whole fruits and vegetables in relationship to chronic disease development is "unjustified" and that policy, which suggests otherwise about fruit and vegetable juices, should be re-examined.

The researchers who authored the paper suggest that more studies in certain area are needed to bolster their findings. __3__. She added that appropriate amounts of juices should be included in the diet of both children and adults, following guidelines established by leading health authorities. __4__.

__5__. The study was published in the International Journal of Food Science and Nutrition TM (2006).

[A] Taylor also points to a large epidemiological study, published in the September 2006 issue of the Journal of *Medicine*, which found that consumption of a variety of 100 percent fruit and vegetable juices was associated with a reduced risk for Alzheimer's disease.

[B] The conclusion is the result of the study designed to question traditional thinking that 100 percent juices play a less significant role in reducing risk for both cancer and cardiovascular disease than whole fruits and vegetables.

[C] In fact, that study found that individuals who drank three or more servings of fruit and vegetable juices per week had a 76 percent lower risk of developing Alzheimer's disease than those who drank juice less than once per week.

[D] Our body can absorb more vitamins and minerals if we drink fresh juices than if we eat the fruits and vegetables whole. By blending fruits and vegetables to make juices and smoothies, we break down the fibers to release the trapped nutrients.

[E] Although this independent review of the literature is not designed to focus on any particular 100 percent juice, it does go a long way in demonstrating that fruit and vegetable juices do play an important role in reducing the risk of various diseases, especially cancer and cardiovascular disease, said Sue Taylor.

[F] As a result, they determined that the positive impact fruits and vegetables offer come not from just the fiber but also from antioxidants which are present in both juice and the whole fruits and vegetables.

[G] By juicing, you extract the juice for your body. In turn this makes it easier for your body to assimilate the nutrition as your body doesn't need to work at breaking down the fruit or vegetable. While juicing saves your body the energy required to extract the juice (nutrition) from the food, it's still important to eat whole vegetables and fruits.

Exercise ❺

Directions: In the following text, some sentences have been removed. For Questions (1—5), choose the most suitable one from the list A-G to fit into each of the numbered blank. There are two extra choices, which do not fit in any of the blanks.

Unidentified Flying Object (UFO), any object or light, reportedly sighted in the sky that cannot be immediately explained by the observer. __1__. Many thousands of such observations have since been reported worldwide.

At least 90 percent of UFO sightings can be identified as conventional objects, although time-consuming investigations are often necessary for such identification. __2__. The remaining sightings most likely can be attributed to other mistaken sightings or to inaccurate reporting, hoaxes, or delusions, although to disprove all claims made about UFOs is impossible.

__3__. The air force concluded that "no UFO reported, investigated, and evaluated by the Air Force has ever given any indication of threat to our national security." Since 1969 no agency of the U. S. government has had any active program of UFO investigation.

__4__. These planes, the Lockheed U-2A and the Lockheed SR-71, accounted for over half of the UFO reports during the late 1950s and 1960s.

Some persons nevertheless believe that UFOs are extraterrestrial spacecraft, even though no scientifically valid evidence supports that belief. The possibility of extraterrestrial civilizations is not the stumbling block; most scientists grant that intelligent life may well exists elsewhere in the universe. A fully convincing UFO photograph of a craft-like object has yet to be taken, however, and the scienfific method requires that highly speculative explanations should not be adopted unless all of the more ordinary explanations can be ruled out.

UFO enthusiasts persist, however, and some persons even claim to have been abducted and taken aboard UFOs. __5__.

[A] In 1997 the U. S. Central Intelligence Agency (CIA) admitted that the U. S. military had deceived the American public in an effort to hide information about high-altitude spy planes.

[B] Because the objects are often shining and in that part of the sky opposite the sun, most investigators, official and unofficial alike, tend to interpret them as reflections of the sun's rays from airplanes. Fireballs, meteors, and other meteorological phenomena account for most of the relatively few UFOs that observers report seeing at night. However, there are some sightings that investigators are unable to explain in terms of known phenomena.

[C] The objects most often mistaken for UFOs are bright planets and stars, aircraft, birds, balloons, kites, aerial flares, peculiar clouds, meteors, and satellites.

[D] Sightings of unusual aerial phenomena date back to ancient times, but UFOs (sometimes called flying saucers) became widely discussed only after the first widely publicized U. S. sighting in 1947.

[E] Throughout history there have been reports of strange objects in the sky. In the 20th century, a number of observers claim to have seen vehicles, or "flying saucers", which some believe are space ships visiting the earth from other planets.

[F] No one has produced scientifically acceptable proof of these claims. Behavioral scientist Carl Sagan once proposed that "certain psychological needs are met by belief in superior beings from other worlds".

[G] From 1947 to 1969 the U. S. Air Force investigated UFOs as a possible threat to national security. A total of 12,618 reports were received, of which 701 reports, or 5. 6 percent, were listed as unexplained.

Exercise ⑥

Directions: In the following text, some sentences have been removed. For Questions (1—5), choose the most suitable one from the list A-G to fit into each of the numbered blank. There are two extra choices, which do not fit in any of the blanks.

This is specially designed education for children who are either partially sighted or blind. __1__. In the United States, approximately 12 out of 1,000 children receive some form of special education because of visual impairments.

__2__. Blind children usually are taught to read *Braille*, a system of raised dots embossed on paper and read by touch. In the past, turning conventional books into pages of *Braille* was very time-consuming, and the large books required enormous storage areas.

__3__. Because *Braille* cannot be read very rapidly, many blind students prefer to listen to books being read on tapes. Some students also use reading machines equipped with cameras that scan lines of print, which computers then convert to synthesized speech. Many blind and partially sighted children receive orientation and mobility training as a part of their education. Specialists teach them how to travel independently in their schools and communities, often with and aid, such as a cane.

Most children with vision impairments are educated in schools within their communities. __4__. The specialists may also teach partially sighted children how to use their remaining vision more effectively and instruct them in the use of adaptive aids. Some children with vision impairments attend special schools designed to meet their particular needs. __5__.

The education of many children with vision impairments is further complicated by their having other disabilities, such as physical disabilities, developmental impairments, or hearing loss. Education for those children might emphasize the development of language and communication, and personal, social, and vocational skills rather than academic skills.

[A] Partially sighted children may use a variety of adaptive aids to see more clearly and to read printed text. These aids include magnifiers, which may be attached to eyeglasses; electronic systems for enlarging print and making it easier to see; and large-print books.

[B] Vision specialists may provide special materials and equipment, help teachers and classmates understand the children's condition, and possibly provide additional instruction.

[C] Vision impairments are diagnosed by medical doctors who examine the physical structures in the eye and evaluate the child's ability to see shapes of different sizes at various distances.

[D] Blind children can do well in school, participate in sports and extracurricular activities, contribute to the community, go to college, and accomplish just about anything their sighted classmates can.

[E] Like boarding schools, these schools often provide residential services as well as educational programs. They also have specially designed facilities, which may not be found in neighborhood schools, for blind children to participate in athletics and other activities.

[F] However, most *Braille* texts are now done electronically. Many students read paperless *Braille* with the aid of machines that mechanically raise the dots in a small panel as the reader progresses through the text.

[G] With proper technical assistance, consultation given to regular classroom teachers, and a broad educational environment, blind children are able to show their true worth; they are then more readily accepted socially by their sighted counterparts.

Exercise ❼

Directions: In the following text, some sentences have been removed. For Questions 1—5, choose the most suitable one from the list A-G to fit into each of the numbered blanks. There are two extra choices which do not fit in any of the gaps.

The United States has rich and productive land that has provided Americans with plentiful resources for a healthy diet. Despite this, Americans did not begin to pay close attention to the variety and quality of the food they ate until the 20th century, when they became concerned about eating too much and becoming overweight. American food also grew more similar around the country as American malls and fast-food outlets tended to standardize eating patterns throughout the nation, especially among young people. Nevertheless, American food has become more complex as it draws from the diverse cuisines that immigrants have brought with them.

Traditional American cuisine has included conventional European foodstuffs such as wheat, dairy products, pork, beef, and poultry. It has also incorporated products that were either known only in the New World or that were grown there first and then introduced to Europe. Such foods include potatoes, corn, codfish, molasses, pumpkin and other squashes, sweet potatoes, and peanuts.

By the late 19th century, immigrants from Europe and Asia were introducing more variations into the American diet. Immigrants from Japan and Italy introduced a range of fresh vegetables that added important nutrients as well as variety to the protein-heavy American diet. Germans and

Italians contributed new skills and refinements to the production of alcoholic beverages, especially beer and sine. Some imports became distinctly American products, such as hot dogs, which are descended from German wurst or sausage. Spaghetti and pizza are from Italy.

America's foods began to affect the rest of the world—not only raw staples such as wheat and corn, but a new American cuisine that spread throughout the world. American emphasis on convenience and rapid consumption is best represented in fast foods such as hamburgers. French fries, and soft drinks, which almost all Americans have eaten. By the 1960s and 1970s fast foods became one of America's strongest exports.

By the late 20th century, Americans had become more conscious of their diets, eating more poultry, fish, and fresh fruits and vegetables and fewer eggs and less beef. They also began appreciating fresh ingredients and livelier flavors, and cooks began to rediscover many world cuisines in forms closer to their original.

As Americans became more concerned about their diets, they also became more ecologically conscious. This consciousness led some Americans to switch to a partially or wholly vegetarian diet, or to emphasize products produced organically (without chemical fertilizers and pesticides). In the latter 20th century, Americans also worried about the effects of newly introduced genetically altered foods and irradiation processes for killing bacteria. They feared that these new processes made their food less natural and therefore harmful.

[A] American cuisine protrudes a convenience and rapid consumption, and then the cuisine becomes the main export.

[B] Immigrants from all over the world introduced all kinds of food, fresh vegetables, drinks and wine and cooking skills.

[C] American food has become more complex including conventional European foodstuffs.

[D] Americans did not begin to pay close attention to the variety and quality of the food they ate until the 20th century, when they became concerned about eating too much and becoming overweight.

[E] American food is not so much complex because it didn't introduce any cuisine into its country, the immigrants don't bring any with them.

[F] Then Americans do like eating fresh ingredients and flavor.

[G] America's foods partly began to affect the whole world not only rice and wheat, but fried chicken and soft drinks.

Exercise ❽

Directions: In the following text, some sentences have been removed. For Questions 1—5, choose the most suitable one from the list A-G to fit into each of the numbered blanks. There are two extra choices which do not fit in any of the gaps.

Reasons such as "seeing the world" still prevail, but some students also want new views of the US role. As college students prepare for a fresh academic year, and the second anniversary of the Sept. 11 attacks approaches, one thing some pundits had predicted is not happening: Young people are not responding to the attacks—or to America's faltering image abroad by turning their back to the world. Instead, young adults are traveling, studying, and volunteering overseas in growing numbers. This steadily rising stream showing that Americans in general shun an isolationist and "go it alone" approach to the world.

Now, study abroad is expected to rise slightly this year, sustaining a five year trend that has seen the numbers of American youths making an overseas experience some part of their academic years jump by 55 percent since 1997, according to the Institute for International Education in New York.

The IIE will publish its annual survey in November, but already some major universities report significant increases in students going abroad—even after the years of growth and an uncertain economy. Michigan State University, which topped last year's IIE survey, expects about a 7 percent rise in students going abroad. Another top spot for study abroad, the University of Texas (UT) at Austin, forecasts about a 4 percent rise.

For some students, the motivation is still just to have fun, to "see the world," or to flee the strictures of home and the paper chase, if only for a semester. But for a substantial number, the new focus is to add some international spice to the sum in a competitive and global job environment.

And for what may be a small but growing number, part of the impetus is a desire to take overseas a different America from the one that, if global surveys are accurate, a large swath of the world increasingly distrusts and even disdains.

"When I first went to London, the big motivation for me was just to have the ability to live overseas, and to get a different perspective on the world and America." Says Elizateth Feltes, a College of William and Mary graduate now at home in Denver, finishing a master's dissertation from the University of London.

"But after Sept. 11 and especially as it became clear we were going to take some kind of action in Iraq, I had a heightened sense of being a representative of America. I realized," she adds, "that we are such important players internationally that we can't afford to isolate ourselves from the world anymore."

[A] In the annual survey of American students, the expectation of going abroad for studying emerges a rise, but there are two universities presenting very obvious.

[B] More American youths expect making an overseas and increase the interest of studying abroad.

[C] The Sept. 11 attacks will not happen in America, which is not interesting in American young people, but the young want to merge into the world through taking part in all kinds of activities.

[D] Some American students expect going to other countries to learn cooking skills, or look for a job, or settle down in another country.

[E] Some students try to get rid of some strictures to see the world which is different from

America.

[F] After I went to another country, I had the ability to live abroad and obtained a different perspective on the world and America.

[G] After the Sept. 11 attacked at America, American young people are afraid of the attacks and want to leave the country as soon as possible.

Exercise ❾

Directions: In the following text, some sentences have been removed. For Questions 1—5, choose the most suitable one from the list A-G to fit into each of the numbered blanks. There are two extra choices which do not fit in any of the gaps.

Not all people like to work but everyone likes to play. All over the world men and women and boys and girls enjoy sports. Since the days of long ago, adults and children have called their friends together to spend hours, even days, playing games.

Sports help people to live happily. They help to keep people healthy and feeling good. When they are playing games, people move a lot. This is good for their health. Having fun with their friends makes them happy.

Many people enjoy sports by watching others play. In small towns, crowds meet to watch the bicycle races or the soccer games. In the big cities, thousands buy tickets to see an ice-skating show or a baseball game.

What are your favorite sports? Is the climate hot where you live? Then swimming is probably one of your sports. Boys and girls in China love to swim. There are wonderful beaches along the seashore and there are beautiful rivers and lakes across the country. The weather is also good for swimming.

Or do you live in a cold climate? Then you would like to ski. There are many skiers in Austria where there are big mountains and cold winters. Does it rain often where you live? Then kite flying would not be one of your sports. It is one of the favorite sports of Thailand.

Surfing is an important sport in Hawaii. The Pacific Ocean sends huge waves up on the beaches, waves that are just right for surfing. But you need to live near an ocean to ride the waves and enjoy surfing.

People in Switzerland lone to climb the wonderful mountains of their country. Mountain climbing and hiking are favorite sports there. But there can be no mountain climbing where there are no mountains.

Sports change with the season. People often do not play the same games in winter as in summer. Sailing is fun in warm weather, but when it gets cold it's time to change to other sports. People talk about sports' seasons. Baseball is only played for a few months of the year. This is called the baseball season."

Games and sports often grow out of the work people do. In Portugal, many people work to catch fish. They fish from boats. Sometimes they use their boats for racing.

The Arab people are famous for their horses. They use horses to travel over the huge plains. Horseback riding is a very exciting sport in countries like Morcocco. Men ride horses at great speeds, often standing up.

[A] There are many different sports programs which people there are favorite in different countries.

[B] For sports are very useful in people's lives, people not only like sports, but take an active part in sports.

[C] Many persons in towns and cities like watching all kinds of sports games, especially in hot summer, they go to swim in the sea, rivers and lakes.

[D] People in some countries like to play games or sports over the water, or to ride horse for sports.

[E] All people in the world like to work and play, generally speaking, all men like to work all day long, but all women like to play or sports.

[F] Work can help people to live happily and feel good, so many people are interested in all kinds of work, and like sports a little.

[G] People in some countries like to talk about sports' season because sports is related to the season.

Exercise ⑪

Directions: In the following text, some sentences have been removed. For Questions 1—5, choose the most suitable one from the list A-G to fit into each of the numbered blanks. There are two extra choices which do not fit in any of the gaps.

Chicken and other poultry are safe to eat if cooked properly, according to a joint statement by the UN Food and Agriculture Organization and the World Health Organization issued to national food safety authorities. However, no birds from flocks with disease should enter the food chain.

In areas where there is no avian influenza outbreak in poultry, there is no risk that consumers will be exposed to the virus via the handling or consumption of poultry products.

Cooking of poultry at or above 70° Celsius throughout the product, so that absolutely no meat remains raw and red, is a safe measure to kill the H5N1 virus. This ensures that there is no active virus remaining if the live bird has been infected and has mistakenly entered the food chain. To date, there is no epidemiological evidence that people have become infected after eating contaminated poultry meat that has been properly cooked.

From the information currently available, a large number of confirmed human cases of avian influenza acquired their infection during the home slaughtering and subsequent handling of diseased or dead birds prior to cooking. In the process of killing and preparing a live bird for food, slaughtering poses the greatest risk of passing the virus from infected or diseased birds to humans.

Most strains of avian influenza virus are mainly found in the respiratory and gastrointestinal tracts of infected birds, and not in meat. However, highly pathogenic viruses, such as the H5N1 strain, spread to virtually all parts of an infected bird, including meat. Proper cooking at temperatures at or above 70° in all parts of the product will inactivate the virus.

It is not always possible to differentiate infected and non-infected birds in outbreak areas. Some avian species, such as domestic ducks, may harbour the virus without displaying symptoms. Therefore, people need to be fully informed about preventive measures, including the use of protective equipment. The practice of slaughtering and eating infected birds, whether diseased or already dead, must be stopped. And these birds should also not be used for animal feed.

[A] Most strains of avian influenza virus are not in meat of birds except for highly pathogenic viruses.

[B] There is no active virus remaining in the birds if only cooking of the bird meat is at or above 70° Celsius.

[C] Chinese and other poultry are properly cooked and are safe to eat except for one kind of situation.

[D] It is impossible to differentiate whether birds are infected or not in outbreak areas because there is virus without displaying symptoms.

[E] The information shows that the diseased or dead birds can not infect humans under any conditions.

[F] It can infect human that killing at home and subsequent handling diseased or dead birds prior to cooking.

[G] It has known to us that we can't prevent the viruses in the diseased or dead birds from entering humans even if measures are taken.

Key to Reading Comprehension
Part B
1)
Text 1
1. C **2.** D **3.** A **4.** F **5.** G

Text 2
1. A **2.** B **3.** D **4.** E **5.** F

Text 3
1. G **2.** B **3.** A **4.** C **5.** D

Text 4
1. B **2.** C **3.** E **4.** F **5.** G

Text 5
1. G **2.** F **3.** E **4.** A **5.** B

2)

Text 6

1. B **2.** A **3.** D **4.** C **5.** E

Text 7

1. E **2.** D **3.** F **4.** A **5.** C

Text 8

1. D **2.** A **3.** C **4.** B **5.** E

Text 9

1. C **2.** B **3.** A **4.** E **5.** D

3)

Exercise 1

1. A **2.** C **3.** E **4.** F **5.** G

Exercise 2

1. C **2.** G **3.** F **4.** D **5.** A

Exercise 3

1. E **2.** C **3.** D **4.** F **5.** B

Exercise 4

1. B **2.** F **3.** E **4.** A **5.** C

Exercise 5

1. D **2.** C **3.** G **4.** A **5.** F

Exercise 6

1. C **2.** A **3.** F **4.** B **5.** E

Exercise 7

1. D **2.** C **3.** B **4.** A **5.** F

Exercise 8

1. C **2.** B **3.** A **4.** E **5.** F

Exercise 9

1. B　2. C　3. A　4. G　5. D

Exercise 10

1. C　2. B　3. F　4. A　5. D

Ⅲ. 阅读与理解 C 节

《大纲》中对于阅读与理解 C 节部分的表述是："主要考查学生准确理解概念或结构较复杂的英语文字材料的能力"。考题结构形式是：需要翻译的部分为 5 个句子，共计大约 150 个词汇。考查考生根据文章上下文准确理解各个句子的词数基本上差不多，句式各异，结构较复杂，内容有一定的难度，并用汉语予以正确表达的能力。具体归纳为两个方面：

1. 语言技能

英译汉考察的要点是放在理解句子和表达能力上，而且主要问题集中在词汇和句法两个方面。

2. 词汇的理解

考生根据文章上下文去理解词汇的意思，因为在试题中有不少词汇具有一词多义的普遍现象。所以只有紧密地结合句子的本身去理解词义、确定词义、引申词义，这样才能够准确地表达词义。

Part C

范文与答案解析

(1)

The Earth is full! Four billion people have crammed into every desirable and fruitful area and have spilled over into all the barren and inhospitable areas. Under the pressure of the fullness, the wilderness is disappearing, competing plants and animals are dying out; the weather is changing and the soil is failing. (1) And yet there is perhaps an even more fundamental danger to humanity in the Earth's fullness than is represented by any sort of physical deterioration. Humanity began as a thin cluster of primitive hominids in East Africa about four million years ago. About two million years ago, the first hominids appeared who were sufficiently close in structure to the human being to be placed into *Genus Homo*. It was not until 150,000 years ago that the hominid brain developed to a size sufficient to produce the first organisms we can classify as *Homo Sapiens*, and it was only 50,000 years ago that "modern man", *Homo Sapiens*, made his appearance on the Earth.

His increase in range was slow indeed. (2) It was not till 30,000 years ago that human beings began to enter Australia and the American continents, and even as late as 300 years ago, those continents were but thinly occupied.

Then came the Industrial Revolution and the Earth filled with what was, on the evolutionary scale, an explosion. (3) In a couple of centuries, the world population quintupled from 0. 8 billion to 4. 2 billion, and now Earth bears all the human load it can manage and, in many places, somewhat more than it can manage.

Consider, then, that we and our hominid ancestors evolved on an essentially empty Earth. (4) There was always the possibility, during times of stress, that one might pick up as much of one's belongings as one could carry and travel to the other side of the hill, where conditions might be better, where a new life might be built and where a new chance might be taken.

This was true even after civilization appeared, very late in human history. The Greeks and Phoenicians colonized the shores of the Mediterranean; the Russians pushed into the Ukraine and Siberia; the Bantus into eastern and southern Africa; the Polynesians from island to island across the Pacific. In modern times, Europeans flooded into the Americas and Australias. In every case, a thin wave of early migrants was replaced by a much denser wave of later ones.

By the 1920's, however, the freedom to migrate vanished. No nation, no region, any longer welcomed newcomers; all nations, all regions, had the power to exclude. (5) Even when migration did take place with permission, migrants had to fit into the full society, too massive to change for them. There was no chance of building a new society.

（1）但对人类来说，与自然环境的恶化相比，人满为患也许是一个更为严重的危险。

分析：本句的主干是 there is a more fundamental danger than…。考查的是比较级句型 more…than… 和 than 后面引导的定语从句的翻译。句子是把 danger in the Earth's fullness（人满为患的危险）和 any sort of physical deterioration 进行比较。而 than is represented by any sort of physical deterioration 即相当于 than the danger that is represented by any sort of physical deterioration. 本句可以翻译为"但对人类来说，人满为患也许比自然环境的恶化是一个更为严重的危险"，但考虑到汉语的行文习惯将译文分成三个部分。

（2）直到三万年之前，人类才进入澳洲和南北美洲，而直到三百年之前，澳洲和美洲大陆的人口密度还很小。

分析：本句考查考生对 it was…that… 和 not until 这两个特殊句型的掌握和对句尾 but 一词的理解。But 在这里不是一个起转折作用的连接词，而是作为副词，表示"仅仅，只有"，起到加强语气的作用。

（3）在两个世纪中，世界人口增加了 5 倍，从 8 亿增加到了 42 亿。现在，地球承受了人类的全部重担，已经到了它能承受的极限；在许多地方，负担之重，甚至已经不堪承受了。

分析：本句考查定语从句的翻译。It（Earth）can manage 和 somewhat more than it can manage 都做 human load 的定语，其中 in many places, somewhat more than it can manage 即相当于 Earth now bears the human load somewhat more than the load that it can manage in many places.

（4）当生活发生困难的时候，他们往往可以收拾能随身携带的行李，爬过山头，来到山的那边；那里的自然条件可能会好些，他们就可以重新开始生活，并获得新的发展机会。

分析：本句的考查点是同位语从句，宾语从句和定语从句。句子的主干是 there was always the possibility that…其中 that 之后的部分作 possibility 的同位语。而同位语从句中，句子的主干部分是 one might pick up…and travel to…，其中 as much…as…作 pick up 的宾语，

where condition might be better, where a new life might be built 和 where a new chance might be taken 作 the other side of the hill 的定语。在把句子翻译成汉语时,可以考虑把同位语从句的主干部分 the possibility that 省略掉,只翻译 that 之后的部分。

(5) 即使允许移民,庞大的社会也不可能为少数移民而改变,只能要求移民完全融入所在国或所在地区的社会。

分析:本句考查重点是 too…to…句型的翻译。在本句中,massive 和 change 的逻辑主语都是 the society,而不是 migrants,因此在翻译成汉语时,可以考虑将 the society 作为句子的主语。

(2)

(1) Science is generally taken as meaning either (a) the exact sciences, such as chemistry, physics, etc., or (b) a method of thought which obtains verifiable results by reasoning logically from observed fact.

If you ask any scientist, or indeed almost any educated person, "what is science?" you are likely to get an answer approximating to (b). In everyday life, however, both in speaking and in writing, when people say "science" they mean (a). Science means something that happens in a laboratory: the very word calls up a picture of graphs, test-tubes, balances, microscopes. A biologist, an astronomer, perhaps a psychologist or a mathematician, is described as a "man of science": no one would think of applying this term to a statesman, a poet, a journalist or even a philosopher. And (2) those who tell us that the young must be scientifically educated mean, almost invariably, that they should be taught more about radioactivity, or the stars, or the physiology of their own bodies, rather than that they should be taught to think more exactly.

This confusion of meaning, which is partly deliberate, has in it a great danger. (3) Implied in the demand for more scientific education is the claim that if one has been scientifically trained one's approach to *all* subjects will be more intelligent than if one had had no such training. A scientist's political opinions, it is assumed, his opinions on sociological questions, on morals, on philosophy, perhaps even on the arts, will be more valuable than those of a layman. The world, in other words, would be a better place if the scientists were in control of it. But a "scientist", as we have just seen, means in practice a specialist in one of the exact sciences. (4) It follows that a chemist or a physicist, as such, is politically more intelligent than a poet or a lawyer, as such. And, in fact, there are already millions of people who do believe this.

But is it really true that a "scientist", in this narrow sense, is any likelier than other people to approach non-scientific problems in an objective way? There is not much reason for thinking so. Take one simple test—the ability to withstand nationalism. (5) It is often loosely said that "science is international", but in practice the scientific workers of all countries line up behind their governments with fewer scruples than are felt by the writers and the artists.

(1) 科学一般被定义为:甲,精确科学,如化学、物理等等;乙,一种通过逻辑推理从观察到的事实得出可验证的结论的思维方式。

分析:本句重点考查的是对 either…or…句型以及 which 引导的定语从句的理解。either…or…的意思是"不是……就是……",二者属于并列关系,由于本句出现项目编号(a)和(b),因此 either…or…不必译出，只要将英文的项目编号用中文的"甲"和"乙"来表示即可。which 引导的定语从句的先行词是"一种思维方式"（a method of thought），由于甲项是一个名词词组，因此译成汉语后的乙项最好也用一个名词词组来表示，以体现两者间的平行关系。

（2）有人告诉我们说年轻人必须得到科学方面的教育，但他们不外乎是说年轻人应该多知道一点辐射、恒星或是人体的生理机能，而并非指应该教年轻人学会更严密地思考。

分析：本句重点考查对定语从句、宾语从句和 rather than 句型的翻译。鉴于原句较长且结构较复杂，在译成汉语时可考虑将这个长句用两个以上的较短的句子来表达。比较合适的译法是把原句从插入语 almost invariably 处分开，将原句的主语单独译成一个句子，而给插入语后面的宾语从句部分补上逻辑主语"他们"译成另一个完整的句子。rather than 句型的意思是"而不是……，而非……"。

（3）加强科学教育的呼吁暗示了一种信念，即如果得到了科学的训练，人们对于所有学科的认识会比没有经过这种训练时要来的明智。

分析：本句重点考查对主语从句、同位语从句、条件句及比较级的翻译。由于本句的结构非常复杂，建议在翻译时将它从连词 that 处分开，译成两个句子。"Implied in the demand… claim"构成一个完整的句子，that 后面条件句构成另一个句子，用于补充说明这种信念的内容。

（4）那么接下去的推论就是这样一个化学家或者物理学家在政治上要比一个诗人或者律师明智。

分析：本句主要考查对 It follows that…句型的翻译。该句型的意思是"由此得出结论……，因而断定……"，as such 的意思是"同样地"。

（5）人们常说"科学无国界"，但在实际上，所有国家的科学工作者在追随本国政府时比起作家和艺术家来更少顾忌。

分析：本句主要考查对 It is said that…句型及比较级的翻译。在该句型中 It 是形式主语，真正的逻辑主语是"science is international"。短语 in practice 的意思是"实际上"，line up behind 的意思是"追随"。另外，为了避免重复，作者将构成比较级的连词"than"后面的 that are felt by the writers and the artists 中的 that 省略掉了，实际上如果补上 that，那么 that 指代的就是上文提到的 scruples（"犹豫、顾虑"），作者是将科学工作者的顾虑与作家和艺术家的顾虑进行比较。

（3）

（1）Although art historians have spent decades demystifying van Gogh's legend, they have done little to diminish his vast popularity. Auction prices still soar; visitors still overpopulate van Gogh exhibitions, and *The Starry Night* remains almost everywhere on dormitory and kitchen walls. So complete is van Gogh's global apotheosis that Japanese tourists now make pilgrimages to Auvers to sprinkle their relatives' ashes on his grave. What accounts for the endless appeal of the van Gogh myth? It has at least two deep and powerful resources. （2）At the most primitive level, it provides a satisfying and nearly universal revenge fantasy disguised as the story of heroic sacrifice to art. Anyone who has ever felt isolated and unappreciated can identify with van Gogh and hope not only for a spectacular redemption but also to put critics and doubting relatives to shame. At the same time, the myth offers an alluringly simplistic conception of great art as the product, not of particular historical circumstances and the artist's painstaking calculations, but of the naive and spontaneous outpourings of a mad, holy fool. (3) The gaping discrepancy between van Gogh's long-suffering life and his remarkable posthumous fame remains a great and undeniable historical irony. But the notion that he was an artistic idiot savant is quickly dispelled by even the most glancing examination of the artist's letters. It also must be dropped after acquainting oneself with the rudimentary facts of van Gogh's family background, upbringing, and early adulthood.

(4) The image of van Gogh as a disturbed and forsaken artist is so strong that one easily reads it back into his childhood and adolescence. But if van Gogh had died at age twenty, no one would have connected him with failure or mental illness. Instead he would have been remembered by those close to him as a competent and dutiful son with a promising career in the family art-dealing business. He was, in fact, poised to surpass his father and to come closer to living up to the much-esteemed van Gogh name.

(5) The van Goghs were an old and distinguished Dutch family who could trace their lineage in Holland back to the sixteen's century. Among Vincent's five uncles, one reached the highest rank of vice-admiral in the Navy and three others prospered as successful art dealers. Van Gogh's grandfather, also named Vincent, had attained an equally illustrious status as an intellectually accomplished Protestant minister. The comparative modest achievement of the artist's father, Theodorus, proved the exception, not the rule.

（1）尽管艺术史家们数十年来一直在淡化梵·高传奇的神秘色彩，但梵·高受欢迎的程度几乎丝毫未减。

分析：本句重点考查对让步状语从句的翻译。需要注意的是主句中的"little"带有否定含义，表示"几乎没有"的意思，而不能翻译成"一些"。

（2）表面上看，梵·高神话是一则为艺术英勇牺牲的故事。但它满足的是人性，激起的是人人皆有的复仇幻想。任何一个感到被人冷落、遭人轻视的人，都能与梵·高心心相印，进而希望能像梵·高那样有朝一日被人肯定，让批评他的人，怀疑他的亲属无地自容。

分析：本句重点考查对定语从句和 not only...but also...句型的翻译。第一句话中，主语 It 指代的是上文提到 the endless appeal of the van Gogh myth，即"梵·高神话"，而该句中定语从句 a satisfying and nearly universal revenge fantasy disguised as...的关系代词被省掉了，实际相当于 a satisfying and nearly universal revenge fantasy that is disguised as...。第二句话中 identify with 的意思是"视……为一体，使……等同于"，而不定式 to put critics and doubting relatives to shame 实际上是作 hope 的宾语，表示 hope 的内容。

（3）梵·高生前长期饱受磨难，死后却如此声名卓著，差别如此之大，无疑是历史上的极大讽刺。

分析：本句比较简单，只要正确理解句中的关键词，就不难把它译成汉语。gaping 的意思是"大而深的"，discrepancy 的意思是"差异"，posthumous 的意思是"身后的"。

（4）在人们的印象中，梵·高是个精神异常，被人遗弃的艺术家，这种根深蒂固的看法自然促使人们将这些不幸归咎他的童年与青少年。

分析：本句重点考查对 so...that...句型的翻译。该句型的意思是"如此……以至于……",也就是说梵·高作为一个精神异常,被人遗弃的艺术家形象在人们心中是如此的根深蒂固,以至于人们很容易将这些不幸归咎他的童年与青少年。短语 read into 的意思是"对……做某种解释",it 指代的是 the image of van Gogh。

(5)梵·高家族是荷兰的名门望族,家史悠久,可以追溯到十六世纪。

分析:本句较简单,重点考查对定语从句的翻译。the van Goghs 指的是整个梵·高家族。短语 trace back to 的意思是"追溯到"。

(4)

The Federal Reserve System was created, in 1913, for many reasons, but the underlying one was that people no longer trusted private bankers to shepherd the financial markets. (1) Prior to the Fed's founding, the government had had no effective weapon to temper the country's economic cycles, nor was there much it could do to ease the periodic crises that afflicted Wall Street. Too often, the government had had to go hat in hand to a private banker for help. By the Progressive Era, with its suspicion of trusts and its faith in regulation, people wanted a bank that would represent the public interest. Ever since, the Fed has been a public servant but one that works in close proximity to private banks and to Wall Street. (2) It is a delicate role, for the Fed is supposed to regulate banking but not to shelter bankers. It must protect the functioning of markets without appearing to be too close—too protective—of the banks it watches over.

(3) The side of the Fed most often seen in public is its governing board, in Washington, which has the high-profile job of adjusting short-term interest rates. The chairman of this body is the country's chief inflation fighter and, in a larger sense, the steward of its economy. Alan Greespan, who has been chairman since 1987, is probably the most respected of all those who have held this job, thanks to the economy's stellar performance during his tenure. If Greespan has perfected a convoluted, often impenetrable style of public utterances, this has only heightened his image as the nation's economic oracle.

(4) More than is commonly realized, Greespan relies on the Fed's individual branches, particularly on the New York Fed, which, among its other roles, functions as Washington's periscope into markets. William McDonough, the beefy president of the New York Fed, kept in close touch with private bankers and reported on what he heard to Greespan. His associate was Peter Fisher, in 1998, a forty-two-year-old bureaucrat who had joined the Fed straight out of Harvard Law School. Fisher ran the Fed's trading desk and oversaw a $450 billion portfolio of government securities. (5) When Greespan wanted to tighten or loosen monetary conditions, Fisher and his staff actually carried out the directive by either buying more securities or selling some.

(1)在美联储建立之前,美国政府根本就没有任何有效的武器来对整个国家经济发展的周期进行掌控,也缺乏有效的政策工具对华尔街周期性发生的危机进行宏观调控。

分析:本题重点考查对连词 Nor 引导的句子的翻译。Nor 的意思是"也不",由它引导的句子虽然形式上是肯定的,但意思上是否定的,而且整个句子需要倒装,就相当于 there wasn't much it could do to ease the periodic crises that afflicted Wall Street,而 it 指代的是 the government。

（2）联储所要起到的作用是非常微妙的：它既要对整个银行系统进行有效的管理，又不能成为银行家们的庇护所；它必须保护整个金融市场的正常运作，又不能与其所监管的银行走得太近，因为这往往会导致过分的保护。

分析：本句重点考查对由 for 引导的状语从句及定语从句的翻译。第一句的主语 It 指代的是上一句提到的美联储的作用，for 相当于 because 表示原因。另外需要注意的是第二句中的副词 too 表示"过多地；过分地"的意思。短语 watch over 是"保护，监管"的意思。

（3）联邦储备系统最为世人所知的，是它位于华盛顿的管理委员会，而管理委员会最主要的工作，就是对利率进行有效的调控。管理委员会的主席是美国"首席通货膨胀斗士"，从某种意义上来说，他也是美国经济的掌控者。

分析：本句主要考查对定语从句的翻译。本题中有两个定语从句：一个是第一句的主语 The side of the Fed most often seen in public，在这句中，关系代词 that 被省掉了，实际相当于 The side of the Fed that is most often seen in public；另一个则是由 which 引导的非限定性定语从句，对于非限定性定语从句的处理办法主要是把它译成并列分句，由于 which 指代的就是 its governing board，因此可以将此句翻译成"管理委员会最主要的工作，就是对利率进行有效的调控"。

（4）比外界所了解的更多的是，格林斯潘对联邦储备的各个分支机构，尤其是对纽约联邦储备银行的依赖非常之大，因为除了其他许多作用之外，纽约联邦储备银行还是华盛顿总部了解市场的信息来源。

分析：本句主要考查对由 which 引导的非限定性定语从句的翻译。如上题所述，对于非限定性定语从句的处理办法主要是把它译成并列分句，在该句中，which 指代的就是 the New York Fed，因此只要明确了从句的主语，再将它单独译成一句就可以了。Periscope 原本是"潜望镜"的意思，这里是个比喻的说法，表示"信息来源"的意思。

（5）当格林斯潘需要收紧或放松银根时，费舍尔及其工作人员就会通过买进或卖出更多的证券来执行格林斯潘的指令。

分析：本句主要考查对时间状语从句及 either…or…句型的翻译。在该句中介词 by 不表示被动关系，而是表示"通过方某种法、手段"的意思。为了避免重复，本句中的 some 实际上指是 some securities。

（5）

All human work, under natural conditions, is a kind of dance. In a large and learned work, supported by an immense amount of evidence, Karl Bucher has argued that (1) work differs from the dance not in kind but only in degree, since they are both essentially rhythmic. There is a good reason why work should be rhythmic, for all great combined efforts, the efforts by which alone great constructions such as those of megalithic days could be carried out, must be harmonized. It has been argued that this necessity is the source of human speech, and we have the so-called Yo-heave-ho theory of language.

(2) It is, however, the dance itself, apart from work and apart from the other arts, which, in the opinion of many today, has had a decisive influence in socializing, that is to say in

moralizing, the human species. Work showed the necessity of harmonious rhythmic co-operation, but the dance developed that rhythmic co-operation and imparted a beneficent impetus to all human activities. It was Grosse, in his *Beginning of Art*, who first clearly set forth the high social significance of the dance in the creation of human civilization. (3) The participants in dance, as all observers of savages have noted, exhibit a wonderful harmony; they are, as it were, fused into a single being stirred by a single impulse. Social unification is thus accomplished. Apart from war, this is the chief factor making for social solidarity in primitive life; it was indeed the best training for war. (4) It has been a twofold influence; on the one hand it aided unity of action and method in evolution; on the other it had the invaluable function—for man is naturally a timid animal—of imparting courage; the universal drum, as Louis Robinson remarks, has been an immense influence in human affairs. Even among the Romans, with their highly developed military system, dancing and war were definitely allied. We may trace a similar influence of dancing in all the co-operative arts of life. All our most advance civilization, Grosse insisted, is based on dancing. It is the dance that socialized man.

Thus, in the large sense, dancing has possessed peculiar value as a method of national education. As civilization grew self-conscious this was realized. One may judge of a king, according to an ancient Chinese maxim, by the state of dancing during his reign. So also among the Greeks; (5) it has been said that dancing and music lay at the foundation of the whole political and military as well as religious organization of a country.

（1）劳动与舞蹈的不同之处并不在于性质,而只是在于程度,因为两者本质上都是有节奏。

分析:本句较简单,主要考查对状语从句的翻译。连词 since 在本句中的作用就相当于 because,表示原因。而 differ from...in...表示"在……方面与……不同"的意思。

（2）然而,姑且不谈劳动,不谈其他艺术,以现今许多人的见解来看,正是舞蹈本身,在促进人类适应社会生活方面具有决定性的影响,即有助于宣传风教。

分析:本句主要考查对强调句的翻译。表示转折的副词 however 在英语中的位置比较灵活,可以在句首,也可以作为插入语置于句中,如本句,但译成汉语时,习惯置于句首。It is...which...是强调句型,在该句中被强调的部分是本句的主语 the dance itself("舞蹈本身"),apart from work and apart from the other arts 和 in the opinion of many today 都是插入语,起补充说明的作用,在翻译时,可考虑将其一律放在强调句的前面。

（3）参与舞蹈的人显示出绝妙的合拍,所有观察生番的人都留意于此;可以说,在单一的冲动激发之下,他们浑然一体了。从而社会统一才得以实现。

分析:本题由三个句型并不复杂的单句组成,只要准确理解了每个词的意思,再译成通顺的汉语就可以了。as it were 的意思是"仿佛,可以说",fuse into 的意思是"合并成"。

（4）它向来具有双重影响:一则促进行动的一致性和进化的方法;一则在鼓足勇气时具有不可估量的作用——因为人天生是胆怯的动物。

分析:本题主要考查对 on the one hand...on the other...句型的翻译及插入语位置的调整。on the one hand...on the other...的意思是"一方面……另一方面……",而 for man is naturally a timid animal 作为插入语,建议在汉译时,可考虑将其放在句末,以便更好地保持句子的连贯性。for 相当于 because 表示原因。

（5）有人说跳舞和音乐位居一个国家全部军政和宗教组织的基础地位。

分析：本题重点考查对 It is said that...句型的翻译。It is said that...句型的意思是"据说、有人说"，至于究竟是谁说的不重要。需要注意的是，这里的 lay 不是动词 lie 的过去时，而是动词 lay 的一般现在时复数形式，意思是"放置，使处于"，as well as 的意思是"也、和……一样"。

（6）

（1）The wages of labor in different employments vary according to the probability or improbability of success in them.

（2）The probability that any particular person should ever be qualified for the employment to which he is educated, is very different in different occupations. In the greater part of mechanic trades, success is almost certain; but very uncertain is the liberal professions. Put your son apprentice to a shoemaker, there is little doubt of his learning to make a pair of shoes: but（3）send him to study the law, it is at least twenty to one if ever he makes such a proficiency as will enable him to live by the business. In a perfectly fair lottery, those who draw the prizes ought to gain all that is lost by those who draw the blanks. In a profession where twenty fail for one that succeeds, that one ought to gain all that should have been gained by the unsuccessful twenty.

（4）The counselor at law, who, perhaps, at near forty years of age, begins to make something by his profession, ought to receive the retribution, not only of his own so tedious and expensive education, but of that of more than twenty others who are never likely to make anything by it. How extravagant soever the fees of counselor at law sometimes appear, their real retribution is never equal to this. Compute in any particular place, what is likely to be annually gained, and what is likely to be annually spent, all the different workmen in any common trade, such as that of shoemakers or weavers, and you will find that the former sum will generally exceed the latter. But make the same computation with regard to all the counselors and students of law, in all different inns of court, and you will find that their annual gains bear but a very small proportion to their annual expense, even though you rate the former as high, and the latter as low, as can well be done. The lottery of the law, therefore, is very far from being a perfectly fair lottery; and that, as well as many other liberal and honorable professions, are, in point of monetary gain, evidently under-recompensed.

Those professions keep their level, however, with other occupations, and not withstanding these discouragements, all the most generous and liberal spirits are eager to crowd into them.（5）Two different causes contribute to recommend them. Firstly, the desire of the reputation which attends upon superior excellence in any of them; and, secondly, the natural confidence which every man has, more or less, not only in his own abilities, but in his own good fortune.

（1）不同行业付出劳动所获的酬报，随该行业所含成功几率的大小而异。

分析：本题较简单。建议将本句中的一组反义词 probability or improbability 合并处理，翻译为"成功的可能性或几率"即可。

（2）任何人在接受相关教育后能否胜任某项工作，根据行业不同而差异万千。

分析：本句重点考查对定语从句的翻译。对于本句定语从句的处理可采用前置法，即把从句 that any particular person should ever be qualified for the employment to which he is educated 译在中心词 The probability 前，加个"的"字就可以了；to which he is educated 相当于 which he is educated to，修饰先行词 employment，起到定语的作用，对于它的处理可采用融合法，即把先行词和定语从句融合恰当，结合前半句一起译成"任何人在接受相关教育后胜任某项工作的可能性"。

（3）但如若送他去学法律，让他对这一行业驾轻就熟并借此谋生，成功率至少是一比二十。

分析：对于本句的处理，首先要判断出两个分句间的存在条件关系，相当于 but if send him to study the law，it is at least twenty to one…，因此在翻译时要通过增词的方式将这种逻辑关系体现出来。If ever 的意思是"如果有的话也"，such…as…的意思是"像这种"，该句可以翻译成"达到能靠此谋生的熟练程度的成功率至少是一比二十"。

（4）年届四十，或许刚在事业上小有成就的律师理应得到些回报，不只是因为当初繁复的学习和昂贵的学费，还因为另外二十几位可能一事无成的同行。

分析：本句重点考查的是对定语从句及并列句型 not only…but…的翻译。对于本题中的两个定语从句，建议都采用前置译法，分别翻译成"那些年届四十，或许刚在事业上小有成就的律师"和"另外二十几位可能一事无成的同行"就可以了。而由于本句的介词宾语是以并列句的形式出现的，比较长，因此可考虑将它们与主句分开处理。

（5）究其原因，主要有两个：首先是对超凡杰出人才及随之而来的名誉的强烈渴望；其次是每个人与生俱来或多或少的自信心，不仅相信自身的能力，也坚信自己能走好运。

分析：本句重点考查对定语从句的翻译。对于本题中的两个定语从句，都可以采用前置法，分别翻译成"超凡杰出人才及随之而来的名誉"和"每个人与生俱来的自信心"。由于第二点原因中的状语是以并列句 not only…but…的形式出现的，比较长，因此可考虑将它们单独提出来，译成两个短句。而将原句中的两个名词词组 confidence in his own abilities 和 confidence in his own good fortune 翻译成汉语的动词词组"相信自身的能力"和"坚信自己能走好运"，则是出于更好地符合汉语表达习惯的考虑。

（7）

This book grows directly out of those conversations on the campaign trail. (1) Not only did my encounters with voters confirm the fundamental decency of the American people, they also reminded me that at the core of the American experience are a set of ideals that continue to stir our collective conscience; a common set of values that bind us together despite our differences; a running thread of hope that makes our improbable experiment in democracy work. (2) These values and ideals find expression not just in the marble slabs of monuments or in the recitation of history books. They remain alive in the hearts and minds of most Americans—and can inspire us to pride, duty, and sacrifice.

I recognize the risks of talking this way. (3) In an era of globalization and dizzying technological change, we don't even seem to possess a shared language with which to discuss our ideals, much less the tools to arrive at some rough consensus about how, as a nation, we might work together to bring those ideals about. Most of us are wise to the ways of admen, pollsters, speechwriters, and pundits. We know how high-flying words can be deployed in the service of cynical aims, and how the noblest sentiments can be subverted in the name of power, expedience, greed, or intolerance. (4) Even the standard high school history textbook notes the degree to which, from its very beginning, the reality of American life has strayed from its myths. In such a climate, any assertion of shared ideals or common values might seem hopelessly naive, if not downright dangerous—an attempt to gloss over serious differences in policy and performance or, worse, a means of muffling the complaints of those who feel ill served by our current institutional arrangements.

My argument, however, is that we have no choice. You don't need a poll to know that the vast majority of Americans—Republican, Democrat, and independent—are weary of the dead zone that politics has become, in which narrow interests vie for advantage and ideological minorities seek to impose their own versions of absolute truth. Whether we're from red states or blue states, we feel in our gut the lack of honesty, rigor, and common sense in our policy debates, and dislike what appears to be a continuous menu of false or cramped choices. Religious or secular, black, white, or brown, (5) we sense—correctly—that the nation's most significant challenges are being ignored, and that if we don't change course soon, we may be the first generation in a very long time that leaves behind a weaker and more fractured America than the one we inherited. Perhaps more than any other time in our recent history, we need a new kind of politics, one that can excavate and build upon those shared understandings that pull us together as Americans.

(1) 从与选民间的对话中,我看到了美利坚民族的道德规范,我更加意识到,正是这些人的理想贯穿了美国历史,并不断鞭策着我们的集体正义感。

分析:本句重点考查的是对宾语从句、定语从句及 not only…but…句型的翻译。当 not only 置于句首时,整句话需要倒装,相当于 my encounters with voters not only confirmed…。that continue to stir our collective conscience 作为 a set of ideals 的定语起到修饰作用,对此定语从句,若按前置法处理译成汉语后定语显得冗长而又不符合汉语表达习惯,因此可考虑采取后置法,即将它译成一个后置的并列分句。

(2) 这些价值观和理想不仅仅是刻在大理石纪念碑上,或者在历史书的背诵中,它们更多地存活于大多数美国人的内心,并感召着我们的自豪感、责任心和献身精神。

分析:本题句子虽然较长但结构并不复杂,且没有什么晦涩难懂的词,只要保存原来的句子结构,采用顺译法处理即可。

(3) 在这个全球化和科技风云变化的时代,我们连一种畅谈理想的共同语言都没有,更不用说让全民族达成一致去致力理想的实现了。

分析:本题重点考查对定语从句和宾语从句的处理。with which to discuss our ideals 相当于 which to discuss our ideals with,在句子中充当先行词 language 的定语,因此可采用前置法,将它汉译为"一种畅谈理想的共同语言"。短语 much less 的意思是"何况、更不用说"。less the tools 和 a shared language 一样都是作 possess 的宾语;而不定式 to arrive at some rough consensus 则作为 tools 的定语,修饰 tools;how, as a nation, we might work together to bring those ideals about 在句中充当介词 about 的宾语,说明要在什么样的问题上达成一致,即"在全民族如何共同努力实现理想的问题上达成一致"。

(4)甚至连标准的中学历史课本上都开宗明义地道出美国现实生活与美国神话有很大的出入。

分析:本句重点考查对定语从句的翻译。对这个定语从句仍然可以考虑按融合法处理,把原句中的主语和定语从句融合在一起译成一个独立的句子。短语 stray from 的意思是"离开、偏离"。

(5)我们都真正地意识到,这个国家的首要任务正在被忽视。如果不尽快调转航向,我们会成为有史以来第一个把由强变弱的美国留给后人的一代。

分析:本句重点考查对宾语从句、条件句和定语从句的翻译。本句中 sense 的宾语有两个:一个是 that the nation's most significant challenges are being ignored,另一个是条件句 that if we don't change course soon...。条件句中由于定语 that leaves behind a weaker and more fractured America than the one we inherited 较冗长,作者为了避免使整个句子显得头重脚轻而没有将它直接放在先行词 generation 后面,而是放在了句末。而对于状语 correctly 的处理应按照汉语的习惯放在动词 sense 的前面。

(8)

My job was on Wall Street. (1) Madison Avenue, by contrast, was the center of the advertising world, the place where smart and manipulative companies burned loads of cash and creative energy to convince us that we needed to use this or that brand of products to wash our hands or brush our teeth. At least (2) I was going to be an analyst whose job it was to evaluate companies on their merits, not someone whose purpose was to seduce America's soap-opera watchers with meaningless slogans and exaggerated promises.

(3) My new job had nothing to do with manipulation and everything to do with balanced, rational thinking. I had made the leap to Wall Street in part because of the money, but also because being an analyst seemed like the perfect job for a serious guy like me who liked to reason his way through life. Sure, emotion and exaggeration sneaked into my line of work occasionally, but in the end, the stock market was rational, analytical, cool. Fooling people wasn't part of this equation.

Or so I thought. In retrospect my naive idea sounded charming or, I can say, silly. (4) *Of course* Wall Street was as much about fooling people as Madison Avenue was, at least if you were one of the corporate executives trying to convince investors and analysts that your company's shares would shoot to the moon. But my job, I hastened to tell myself, was all about shooting straight. I` had been in a sales role before, and I'd never liked it. Now I'd have a chance to focus entirely on the facts.

I grabbed on to that belief as if it were a life preserver and clutched it as I walked up Madison, then west on Forty-eighth Street and north on Sixth Avenue until I reached the headquarters of Morgan Stanley at Fiftieth and Sixth. I was 36 years old, it was my first day on Wall Street, and I was scared out of my mind.

Not that I had fallen off the turnip truck or anything. I had moved here from Washington, D. C. , where I had been director of business analysis at MCI, the brash upstart that was shaking up the telecommunications business. (5)I had interacted with Wall Street and its analysts and bankers for the past two years, trying to make them see my company as positively as I did. What I loved the most was the intellectual sparring as we debated the future of MCI and the telecom industry. It had been a great gig.

（1）和华尔街比起来，麦迪逊大道是广告世界的中心，那些聪明伶俐的公司在这里大量烧钱，并且发挥创造的能量来劝说我们大众，我们要用这个牌子的洗手液洗手或者那个牌子的牙膏来刷牙。

分析：本题主要考查对定语从句和宾语从句的翻译。由于 where smart and manipulative companies...作为修饰先行词 the place 的定语较冗长，因此可考虑将它单独译成一个分句；而 that we needed to use this or that brand of products to wash our hands or brush our teeth 作为 convince 的宾语，处于同样的原因，也可作分句处理。

（2）我将成为一名证券分析师，这份工作是根据各家公司的优点来评估其投资价值，而不是像有些人那样用毫无意义的口号与夸大的承诺来减少美国肥皂剧的观众。

分析：本题主要考查对定语从句的翻译。本句由两个并列分句组成，由于结构较简单，可考虑保留原句的结构，顺译成汉语，再稍作调整即可。由于 whose job it was to evaluate companies on their merits 作为先行词 analyst 的定语较冗长，因此可考虑将它单独翻译成一个分句；而对于 whose purpose was to...则可运用融合法，把它和主语 someone 合在一起译成一个独立的句子，以符合汉语的表达习惯。

（3）我的新工作就是进行公正的研究，我想，跟人工操纵没有任何关系，每一件事都与平衡的、理性的思考有关。

分析：本句主要考查对词组 have nothing/everything to do 的翻译。由于本句结构较简单，可保留原句的结构，顺译成汉语即可。have nothing to do 的意思是"与……无关"，而 have everything to do 的意思是"与……有关"。

（4）华尔街欺骗大众的程度肯定不轻于麦迪逊大道，至少，如果你是公司的一名执行官，你就会努力让投资者——以及分析师——相信，你们公司的股票将牛气冲天。

分析：本题第一个分句中 as much as 是个同级比较，表达"与……一般多、差不多"的意思；第二个分句中的现在分词短语 trying to convince investors and analysts that... 作后置定语，起到修饰 the corporate executives 的作用，由于定语较长，采用前置法会使句子显得头重脚轻，故最好单独译成一个分句。

（5）我过去两年都在同华尔街，同华尔街的分析师和银行家们打交道，一直想让他们像我一样对我服务的公司持正面看法。

分析：本句较简单，建议基本保留原句结构，采用顺译的方法译成汉语即可。在该句中，现在分词短语 trying to make them see my company as positively as I did 作为状语，表示目的。

（9）

Now let us see what intellectual virtues philosophy can provide in the subjects of ethics. The pursuit of philosophy is founded on the belief that knowledge is good, even if what is known is painful. (1) A man imbued with philosophic spirit, whether a professional philosopher or not, will wish his beliefs to be as true as he can make them, and will, in equal measure, love to know, and hate to be in error. This principle has a wider scope than may be apparent at first sight. Our beliefs spring from a great variety of causes and any one of these causes may or may not lead us to true beliefs. (2) Intellectual sobriety, therefore, will lead us to scrutinize our beliefs closely, with a view to discovering which of them there is any reason to believe true. If we are wise, we shall apply solvent criticism especially to the beliefs that we find it most painful to doubt, and to those most likely to involve us in violent conflict with men who hold opposite but equally groundless beliefs. If this attitude could become common, the gain in diminishing the acerbity of disputes would be incalculable.

There is another intellectual virtue, which is that of generality or impartiality. I recommend the following exercise: In a sentence involving words that arouse powerful but different emotions in different readers, try replacing them by symbols, A, B, C, and so on, and forgetting the particular significance of the symbols. When, in elementary algebra, you do problems about A, B and C going up a mountain, you have no emotional interest in the gentlemen concerned, and you do your best to work out the solution with impersonal correctness. But if you thought that A was yourself, B your hated rival and C the schoolmaster who set the problem, your calculation would go askew, and you would be sure to find that A was first and C was last. (3) In thinking about problems where emotional bias is bound to be present, only care and practice can enable you to think as objectively as you do in the algebraic problem.

It is not to be supposed that young men and women who are busy acquiring valuable specialized knowledge can spare a great deal of time for the study of philosophy, but even in the time that can easily be spared without injury to the learning of technical skills, philosophy can give certain things that will greatly increase the student's value as a human being and as a citizen. (4) It can give a habit of exact and careful thought, not only in mathematics and science, but in questions of large practical import. It can give an impersonal breadth and scope to the conception of the ends of life. (5) It can give to the individual a just measure of himself in relation to society, of man in the present to man in the past and in the future, and of the whole history of man in relation to the astronomical cosmos. By enlarging the objects of his thoughts it supplies an antidote to the anxieties and anguish of the present, and makes possible the nearest approach to serenity that is available to a sensitive mind in our tortured and uncertain world.

（1）凡具有哲学精神的人——不管他是不是职业哲学家——总是会在力所能及的范围内使自己的信念成为真理,总是会同等程度地热爱真知、憎恨谬误。

分析:本句主要由两个并列分句组成,句式较简单,可基本保留原句结构,稍作调整即可。过去分词短语imbued with philosophic spirit是中心词a man的后置定语,汉译时,应按照中文的表达习惯,把它放在a man的前面,翻译成"一个具有哲学精神的人"。对于插入语whether a professional philosopher or not的处理,则应考虑到译文结构的需要添加上原文省略掉的主语和谓语,即whether he is a professional philosopher or not。as true as是一个同级比较,表达"和……一样真"的意思;in equal measure 的意思是"同等程度地"。

(2) 因此,只有清醒的理智才会引导我们仔细考查我们的信念,让我们发现其中哪些信念有理由使人相信它们是真理。

分析:本句重点考查对宾语从句的翻译。副词 therefore 在英语中的位置较灵活,而在汉译时则应按照汉语的习惯,置于句首。with a view to 的意思是"以……为目的、考虑到"。which of them there is any reason to believe true 中的 them 指代的是前半句提到的 our beliefs。

(3) 在思考难免会受情感性偏见纠缠问题时,就像你解代数题一样,只有小心谨慎和循序渐进才能使你客观地思考。

分析:本句重点考查对定语从句和比较级的翻译。该句中,介词短语 In thinking about problems where emotional bias is bound to be present 充当了整个句子的状语成分。where emotional bias is bound to be present 作为中心词 problems 的定语较长,汉译时最好采用前置法放在中心词的前面;as objectively as you do in the algebraic problem 是个同级比较,意思是"和你解代数题一样客观地",作为方式状语,它略显冗长,因此也可考虑将它单独译成一个分句,放在主句的前面。

(4) 哲学有助于陶冶精确审慎思考的习惯,这不仅有益于数学和科学思考,也有益于若干实际重大问题的思考。

分析:本题主要考查对并列句型 not only...but also...的翻译。主语 It 指代的是上文提到的 philosophy。出于译文结构的考虑,在处理两个并列短语时,应增加原文中省略的中心词"思考",即"数学和科学的思考"和"实际重大问题的思考"。

(5) 哲学可以让个人正确地权衡自己与社会的关系,正确地评价当代人类、古代人类和未来人类,正确地认识人类的全部历史和天文宇宙的关系。

分析:本句重点考查对平行结构的翻译。of himself in relation to society、of man in the present to man in the past and in the future 和 of the whole history of man in relation to the astronomical cosmos 都是作为 a just measure 的定语,起到修饰它的作用。由于定语很长,最好按照汉语的习惯将它分做三个排比句来处理。另外,由于英语倾向于用名词或名词词组来表述动作或行为的概念,因此汉译时常常要把英语名词转换为汉语动词,从而译出符合汉语习惯表达的译文来,就像在翻译该句中的 a just measure,可考虑将它动词化,译成"正确地权衡……"。

(10)

Asked whether they want more stuff, consumers in rich countries have responded with an emphatic "No". (1) The breathtaking speed with which retail sales have plummeted in both America and Europe has caught retailers and manufacturers by surprise. In response, companies have tried desperately to prop up revenues using a variety of promotions, advertising and other marketing ploys, often to no avail.

But as they battle with these immediate problems, marketers are also pondering what longer-term changes in consumer behavior have been triggered by the recession. It is tempting to conclude that, once economies rebound, customers will start spending again as they did before. Yet (2) there are good reasons to think that what promises to be the worst downturn since the

Depression will spark profound shifts in shoppers' psychology.

The biggest changes will take place in America and parts of Europe, where housing and stock market bubbles have imploded and unemployment has soared. (3) As well as seeing their incomes fall as employers cut wages and jobs, households have also seen the value of their homes and retirement savings shrink dramatically. Although the threat to wages will fade as growth picks up, the damage done to housing and other assets will linger.

This has already led to a swift tightening of purse strings by shoppers and a wave of discounting by companies. Inmar, an American firm that processes discount coupons, says that redemptions in America were 17% higher in the first quarter of 2009 than in the same period last year, as consumers hunted for bargains. (4) Many companies have launched lower-priced products in order to avoid losing customers as they trade down. Danone, a French food group, has created a line of low-cost yogurts in Europe, called "co Packs", that come in smaller tubs and fewer flavors than its standard products.

The trend towards thrift will not disappear when the economy picks up. (5) For one thing, those banks left standing after the bust will be far more parsimonious with consumer credit. For another, many people will still be intent on rebuilding their nest-eggs, which is reflected in sharply rising rates of saving. Sociologists also detect a distinct change in people's behavior. Until the downturn, folk had come to assume that "affluence" was the norm, even if they had to go deeply into debt to pay for gadgets and baubles. Now many people no longer seem consumed by the desire to consume; instead, they are planning to live within their means, and there has been a backlash against bling.

So for years to come, many more households will be firmly focused on saving, splashing out only occasionally on a big-ticket item.

(1) 在美国和欧洲,零售商品销量下滑的速度令零售商和制造商们大为吃惊。作为回应,企业拼命地试图使用各种各样的促销、广告和其他市场策略来支撑收入,但往往劳而无功。

分析:在该句中,从句 with which retail sales have plummeted 作为先行词 the breathtaking speed 的定语,在汉译时可采用前置法放在中心词之前,即"零售商品销量下滑的速度";现在分词短语 using a variety of promotions, advertising and other marketing ploys 作为方式状语,按照汉语的习惯,应放在动词 prop up revenues 的前面,而把结果状语 often to no avail 置于句末。短语 to no avail 的意思是"完全无用"。

(2) 然而,更为理性的观点则认为,这场自大萧条时期以来最为糟糕的衰退将引发消费者心理产生深刻的改变。

分析:本句重要考查对宾语从句和主语从句的翻译。由 that 引导的宾语从句在汉译时不需要改变它在原句中的位置,而由 what 引导的主语从句则在句子中充当动词 think 的宾语。since the Depression 作为时间状语,在翻译时可考虑按照汉语的习惯放在主语从句的句首位置。

(3) 因为雇主削减工资和职位,很多家庭正在面临收入下降,住房价值以及退休储蓄大幅缩水的状况。尽管经济恢复增长时工资下跌的威胁将会褪去,但住房和其他资产所受到的损害还将存在更长的时间。

分析：本题重点考查对介词 as 不同意思的理解。短语 as well as 是"同……一样"的意思；as employers cut wages and jobs 中的 as 相当于 because，表示原因；让步状语从句 Although the threat to wages will fade as growth picks up 中的 as 相当于 when，表示"随着"的意思。在第一句中，由于两个分句的主语和谓语是一样的，因此对于第一句的处理，可采用合句的办法，即把原文的两个分句作为并列成分合译在一个汉语句子，即"很多家庭正在面临收入下降、住房价值以及退休储蓄大幅缩水的状况"。第二句中，过去分词短语 done to housing and other assets 作为中心词 the damage 的定语，汉译时应置于中心词的前面，翻译成"住房和其他资产所受到的损害"。

（4）当交易下降时，为了避免失去顾客，许多公司开始降低商品价格。

分析：本句较简单，主要考查对多状语的处理。in order to avoid losing customers 是本句的目的状语，而 as they trade down 是时间状语。按照中文的表达习惯，时间状语应在目的状语之前，因此汉译时只要对原句中状语的顺序略作调整即可。

（5）首先，经此一役之后，那些存活下来的银行对于消费信贷将会越发审慎。其次，许多人仍将专注于重建其储蓄，这一点已经被急剧上升的储蓄率所反映。

分析：根据 for one thing… for another…可以判断出，本题所含的两个句子属于并列关系。在前一句中，过去分词短语 left standing after the bust 作为 those banks 的后置定语，在汉译时应当做前置处理，翻译成"那些存活下来的银行"。在后一句中，由于 which 引导的非限定性定语从句对主句不起限制作用，而只起到解释说明的作用，因此在汉译时将它译成与主句并列的分句即可。

练习题及参考译文

（1）

I have to stress the fact once again that the world is flat and that in this flat world the frontiers of knowledge get pushed out farther and farther, faster and faster. Therefore, （1） <u>companies need the brainpower that cannot only reach the new frontiers but push them still farther.</u> That is where the breakthrough drugs and software and hardware products are going to be found. And （2） <u>America either needs to be training that brainpower itself or importing it from somewhere else, or ideally both</u>, if it wants to dominate the twenty-first century the way it dominated the twentieth-- and that simply is not happening.

"There are two things that worry me right now," said Richard A. Rashid, the director of research for Microsoft. "One is the fact that we have really dramatically shut down the pipeline of very smart people coming to the United States. If you believe that we have the greatest research universities and opportunities, it all has to be driven by IQ. （3） <u>In trying to create processes that protect the country from undesirables, the government has done a much better job of keeping out desirables.</u> A really significant fraction of the top people graduated from our universities in science and engineering were not born here, but stayed here and created the businesses, and became the professors, that were engines for our economic growth. We want these people. In a world where IQ

is one of the most important commodities, you want to get as many smart people as you can."
Second, said Rashid, "(4) We have done a very poor job of conveying to kids the value of science and technology as a career choice that will make the world a better place. Engineering and science is what led to so many improvements in our lives. But you talk to kids about changing the world and they don't look at computer science as a career that is going to be a great thing. The amazing thing is that it is hard to get women into computer science now, and getting worse. Young women in junior high are told this is a really wretched lifestyle. (5) As a result, we are not getting enough students through our systems who want to be computer scientists and engineers, and if we cut off the flow from abroad, the confluence of those two will potentially put us in a very difficult position ten or fifteen years from now. It is a pipeline process. It won't come to roost right away, but fifteen or twenty years from now, you'll find you don't have the people and the energy in these areas where you need them."

参考译文:

(1) 企业需要的人才,不只要能触到新的前沿,还要再把这个前沿往前推。

(2) 美国如果还想像曾经主宰 20 世纪那样主宰 21 世纪,就必须自己培养人才,或者从外国引进,理想是双管齐下。但目前美国却没有那样做。

(3) 美国政府的一些政策本来是想保护国家免受不良分子渗透的,但最后搞出来的却反而阻挡了我们最需要的优良分子。

(4) 我们没把科学和技术的价值灌输给孩子,让孩子知道科技是一种可以把世界变美好的职业选择。

(5) 结果,我们的教育就没有产出足够的计算机科学家与工程师。如果我们再切断海外的人才来源,未来十到十五年我们可能就惨了。

(2)

In their new book, *God Is Back*, John Micklethwait, editor in chief of *The Economist*, and Adrian Wooldridge, that magazine's Washington bureau chief, argue that religion is "returning to public life" around the world, that "the great forces of modernity—technology and democracy, choice and freedom—are all strengthening religion rather than undermining it", that these days "religion is playing a much more important role in public and intellectual life". (1) They assert that "religion is becoming a matter of choice", something that individuals themselves decide to believe in instead of something imposed upon them, and that "the surge of religion is being driven by the same two things that have driven the success of market capitalism: competition and choice."

(2) One problem with this book is that the authors selected information and examples that supported their thesis, while ignoring or diminishing data that contradicted it. In arguing that "religion's power" has "continued to increase", they contradict considerable evidence to the contrary. ((3) According to a survey released this month, "the U. S. population continues to show signs of becoming less religious, with one out of every five Americans failing to indicate a religious identity in 2008.") In arguing that religion is increasingly a matter of choice, they ignore

the plight of people (like women under Taliban rule) who are forced to live by strict religious codes they themselves may not believe in.

(4) <u>What this book does best is give the reader some glimpses of the new forms that religion is taking around the world, while explicating some of the reasons that religion might appeal to people in modern times</u>: as a source of community in an increasingly atomized world; as a source of certainty in an era of rapid technological and social change; as a source of identity for immigrants far away from home; and as a source of social assistance (like food for the poor, educational programs and medical assistance) in economically challenging times.

(5) <u>Some of the churches described in this book sound more like huge suburban malls or recreation centers than places of worship, offering self-help advice, social services and entertainment in place of spiritual sustenance.</u> The Second Baptist Church in Houston, the authors report, boasts a school for over 12,000 students, a day-care center, basketball and racquetball courts, an air-conditioned walking track, a bowling alley, a bookshop, a cafeteria and a football field complete with floodlights.

And the last section heading in the last chapter of this unpersuasive book reads, "God Is Back, for Better," which, in retrospect, seems like an apt summary of this volume's poorly argued thesis, as well as its nonagnostic point of view.

参考译文:

(1) 他们声称"宗教正在变成一个选择问题",一个由个体决定是否相信的而非强加于他们身上的问题,"宗教的浪潮正在被曾经成功驱使市场资本主义的那两种东西所驱使:竞争和选择。"

(2) 本书的问题之一是作者挑选的信息和例证都是支持他们的论题的,而忽略或者减少了否定其论题的数据。

(3) 本月出炉的一份调查发现,"美国人口继续呈现出宗教信仰者数量开始下降的趋势,2008 年每五个人当中就有一个人不能表明其宗教身份。"

(4) 这本书最大的优点在于,它略告诉了读者一些宗教正在全世界起作用的新形式,解释了宗教在现代可能对人们产生吸引力的一些原因。

(5) 本书中描写的一些教堂更像是大型郊区购物中心或是娱乐中心,而不是进行礼拜、给予自我救赎的建议、提供社会服务和代替精神食粮的娱乐活动的场所。

(3)

Chances are you believe in free will—I do too. To me it seems that one moment I want cereal and soon I have it. Next I want to ride my bicycle and soon I am. Later I have an itchy nose, and, in no time at all, it is scratched.

But, say some scientists and philosophers, this sense of agency is an illusion: you were hungry and that's why you "wanted" cereal; you were bored and fed up of being inside so you "decided" to get some exercise; and as for itchy noses, well there is a biological cause for that as well. (1) <u>From a determinist viewpoint each of these actions, and their causes, as well as their causes and their causes can be traced right back to my birth, then back through my parents' lives,</u>

then right back, like clockwork, to the beginning of the universe.

（2）The strong determinist view—that we're locked in an unchanging web of cause and effect going right back to the big bang—is repulsive to many. And quite naturally so, as free will forms the backbone of so many of society's structures. （3）The criminal justice system is built on the idea that people can choose whether to obey the law or not, therefore people who don't obey should be punished.

Similarly many religious and/or philosophical systems of thought have the notion of free will at their heart. Existentialist philosopher Jean-Paul Sartre emphasized the connection between freedom and responsibility. He thought we must take responsibility for our choices, and that taking responsibility was at the heart of a life well lived.

（4）This debate about free will is so interesting—and knotted—that philosophers can't keep away from it; but psychologists, on the other hand, perhaps sensing no end to the argument, can't help their minds wandering away to more practical points. They have focused more on how beliefs in free will might affect our behavior and whether, more generally, there might be some reason why we seem predisposed to think we have it.

In new research published in the Personality and Social Psychology Bulletin, Baumeister, Masicampo and DeWall (2009) theorize that （5）a belief in free will may be partly what oils the wheels of society, what encourages us to treat each other respectfully. They explore this theory with three studies, two on helping behaviors and one on aggression.

参考译文：

（1）从一个决定论者的观点看,每一个行为以及它们的原因,以及它们原因的原因,还有原因的原因的原因,都可以直接追溯到我出生的时候去,然后追溯到我父母的生活,然后一直推算回去,就像一个钟一样,到宇宙的开端。

（2）强大的决定论观点认为,我们是被锁在一个从大爆炸开始就不变的因果体系网络中的。这种观点让很多人难以接受。

（3）刑事司法体系就是建立在这样一种观点上,人们可以选择是否遵守法律,所以不遵守法律的人会受到惩罚。

（4）对自由意志的争论是那么有趣,也是那么棘手,哲学家无法摆脱它;然而心理学家,或许看到这场争论没有结局,不由自主地联想到其他更实际的观点。

（5）自由意志的信念或许部分推动了社会前进的车轮,鼓励我们尊重地对待彼此。

（4）

（1）In recent months many economists and policymakers have put "global imbalances"—the huge current-account surpluses run by countries like China, alongside America's huge deficit—at the root of the financial crisis. But the IMF disagrees. It argues that the main reason was deficient regulation of the financial system, together with a failure of market discipline, and that global imbalances contributed only "indirectly" to the crisis. This may sound like buck-passing by the world's main international macroeconomic organization. （2）But the distinction has important consequences for whether macroeconomic policy or more regulation of financial markets will provide the solutions to the mess.

In broad strokes, the global imbalances view of the crisis argues that a glut of money from countries with high savings rates, such as China and the oil-producing states, came flooding into America. (3) This kept interest rates low and fuelled the credit boom and the related boom in the prices of assets, such as houses and equity, whose collapse precipitated the financial crisis. A workable long-term fix for the problems of the world economy would, therefore, involve figuring out what to do about these imbalances.

But the IMF argues that (4) imbalances could not have caused the crisis without the creative ability of financial institutions to develop new structures and instruments to cater to investors' demand for higher yields. These instruments turned out to be more risky than they appeared. Investors, overly optimistic about continued rises in asset prices, did not look closely into the nature of the assets that they bought, preferring to rely on the analysis of credit-rating agencies which were, in some cases, also selling advice on how to game the ratings system. This "failure of market discipline", the fund argues, played a big role in the crisis.

As big a problem, according to the IMF, was that financial regulation was flawed, ineffective and too limited in scope. What it calls the "shadow banking system"—the loosely regulated but highly interconnected network of investment banks, hedge funds, mortgage originators, and the like—was not subject to the sorts of prudential regulation (capital-adequacy norms, for example) that applied to banks.

In part, the fund argues, this was because they were not thought to be systemically important, in the sense that banks were understood to be. But their being unregulated made it more attractive for banks (whose affiliates the non-banks often were) to evade capital requirements by pushing risk into these entities. In time, (5) this network of institutions grew so large that they were indeed systemically important: in the now-familiar phrase, they were "too big" or "too interconnected" to fail.

参考译文：

（1）最近几个月，许多经济学家和决策者将金融危机的根源归咎于"全球失衡"，即一边是像中国这种国家产生的巨大的经常性账户盈余，另一边则是像美国那样产生巨大的贸易赤字。

（2）这种区分对于到底采取宏观经济政策还是金融市场规管来解决眼下这场混乱却至关重要。

（3）这使得利率维持在了较低的水平，并燃起信贷及其相关的资产价格——例如房屋和产权——的繁荣，它们的崩溃加速了金融危机的发生。因此，对于修补世界经济问题的一个长期可行的方法需要考虑的问题是如何处理这种失衡。

（4）如果金融机构没有为了迎合投资者对更高利润的追求，而在开发新型金融工具和手段方面表现出了创造性的才能，单凭贸易失衡并无法造成金融危机的产生。

（5）这些机构形成的网络发育得如此庞大，以至于真的成为整个系统的重心所在：用现在流行的话说，它们已经"大得不能倒"或者"复杂的不能倒"。

Said Intel chairman Craig Barrett, "(1) U. S. technological leadership, innovation, and jobs of tomorrow require a commitment to basic research funding today." According to a 2004 study by the Task Force on the Future of American Innovation, (2) basic research performed at leading U. S. universities—research in chemistry, physics, nanotechnology, and semiconductor manufacturing has created four thousand spin-off companies that hired 1.1 million employees and have annual world sales of ＄232 billion. But to keep moving ahead, the study said, there must be a 10 to 12 percent increase each year for the next five to seven years in the budgets of those key research-funding agencies.

Unfortunately, federal funding for research in physical and mathematical sciences and engineering, as a share of GDP, actually declined by 37 percent between 1970 and 2004, the task force found. (3) At a time when we need to be doubling our investments in basic research to overcome the ambition and education gaps, we are actually cutting that funding.

In the wake of the Bush administration and the Republican Congress's decision to cut the National Science Foundation funding for 2005, Republican congressman Vern Ehlers of Missouri, a voice in the wilderness, made the following statement: "(4) While I understand the need to make hard choices in the face of fiscal constraint, I do not see the wisdom in putting science funding behind other priorities. We have cut NSF despite the fact that this omnibus bill increases spending for the 2005 fiscal year, so clearly we could find room to grow basic research while maintaining fiscal constraint. But not only are we not keeping pace with inflationary growth, we are actually cutting the portion basic research receives in the overall budget. (5) This decision shows dangerous disregard for our nation's future, and I am both concerned and astonished that we would make this decision at a time when other nations continue to surpass our students in math and science and consistently increase their funding of basic research. We cannot hope to fight jobs lost to international competition without a well-trained and educated workforce."

No, we cannot, and the effects are starting to show. According to the National Science Board, the percentage of scientific papers written by Americans has fallen 10 percent since 1992. The percentage of American papers published in the top physics journal, *Physical Review*, has fallen from 61 percent to 29 percent since 1983. And now we are starting to see a surge in patents awarded to Asian countries. From 1980 to 2003, Japan's share of world industrial patents rose from 12 percent to 21 percent, and Taiwan's from 0 percent to 3 percent. By contrast, the U. S. share of patents has fallen from 60 percent to 52 percent since 1980.

参考译文：

（1）美国若想在科技上继续领先，继续创新，创造就业机会，现在就应该对基础研究做出投资承诺。

（2）美国一流大学在化学、物理、纳米技术、半导体生产等领域的基础研究，已经创造出4,000家公司，110万个工作机会，2,320亿美元的全球年营业额。

（3）就在基础研究应该加倍投资以缩小与其他国家之间目标差距和教育差距的当口，

美国却反而削减了投资。

（4）我虽然了解财政紧缩之时必须做出痛苦的取舍，我却不认为看轻科研是明智之举。

（5）这项决定表明我们对国家前途的漠视已经到了危险的程度。就在其他国家的学生的数理表现持续超越我国，其他国家的科研预算也持续在增加的时候，我们竟会做出这种决定，我真是既忧心又震惊。

（6）

According to a much-reported survey carried out in 2002, Britain then had 4. 3 m closed-circuit television (CCTV) cameras—one for every 14 people in the country. (1) That figure has since been questioned, but few doubt that Britons are closely scrutinized when they walk the streets. This scrutiny is supposed to deter and detect crime. Even the government's statistics, though, suggest that the cameras have done little to reduce the worst sort of criminal activity, violence.

That may, however, be about to change, and in an unexpected way. (2) It is not that the cameras and their operators will become any more effective. Rather, they have accidentally gathered a huge body of data on how people behave, and particularly on how they behave in situations where violence is in the air. This means that hypotheses about violent behavior which could not be tested experimentally for practical or ethical reasons, can now be examined in a scientific way. And it is that which may help violence to be controlled.

One researcher who is interested in this approach is Mark Levine, a social psychologist at Lancaster University in Britain who studies crowds. (3) Crowds have a bad press. They have been blamed for antisocial behavior through mechanisms that include peer pressure, mass hysteria and the diffusion of responsibility—the idea that "someone else will do something, so I don't have to". But Dr Levine thinks that crowds can also diffuse potentially violent situations and that crime would be much higher if it were not for crowds. As he told a symposium called "Understanding Violence", which was organized by the Ecole Polytechnique Fédérale de Lausanne in Switzerland earlier this month, (4) he has been using CCTV data to examine the bystander effect, an alleged phenomenon whereby people who would help a stranger in distress if they were alone, fail to do so in the presence of others. His conclusion is that it isn't so. In fact, he thinks, having a crowd around often makes things better.

According to the observation of Dr Levine, bystanders frequently intervene in incipient fights. (5) The number of escalating gestures did not rise significantly as the size of the group increased, contrary to what the bystander effect would predict. Instead, it was the number of de-escalating gestures that grew. A bigger crowd, in other words, was more likely to suppress a fight.

参考译文：

（1）这个数据一直遭到人们的质疑，但在街上来来往往的英国公民被闭路电视严密监视的事实却鲜有疑问。设计这种监控的初衷是为了能及时发现和制止犯罪行为。

（2）倒不是摄像机和这些机器的操作员变得更有效率了。而是人们无意中通过闭路电视收集到的大量的数据反映了人们的行为方式，特别是他们在暴力即将发生时的行为方式。

（3）人们有着不怎么光彩的名声。包括趋同心理压力、群体歇斯底里以及责任分散效应（人们常说的"反正总会有别人去做的，所以我就不用去做了"就是责任分散效应的体现）等在内的一些机制通常会使人们被扣上"反社会行为"的帽子。

（4）他通过闭路电视监控数据对旁观者效应进行检验。所谓旁观者效应是指人们会在没有他人在场的情况下去帮助处于危险境地的陌生人，而在有其他人在场的情况下反而会袖手旁观的现象。

（5）跟所谓的"旁观者效应"刚好相反，"激化行为"并没有随着人数的增多而显著地增加。

（7）

Although she was never an ardent follower of any formal religion, my mother's (Audrey Hepburn) own faith endured throughout her life: her faith in love, her faith in the miracle of nature, and her faith in the goodness of life. She honored this second chance at life at every opportunity that presented itself and most of all at the end of her life, through her work for UNICEF.

（1）Sometimes a near-death experience can free us of the shackles that life slowly trains us to wear. We come to realize what's worth the sweat and what isn't. Although she had no memory of her childhood near-death experience, the knowledge of it, coupled with the fertile ground of an already self-effacing nature, were the roots of the humility that graced her entire life.

I never heard her say, "I did this," or "I've done that." Toward the end of her life, throughout the UNICEF years, I would hear her say regularly, as the world listened to her, "I can do very little." I never heard her say that she liked any of her performances. （2）When people complimented her, she would always shy away and ultimately explain how those who surrounded her were the reason for her success.

Bessie Anderson Stanley wrote, "（3）To laugh often and much, to win the respect of intelligent people and affection of children, to earn the appreciation of honest critics and endure the betrayal of false friends, to appreciate beauty, to find the best in others, to leave the world a bit better whether by a healthy child, a garden patch or a redeemed social condition, to know even one life has breathed easier because you have lived, this is to have succeeded." By Ms. Stanley's standards, my mother's life was a success: She was graced with good choices. The first choice she made was her career. Then she chose her family. And when we, her children, were grown and had started our lives, she chose the less fortunate children of the world. She chose to give back. （4）In that important choice lay the key to healing and understanding something that had affected her throughout her entire life: the sadness that had always been there.

（5）Her choices healed the sadness of a little girl who didn't know her father for most of her life and yet who yearned and longed for that warm embrace, that reassurance that you are loved and that you matter. When I look back, that is just what she gave to Luca and me: the reassurance that we were loved and that we mattered. This was the most valuable essence, the roots that live and grow forever inside you. She truly was a wonderful mother and friend.

参考译文：

（1）尽管生活的磨砺慢慢使我们习惯于戴上枷锁，但有时一次濒死的经历就足以让我们从这些枷锁中解脱出来。我们逐渐认识到什么东西值得孜孜以求，什么不值。

（2）当人们赞美她时，她总是惟恐避之不及；最终，她会解释说，她的成功其实全仗她周围人的努力。

（3）若能笑口常开，若能赢得有才智的人的尊敬和孩子的喜爱，若能赢得诚实的批评家的赞赏并承受虚朋假友的背叛，若能欣赏美，若能发现他人的长处，若能使世界变好一点（不管是使某个孩子健康、修整某一片花园、还是改良社会状况），甚至若能得知因为你的存在而使某一个人呼吸得更舒畅，这都是成功。

（4）她的整个生活曾深受创伤——积久的创伤——的影响，而她这个重要的选择正是理解和愈合这创伤的灵丹妙药。

（5）她的选择抚平了一个小女孩心灵的伤痕。这个小女孩在大半生中不知道自己的父亲是谁，尽管她渴望温暖的拥抱，渴望确切地知道自己被爱，确切地知道自己的价值。

（8）

After their demise, artists are at the mercy of history. (1) The ones who survive are the ones who are adaptable, who can ride the shifting tides of ideology, ideals, theory, fashion and catastrophe that constitute the spirit of the time. The survivors, however, don't always ride those tides unscathed. Two cases in point are JS Bach and Mozart. (2) Bach was created by his time, but outlived it; Mozart was in tune with his time, but his legacy took surprising turns in the next generations.

What, above all, helped Bach be Bach was a family tradition of composers going back generations, as well as the Lutheran church, in which music was woven into services. (3) Bach came of age as a composer at the height of the baroque period, a time of grandiose, richly ornamented architecture and music. By the latter part of his career, however, baroque was giving way to the lightness and preciousness of the early classical style, soon to become the high-classical style of Mozart and Haydn. To add to the posthumous insult, the leading voices of the new generation were JS Bach's own sons WF, JC (a mentor to Mozart) and CPE. These sons honored their father and helped keep his name alive, but among themselves they called dad "the Old Wig".

It was the dawning classical spirit that gave rise to one of history's famous lousy reviews, in 1737, by one-time Bach pupil JA Scheibe: "(4) [Bach] would be the admiration of whole nations if he had more amiability, if he did not take away the natural element in his pieces by giving them a confused style, and if he did not darken their beauty by an excess of art." What the new spirit at that time defined as "natural" was gallant, easy on the ears, popular, quasi-artless - amiable, even. (5) Contrary to later myth, Bach was never forgotten before his revival in the 19th century, but he was more admired than performed. The peculiar thing is that this charge of "an excess of art", which was used to cudgel Bach in his last years, was one that dogged Mozart throughout his maturity. The famous complaint of Emperor Joseph II about *The Marriage of Figaro*—"too many notes, Mozart"—is generally perceived to be a gaffe by a blockhead. In fact, Joseph was echoing what nearly everybody, including his admirers, said about Mozart: he was so imaginative that he couldn't turn it off, and that made his music at times intense, even demonic. Hence Mozart's bad, or cautionary, reviews: "too strongly spiced"; "impenetrable labyrinths"; "bizarre flights of the soul"; "overloaded and overstuffed".

参考译文：

（1）能够幸免于此的也只能是那些具有适应性很强、能顺应时代观念、理想、学说、时尚甚至灾祸这些时代精神转变的人们。

（2）时代造就了巴赫，但他的声望却超越了他所在的时代。莫扎特与他所在的时代潮流相契合，而对他遗产的评说却在一代代人中发生了令人惊讶的变化。

（3）在崇尚宏大、丰美、装饰繁复的艺术和音乐的巴洛克风格的鼎盛时期，巴赫作为一名音乐家脱颖而出。

（4）如果巴赫作品里多一点温和友善，如果他不是用那些晦涩的东西代替自然简朴的音乐元素，如果他不是用过分的专业技艺降低其音乐的优美性，那么，他还有可能获得整个民族的敬仰。

（5）与后世的传说相反的是，在19世纪巴赫复兴之前的时光里，他从来没有被遗忘过。然而，景仰的人多，演奏的人少。

（9）

（1）Any attempt to put an economic value on fresh air, clean water or tropical rainforests can offend the delicate sensibilities of those who argue that the conservation of nature is a moral duty. Yet although the best things in life appear to be free, that does not mean they are without financial value. It simply means that nobody asks you to pay when, for example, you watch a beautiful sunset over the hills.

Putting a financial value on the environment, however, may be the most important thing that people can do to help nature conservation. When governments allocate money, they do so according to where it will bring benefit. （2）If a government is unaware of the value of a landscape to its tourism, or of a swamp to its fishing industry—and thus its foreign-exchange income—then it will invest too little in managing these resources. Worse, if the true value of a forest or swamp is hidden, governments may destroy it by subsidizing the conversion of the land to agriculture. （3）The costs are unknown for now, but may appear eventually as the price of building a filtration plant to remove the sediment from the water that the forest once took care of, or the price of importing food when fish vanish.

（4）Some estimates of the annual contribution of coastal and marine ecosystems to the global economy exceed $20 trillion, over a third of the total gross national product (GNP) of all the countries of the world. Even so, says Katherine Sierra of the World Bank, such ecosystems are typically much undervalued when governments made decisions about development.

Glenn-Marie Lange, also of the World Bank, attended a meeting in Washington DC organized by her employer to launch its report "Environment Matters" on April 6th. She told participants that one of the reasons why ecosystems become degraded is that their value to local people is often small. As a result, these people do not have much reason to manage their resources carefully. She estimates, for example, that only 36% of the income generated by the coastal and marine environments in Zanzibar goes to locals. Most of this comes from fishing; only a tiny fraction of the money from tourism ends up local hands.

More broadly, Dr Lange wants the value of the environment to be integrated into national and local accounting. She argues that governments should identify the contributions that marine ecosystems make to their countries' GNPs and foreign-exchange earnings. She also wants them to examine whether or not they are running down their countries' "natural capital".

(5) For too long, an absence of proper green accounting has allowed people to privatize the gains from the environment but socialize the costs, to paraphrase Carl Safina, an American scientist and environmentalist at the meeting. As Dr Safina puts it, "conservation is not a trade-off between the economy and the environment. It is a trade-off between the short and long term."

参考译文：

（1）任何企图给新鲜空气、清洁水源或者热带雨林赋予经济价值的尝试都会冒犯某些脆弱敏感的人，因为他们认为保护自然是人类的一种道德责任。

（2）如果政府并没意识到一片风景对于旅游业的价值，或一块湿地对于渔业的价值，以及因此而产生的外汇收入，可能就会在管理这些资源方面投资过少。

（3）其代价暂未可知，但随着森林砍伐殆尽，高价建造过滤装置以消除水源中的沉积物，或者随着鱼类消失，进口食物价格上涨，其代价就会逐渐显露出来。

（4）有人估计沿海及海洋生态系统对全球经济的年贡献为 20 万亿美元。超过全球所有国家国民生产总值（GNP）的 1/3。

（5）长期以来，绿色核算账户的缺失使得人们将从环境中获得的收益个人化，其成本社会化。

（10）

（1）It is a book that will take you into the inner backroom of Wall Street, a book that I hope will open a door to a new world in the same way a new world opened up to me when I took my first job as a Wall Street analyst in 1989 and soon received the first of many cryptic calls：

"Come immediately to a meeting, Dan. Don't let anyone, not even your staff or your family, know where you're going."

At such meeting, it would become clear that a company was about to undertake a major move such as a merger, an acquisition, or a big financing with the help of my investment bank, and that the company wanted my advice. On Wall Street, this experience was called going "over the Wall", referring to the "Chinese Wall". （2）It was supposed to keep confidential, inside information obtained by an investment banker from falling into the hands of someone who could use it for unfair gain. I went over the Wall many times in my career. And this book will bring you over the Wall, too—the wall that conceals and protects how Wall Street really works.

As I write, the telecom and financial worlds are showing signs of life. A few stocks, such as Google, the Internet search engine, are defying gravity once again. (3) Investment banks have restructured in an attempt to keep analysts from the types of temptations and conflicts of interest that brought their firms numerous lawsuits and billions in fines. Boards of directors have been reshuffled. Ethics policies have been implemented and laws changed. Some of the most lurid corporate scandals of the early twenty-first century, from Tyco and Adelphia to WorldCom and Enron, have finally reached all the way to the tops of those organizations, thanks in part to the zealous efforts of government prosecutors. And mega-billion-dollar mergers in the telecom industry once again headline the news.

It seems like a whole new world. And indeed, it is certainly true that the Street has changed in some ways, ways that make it a little less vulnerable to overt fraud. (4) It is also true that some executives of some corrupt companies are finally being brought to account and that investment banks and the analysts who work for them are under much more scrutiny than ever before.

But let's not be fooled. There remain many conflicts, leaks, and abuses of the law—and of investors' trust—that have never been exposed. (5) No one has fully explained why the remedies offered and prosecutions undertaken thus far will not solve the problems inherent on Wall Street. No one has fully explained how investors play on an unbalanced and unfair playing field, a field that individuals and even many professional investors have no business playing on at all. And no one has explained how crime paid—and paid big—for the majority of people who broke the rules.

参考译文：

（1）这本书将引导你进入华尔街的内部"密室"，我希望它将为你打开通向一个全新世界的大门，就像我在1989年接受第一份华尔街证券分析师的工作，这个全新的世界向我敞开了一样。

（2）设墙的目的是防止被投资银行家掌握的内部消息落到了那些可以利用其进行不公平交易的人手里。

（3）投资银行已经重组，试图让证券分析师们远离各种各样的诱惑与利益冲突，这些东西曾经使得银行被大量的官司缠身，在罚金上损失了几十亿。

（4）确定的变化还有，一些腐败公司的执行官们最终被质询，为这些公司工作的投资银行和分析师们被置于比以前严格得多的监督之下。

（5）没有人透彻地解释为什么实行的纠正措施和执行的起诉程序远不能解决华尔街内部的痼疾。

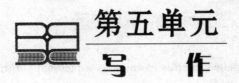

第五单元
写 作

　　写作题归为主观题,分 A、B 两节,即英语应用文和英语短文。主要考查考生运用英语语言撰写不同类型的应用文和短文的能力。

　　应用文包括私人和公务信函,如:书信、邀请函、介绍信、推荐信、祝贺信、请求信、确认信、求职信、劝告信、调查信、拒绝信等以及证明、报告、注意事项、通告、请帖、告示、便务、启示、公约、守则、备忘录和摘要等。除了少数应用文外,字数要求 100 词左右。要求考生把握其写作特点、方法和格式。

I. 应用文写作

Ⅰ) 书信类应用文

1. 私人信

　　要点提示:书信类应用文撰写的格式基本上是相同的,但它有不同的语体,如:正式与非正式语体,书面语体与口语化语体等。

　　格式大致相同:

　　1) 信头(Heading)

　　2) 信内地址及日期(Address and Date inside it)

　　3) 内容提纲(Headline)

　　4) 称呼(Salutation)

　　5) 正文(Body)

　　6) 客套结尾(Complimentary close)

　　7) 签名(Signature)

　　(注意:不要求考生写信头、信内地址及写信日期,只从称呼开始,然后是正文,客套结尾,签名。)

Model 1:(私信)

A student received a teacher's letter and knew that the teacher would come to be a teacher.

Write a letter to his/her teacher.

1) glad to receive his teacher's letter

2) wish to see his teacher

3) introduce his life and study to his teacher

4) Inquire something from his teacher.

Don't write your own name at the end of the letter. Use "Wang Ming" instead.

Don't write the address.   (10 points)

Dear Miss Martha,

Your letter of May 5 reached me this morning as a pleasant surprise. I had been missing you all the time, dear teacher. Glad to know that you are planning to come to Nanjing for a private visit this summer. I eagerly look forward to seeing you as soon as possible.

I've been in Nanjing for almost a year. I am now quite used to life here. This term I take four courses: English, history, international law and commercial course. They are all very interesting and have benefited me greatly. I like them awfully.

Are you still teaching our class? What English textbooks are you suing this year? I will never forget your English classes, which were so lively and interesting, and helped me immensely.

Love to your family!

Yours gratefully,
Wang Ming

Model 2:（私信）

You are preparing for English graduate entrance examination and are in need of some reference books. Write a letter to the sales department of a bookstore to ask for:

1) detailed information about the books you wanted

2) methods of payment

3) time and way of delivery

Write a letter to ask for EGEE books.

Dear Sir/Madam,

As a student preparing for EGEE in the coming January, I am writing to ask if you have approaches to EGEE compiled by Professor Yang Zhi and published by Southeast University Press in 2008.

If you have the book for sale, I'd like to mail to order it. Please let me know if I can pay for it by money order or do you accept Credit Card?

I'd appreciate it if you might send me the book at your earliest convenience by EMS to the following address:

Foreign Languages Department of CUP, Nanjing

Sincerely Yours,
Mao Ying

2. 邀请信

要点提示：邀请信有两种：一种是正式的,称之为请柬;另一种为非正式的,就是一般社交场合所用的邀请函。这里介绍非正式的一般社交场合邀请函,它要求写作语言十分简短,写得有头有尾,令人一读皆知。同时要求写得明确具体,不可含糊其辞。邀请别人去做什么,在何场合,具体的时间等都应清清楚楚。

Model:

An Invitation Letter to Dinner(邀请赴宴)

Dear Ruth,

Li and I are having some very special friends here for dinner on Sunday, October second. Naturally the party wouldn't be complete without you.

I hope you can come, as we are planning to show the movies we made in Hong Kong, and I know you are thinking of going there this summer.

Dinner is at seven, as usual. I'll be looking forward for you the charming person at that time, so don't disappoint us!

Affectionately Yours,

Xiao Hui

3. 私人介绍信

要点提示:用语较随便,介绍某人去结识某人。被介绍人的性格、为人和学业等情况都应作一个具体简要的介绍,以便让收信人对被介绍者首先有一个感官认识和大概印象。

Model:

A Private Letter of Introduction(私人介绍信)

Dear Prof. John:

This is to introduce Bill to you, whose parents are both my good friends. He is now going to Zhuhai and will spend his summer holiday there, doing some research work on the marine environment at Zhuhai University. He hopes to obtain your advice and guidance in theoretical studies and laboratory tests. Bill has amiable manners and good study style, always respectful and modest. I'm sure that you would be pleased to meet and help him.

It is possible and convenient for you if he comes to see you once a week? Many thanks for the trouble you will have to take for Bill.

Yours sincerely,

Li Feiyang

4. 业务介绍信

要点提示:信中对被介绍者的性格、为人和工作等情况可不必提及,着重介绍被介绍者熟悉中国市场,讨论营销计划等情况,恳求对方热情照顾和帮助。

Model:

A Business Letter of Introduction(业务介绍信)

Dear Mr. Miller:

We have recently appointed a new Overseas Sales Manager Mr. Zhang, who will be visiting Russia, and especially Moscow at the end of next month. We are writing this letter to introduce him to you and we should be much obliged if you would extend to him the courtesy and help which you invariably gave to his predecessor, Mr. J. Shefu.

Mr. Zhang is thoroughly conversant with the Chinese market and would like to discuss various schemes which might be to our mutual benefit.

Yours sincerely,

Fang Li

5. 求职推荐信

要点提示：信的内容可以包括你的工作能力、学历、工作表现、品格特性、健康状况等。信的目的是让对方了解你、看好你、聘用你。文字简洁朴实，内容明确，表达流畅。

Model：

Recommendation Letter for Applying for a Position（求职推荐信）

Dear Mr. Wang：

Comrade Li has been known to me personally for a long time, and I have had an opportunity to observe closely his personality and his work.

He is a well-trained college student who has used his brains in whatever he undertakes. His studies show special excellence. His family connections have given him an opportunity to associate with men and women of ideas. He is democratic, likeable and accustomed to meeting persons who are influential in business and political circles.

At college, he showed himself a natural disciplinarian whose generous, wholesome personality made him the confidence and adviser of the students.

His character is beyond question, his judgment is good, and he has the qualities necessary to make him a successful employee in the future work.

Very truly yours,

Zheng Chunling

6. 庆贺信

要点提示：庆贺信是一种社交书信，是对别人好事、喜事等表示恭贺道喜。此信要尽情发挥，表达自己的喜悦之情。文字的长短不限，格式不拘，但要写得真诚自然，亲切有加。

Model：

Congratulating One's Birthday（庆贺信）

Dear Mr. Zhang：

So you're a year older today—or don't you want to be reminded? Anyway, congratulations and best wishes and all that sort of thing.

If you feel in the mood for celebrating, will you let me take you to dinner and the movies, as a sort of birthday treat? You name the day, and meanwhile, a lot of happy returns!

Cordially,

Liu Bicheng

7. 求职信

要点提示：求职信是展示自己的观点、抱负、精力、热情、特长等知识的机会。其内容包括年龄、性别、自己的工作能力、受过的教育和训练以及资历、成就、希望和抱负等内容。写作时要力求简明有趣、不落俗套，防止写得古怪异常、哗众取宠。同时也要注意：要客观陈述事实经历，避免表达主观见解；切忌批评抱怨前任雇主；不要过分地渲染自己；行文语气得当等。

Model：

Applying for Market Investigation（求职信）

Dear Sir，

For a few years I have been a staff in another company, and now wish to make a change. My only reason is to richen my market experience and at the same time improve my prospects. It occurred to me that a large and well-known company such as yours might be able to use my services.

I am thirty-one years of age and in good health. I thoroughly enjoy working on investigations, particularly when the statistical work is involved. At Southeast University I specialized in merchandising and advertising and was awarded a Ph. D. for my thesis on the Abuses of Statistical Investigation.

Although I had no more experience in consumer research, I am familiar with some methods employed and fully understand their importance in the recording of buying habits and trends, I should like to feel that there is an opportunity to use my services in this type of research and that you will invite me to call on you. I could then give you further information and bring testimonials.

Yours faithfully，

He Changping

Ⅱ）告示类及其他类型应用文

1. 证明

1）求职证明信

要点提示：写作简明扼要，用词正规。着眼点主要放在雇员任职期间内的工作能力、工作职责和工作表现。开头可用 To Whom It May Concern，也可用 Dear Sir，末尾的签名要写上公司全称以及证明人的职位和头衔。

Model：

Certificate of Application（求职证明信）

To Whom It May Concern，

This is to certify that Comrade Zhou was employed by this company as production assistant from 1st July, 2005 to 20th November, 2008 when he resigned of his own accord.

Comrade Zhou is regarded as one of our best production assistants. Apart from his experience in production, he also has profound knowledge on book-design, proof-reading and other techniques or skills. He has always been honest, industrious and conscientious, and can be really believed with no supervision.

We are very sorry to lose him, and we have no hesitation in recommending him to any publisher or printer.

Jia Daolin

2）健康证明

要点提示：内容简洁,文字精练,抓住要点,避免无关紧要的语言,说明问题即可。

Model：

Health Verification(健康证明)

To Whom It May Concern,

    This is to certify that Mr. Hu Xiaoming is physically and mentally healthy. This statement is based on his health history and physical checkup. My observation of his health condition is that he is capable of doing extensively hard work, both manually and intellectually.

Sincerely yours,

Surgical Dept.

Zhongxin Hospital

2. 报告

要点提示：报告一般以客观事实为基础,得出结论或提出建议。语言要准确实用,文体简洁并做到：内容完整充实,无片面性和私人感情,句子语言结构简易,防止华而不实。报告种类繁多,这里仅列出一例供考生借鉴。

Model：

Investigation Report(调查报告)

Oct. 20

To：Mr. Zheng, President of Northeast University

Subject：Buying English Books

Dear President,

    Under the request of foreign languages school, we have investigated and discussed the necessity of buying English books. We found that teachers and students are quite interested in all kinds of English books, especially in English reference books and we think that it is a good way to help teachers with doing scientific research and to train students' knowing the original books. So we suggest that 10,000 English books should be bought and allotted to the library of Foreign Languages School.

Lin Xiang

Dean of Studies

3. 介绍商品

要点提示：通过正常的渠道向外推销、介绍产品的质量和性能以及良好的售后服务。语言简练朴实,实事求是。

Model:

Introducing Commodities(介绍商品)

Dear Sir,

We learn through our institution stationed abroad, that you are interested in TV sets of Chinese manufacture and enclose here our illustrated catalogue and pricelist.

All our TV sets can be used in home and the public places, and can be supplied with best packing boxes and maintaining accessories. They are the product of the finest materials and workmanship and we can offer a worldwide after-sales service.

We hope that you will send us a trial order so that you can test our claim against the facts.

Yours faithfully

4. 通告

要点提示:通常采用书信、明信片的方式通告,打上客户的地址和姓名。文字简洁,表意清楚。

Model 1:

Change of Name(更名)　　　　　　　(Letter Form)

May 10, 2008

Dear Sirs,

We inform you that the business hitherto carried on the name of R. N. & Co. will be continued under the style of W. M. & Company, Limited.

Very truly yours

Model 2:

Change of Name(更名)　　　　(Visiting Card Form)

Red Sun Trading Limited

Nanjing, China

Change of Name

Please be advised that the Name of Dadi Co.

Ltd. Will be changed to Red Sun Trading Limited

With immediate effect

Our telephone and telex numbers remain unchanged

5. 请帖

要点提示:1) 正式请帖的用词必须是标准的;

2) 镌版印刷的请帖字体可以自由选择;

3) 正式请帖有两种形式(用镌版全文印刷和在请帖中留空),可根据本人兴趣选用;

4) 在镌版印刷的请帖中不用缩写词、混名、绰号以及不正规的短语;

5) 全部写出人名,地名;

6) 年月日,星期几,几点钟使用英文拼写,不用阿拉伯字母代替;

7) 在宴会、舞会请帖上常使用"request the pleasure of your company",在婚礼请帖上常见"request the honour of your presence";

8）正规的宴会、舞会请帖应提前时间发出，如客人出席，主人方便有时间安排；

9）凡是正规的请帖都一定邀请夫妻双方；

10）发出请帖可请对方回复，也可以不必回复。

Model 1：

Dr. and Mrs. Li Ming

request the pleasure of your company

at dinner

on Saturday, the first of May

at six o'clock

Nanjing Jinling Hotel

Model 2：

Mr. and Mrs. Wang Jun

request the pleasure of your company

at party

on the Twenty Anniversary of their marriage

on Sunday, the second of July

at six o'clock

15 Zhong Yang Avenue

Model 3：

Mr. and Mrs. Zhang Lin

request the pleasure of your company

at luncheon

on Sunday, the fifth of October

at twelve

at the People's Club

Please send reply to

25 Zhong Shan Avenue

Model 4：

Mr. and Mrs. Zhan Lin

accept with pleasure

Dr. and Mrs. Zheng Qin's

invitation to dinner

on Saturday, the sixth of August

at seven o'clock

Hilton Hotel

Nanjing

6. 告示/公告

要点提示：公告/告示指政府机关、团体、单位等部门向公众发出的通告，它的书写格式与一般告示基本相同,根据内容可长可短,文字简练明了。

Model 1:

Proclamation of Election Results(公示选举结果)

It is hereby proclaimed that Comrade Li Xiang has been elected on May 5, 2008 to the director of our office.

Foreign Languages School

May 8, 2008

Model 2:

Notice of Appointment(任命公告)

On the proposal of the government of Jiangsu Province, the First Session of the Seventh National People's Congress of the Jiangsu Province decided on July 15, 2007, to appoint Comrade X X X director of the Provincial government.

The first Session of the Seventh
National People's Congress of
the Jiangsu Province

July 18, 2007

7. 请假条

要点提示:请假条包括病事假及续假条。写清楚原因和时间,请假的理由要写充分,并可付上有关证明、电报等。主要是本人写或代写。

1)本人写:

Model:

Sept. 5, 2008

Dear Mr. Hu:

I am very sorry to apprise you that I can not attend your class this morning owing to a bad cold, I enclose doctor's certificate and ask you for sick leave of two days.

Your student Fang Meimei

Encl: doctor's certificate for sick leave

2)代写

June 20, 2009

Dear Sir,

Please excuse Li Ping's absence from school today. He caught a bad cold yesterday and could not fall asleep until well into the night, so I am writing to ask you for two days' sick leave and will let him resume his study if he feels better the day after tomorrow.

Very truly yours,

Wang Ming

8. 启事

要点提示:用于机关、团体或个人,如有需要向公众说明或请求什么帮助等时,均可用它来把要说的事情简要地写成启事张贴出去。如有需要还可以登报。

最常见的启事是：失物启事和招领启事。其写作特点是把内容作为标题写在上方正中。日期写在右上方，署名放在右下方。如文中已写明启事者，亦可不署名。一般不用称呼，如有确切的对象也可用称呼。

Model 1：

A Mobile Phone（手机）

August 6，2009

In the classroom, in the morning, August 6, a mobile phone lost. Finder please returns it to the owner, Li Chen, Room 5, Dormitory 6.

Model 2：

Found

1）A Wrist Watch, in the office on the afternoon of July, 3

2）A skirt, red in color, on the sports ground, on the morning of July, 10

3）A golden pen, in the reading room, on the evening of July, 18

Please apply at the lost Property Office, Room 202, on the 2nd floor of the office building. Open from 8：00 a. m. and 2：00 to 6：00 p. m.

Lost Property Office

July 20，2009

Model 3：

To Let or for Sale

Cuiping Dongnan Court, 25 Jiang Jun Road Eighth floor, $140m^2$, 4 bedrooms with a dining-room. Sale at ￥400,000. Rent ￥1,400. Tel：85240321, office time.

9. 学生守则

要点提示：书写的格式是条文式的，文字简洁，条文清楚，内容全面，不需要抬头和落款。

Model：

Rules for Students

1）Love the motherland and the people, support the Communist Party of China.

2）Study diligently and be ready to make contribution to socialist modernization drive.

3）Come to school on time and don't be late for class, don't leave before a period ends and don't be absent from class with no permission.

4）Have an ear to listen to the teachers' lectures and be good at thinking independently about what you learn, and try to finish your exercises earnestly.

5）Persist in physical training so as to keep fit and take an active part in recreational activities.

6）Pay attention to hygiene, do not smoke or drink alcohol and do not spit everywhere you like.

7）Take an active part in physical labour, and be thrifty and simple in daily life.

8）Observe any disciplines and public order and laws and decrees of the state.

9）Respect the teachers and elders and maintain close relations with your schoolmates.

10）Be polite to others and do not swear at or start a fight with others.

11）Love the collective and protect state property.

12）Be modest and honest and correct any mistakes you make.

10. 摘要

要点提示：用一种简洁的语言概述一个问题、事件或观点。可分为两种：一种称为信息摘要（information abstract）；另一种称为描述摘要（descriptive abstract）。

前者是将文章的主要内容用最简洁的语言表达出来，一般置于文后，后者一般独立存在，用语言简洁的方式概述文章内容，通常置于文前。它们的主要写作特点就是简明扼要，抓住重点，突出新观点。强调文章的目的和主要结论。

Model 1：（Information Abstract）

Abstract

Body（正文省略）---

Three Chinese astronauts told about their life and work in a sky laboratory and showed how they can observe the heavenly bodies from the sky laboratory and do the scientific experiments on plant-growing and the military telecommunication under weightless conditions.

点评：内容简洁，只概述一个问题：中国三个宇航员的生活和工作情况。

Model 2：（Descriptive Abstract）

Abstract

Idioms early originated from the idioms in Greek, including, in a broad sense, set-phrases, proverbs, common sayings, allusions, slang as well as a two-part allegorical sayings and so on. They were extracted from the long social practice, with uniqueness and fixation in the course of English and Chinese have differences in such aspects as geography, religious belief, way of life and habits and customs, their idioms, as an enriched expression way of languages, bear the abundant cultural features and cultural information from different nationalities, and accumulate profound cultural details, which are difficult for us to understand and translate these idioms. This treatise inquires into the reciprocal information in two cultures and transforms into T. L expression ways of cultural information.

Key words：idiom, foreignization, domestication, transliteration, foot-notes

Body（正文省略）---

11. 备忘录

要点提示：这是一种公文，用来提醒或督促对方以及表示自己的看法。常见以下几个方面的内容：

1）书端（Heading）

2）对方的姓名、头衔、地址（Name, Introductory, Address）

3）称呼用语（Salutation）

4）事由（Docket）

5）正文（Body）

6）结束语（Complimentary Close）

7）签名（Signature）

Model 1:

Memorandum No. 1

June 20, 2009

To Mr. Wang

From Mr. Li Jie

Subject: Computer

Dear Sir,

    I would like to remind you that our office of Foreign Teaching Section is badly in need of a computer. I hope that you will pay attention to this matter and solve it as soon as possible.

    Regards!

Yours,

Li Jie

Model 2:

Memorandum No. 2

Southeast University

118 Road Zhong Shan

Nanjing, Jiangsu

October 18, 2008

To:

The President of Southeast University

Sir,

    I have the honor to inform you that I am going back to our university next month to take on the teaching task. Before returning to our university, I hope that my work will be well arranged so that I will not affect my work in teaching and scientific research.

    I avail myself of this opportunity to extend to you my best regards.

Yours truly,

Da Wei

12. 个人简历

要点提示：简历通常包括以下几个部分：

1）姓名、地址、电话等。

2）受教育情况，从最近写起，往回写（与中文相反），与求职有关的课程可提及。

3）工作经历，写法与上面一样，也是从最近的工作往回写。

4）个人情况，包括年龄、健康状况、婚姻、性别等，个人的特长、爱好也可以写进去。

5）证明人可以选择可靠的人，权威人士更好，写清楚他们的姓名、单位、职务、联系电话等。

Model:

Resume of Liu Chen

858 Tong Jia Lane

Nanjing, Jiangsu

Objective

Graduate of English Specialty

Specialized in English translation

Experience

course of the graduate with Master

July 2008 to present

Degree, and only graduate of the year

Award achieved great successes both in serving students and in examination of all subjects.

July 2007 to June 2008

<u>Monitor of the first class</u>, Supervised 15 schoolmates. Charged with responsibility of keeping normal teaching discipline and being ready to widening reading and collecting data for writing papers.

May 2006 to May 2007

<u>Committee Member in charge of study.</u> Be responsible for supervising study discipline and know the conditions in the study of the whole class and report them to our assistant.

Education

June 2006 to present

Nanjing Normal University

Foreign Languages School

Seeking Master Degree in English major with doing exceedingly well in all examination, expected to be graduated July 2009.

July 2003 to June 2006

Foreign Languages School

Suzhou University

Graduated with honors from English specialty of Foreign Languages School, Suzhou University.

July 1998 to June 2003

Grant Middle School

Changzhou City

Graduated from Grant Middle School of Changzhou City.

Personal

Age: 26

Marital Status: Single

Languages: Fluent English

Strong Points: sports and

Some French

drawing

II. 短文写作

1. 短文写作要点

根据试卷中提供的信息,写出一篇 160—200 词的短文。提示的信息主要有主题句、写作提纲、规定的情景及图表等。近几年来命题形式多采用了图画及图表提示,因此考生要特别注意:

1）从图画和图表中悟出其中的寓意。

2）图画和图表中都反映出比较突出的,与人们生活息息相关的社会现象和普遍的问题。

3）图画和图表式的作文均以议论文为主,伴有描写与议论或夹叙夹议的表现形式。

4）作文的要求是:切题、清楚、连贯、规范,内容是否切题是衡量作文标准的首要问题。

英语短文常见结构和格式如下图所示:

题目:……

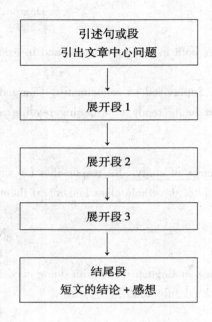

2. 图表作文

要点提示:要求考生将给出的画面或图表中的景物、情节和数据等叙述或描写出来。实际上是针对一幅图或一张图表写一篇说明文。所以在写作时,可以写直观的情景,此时可以补充一些其他内容。其表达方式可以单纯地解释、说明,亦可在说明中伴有叙述、描写和评论,或者把图画中的内容编成故事写出来。

可见,看图作文就是将图表中的数字和图像写成说明文性质的短文。一般写作方式采用三段式:

第一段:写图表中的总情况;

第二段:分析比较图表中的数字,写出增减比率;

第三段:写出自己的感想或评论;

Model 1:

Direction:

Write an essay of 160—200 words based on the following graph. In your essay, you should:

1）describe the graph briefly

2）explain its intended meaning

3）give your views

（图表中是"模拟数字"）

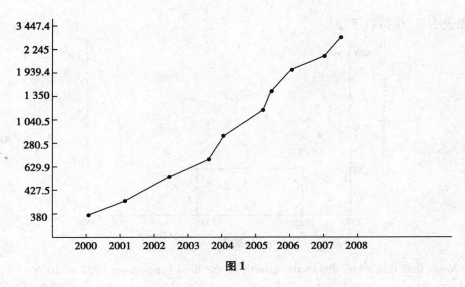

图1

Note: Only imitation count in above list

Average personal incomes of the Chinese peasants from 2000 to 2008.

The personal incomes of the Chinese peasants went up steadily from 2000 to 2008.

We know that at the end of 20 th century, the Chinese peasants' incomes were rather low. It was counted that their average annual incomes were approximately 380 *yuan*. But then a great reform of the agricultural policy of China took place, and the Chinese government has continuously carried on the "Three Agricultures" policy, which has brought peasants a lot of the material benefits so that the preferential policy brought about a great increase in the peasants' incomes. In 2002, the average personal income increased about 30%, reaching 629.9 *yuan*, their personal incomes increased over 2 times in 2005. After that there appeared an even more consistent tendency for their incomes to rise. In 2006, a peasant earned an average of 1,939.4 *yuan*. In 2008, their incomes reached 3,447.4 *yuan* and increased many times. Between 2001 and 2008, the peasants' incomes had been rising at a rate of 30% each year.

It is obvious that the life of the Chinese peasants has been improved with their incomes increase and will become better and better in the coming days.

点评:本文首先用图表展示出文章的内容,接着以年份和收入数字作为叙述的内容,作者采用叙述、对比、分析的写作方法表达出本文的主题。最后提出了自己的看法和观点作为文章的结尾。

Model 2:

Write an essay about the changes of the floor space as shown in the following graph. In your essay, you should:

1) describe the graph briefly

2) explain its intended meaning

3) give your comments

Architectural Graph of Houses in a city.

（图表中是"模拟数字"）

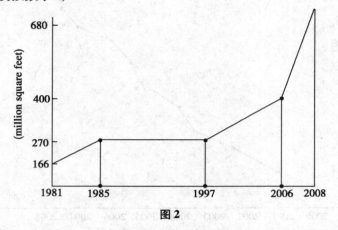

图2

We know that this graph shows the growth of the floor space from 1981 to 2008.

In 1981, there were 166 million square feet of the floor space in this city. With the growth of our national economy, in 1985, the additions to the floor space went up rapidly to 270 million square feet, which was 2.23 times of that in 1981. From 1985 to 1997, no increase is shown in the graph. The floor space reached 400 million square feet in 2006 (an increase of 130 million square feet over the previous years). With the rapid development of our national economy and the increase of the people's incomes, then came a sharp increase of 280 million in the three years spanning from 2006 through 2008.

It is believed that with the steady rise of the gross national product, the amount of the floor space will swiftly go up, too.

点评：本文首先简述了该曲线图的内容，然后按年份和数字进行叙述、分析、说明、比较，其中也有作者的观点和看法。

Model 3：

Write an essay about the following picture, in your essay, you should：

1) describe the graph briefly

2) explain its intended meaning

3) give your comments

图3

It can be seen from the picture that night has fallen over the country. From behind the two big trees rises a bright and full moon like the size of a silver dish, shedding its light in the sky.

The trees, the lake and many stones are all seen but dimly, as if they were seen in one's dreams. It is evident that the colorful flowers can't be nearly seen but we find that they actually exist there. The clear shadows of the trees are like black hulks, which is really a beautiful scenery on the lake. In the middle of the lake floats freely a small boat in which there is a couple of lovers, talking and smiling. The young man is rowing the boat with his might. The ripples in little eddies at the stern make incessant pleasant sound. How about the girl? She seems to be gazing at the night sky, enjoying the beautiful scenery of the night humming the song *Row, Row, Row Your Boat, Gently Down the Stream…*", she looks as if being immersed in happiness.

点评：本文以图作为背景材料展开描写，先写月亮，再写树，然后写湖泊、石头、小舟等。细致地描述了图中景物的状态。其中作者采用了比喻的手法把景物生动地表现出来，使人有身临其境之感。写小舟时，作者发挥了自己的想象力，使文章具有活力和生动性。

3. 描写文

要点提示：此类文体通常用生动、形象的语言对人物、事件、环境等进行描写刻画，使之生动传神，如闻其声，如临其境，可以说是一种形象化的叙述。其特点如下：

1）描写人物时，则描写人物的肖像、语言和举止行为，心理活动和生活细节。其目的就是要塑造出栩栩如生的人物形象，使之感染读者。

2）描写景物时，则写自然风景、社会环境及各种场景。其目的就是要写出环境对人的影响以及人与自然之间的相互关系。

3）描写自然风景时，往往是描写河山风光、草木花鸟、烈日星空、风花雪月、田园风光等。其目的是要写出大自然之美，抒发出作者热爱大自然、赞美大自然的思想情怀。

4）描写社会环境时，就是要写出人物活动的背景。即对活动空间、劳动和工作的场面、战斗场面以及各种会议场面等的描写。通过这样的描写，表现出人的性格和精神面貌。

Model 1：

Write an description about "My Teacher in My Memory". In your essay, you should：

1）describe his/her figure briefly

2）describe his/her advantages

3）give your views

My English teacher Mr. Guo, was a tall man of fifty, with a dark complexion and a thick beard. His face looked very wise and he was often dressed up like a dog's dinner. He was all smiles and looked very warm. But he was always strict to his students.

I showed a great respect for him. When asked about his wage and life, he said, "The main object to my life is not for earning more money, and there is something better than money. The standard of my living is not so high." And said, "If your work is first with you, your fee will be second." In class, he would ask us to do endless questions full of the novel knowledge and lead the conversations around in such a way that at the end of them we classmates would suddenly see for ourselves what is really true and right.

I haven't seen Mr. Guo for over 10 years. Yet the best impression Mr. Guo left on everyone of us shall never perish and be remembered for good and all. I always feel it a pleasure to pay a tribute to a revered teacher like Mr. Guo.

点评：此文用生动、形象的语言，精细入微地描写这位老师的外貌、生活态度和工作目标，并描写了学生对他的尊敬和永远留念之情。

Model 2：

Write a description about "An Autumn". In your essay, you should：

1）describe the autumn scenery briefly

2）describe the peasants' being busy with farm work

3）give your views

The weather in autumn is fairly comfortable, neither too cold nor too hot. It is one of the most comfortable and emotional season in a year. People feel very happy. In the sky of autumn season, the endless lines of wild geese are flying toward the south in the pattern of the Chinese character meaning "person". They are a sign of autumn. People can enjoy the countless red leaves and all kinds of flowers everywhere, which makes people relaxed and joyful.

Autumn is also the season of harvest in a year. You can see many fruit trees along the banks of the stream. They may be pear trees. The fruit on the trees are big and they look like pears or other kinds of apples. Under the trees, some peasants sit on the rock for a good rest. May be they have just finished the day's farm work and are coming home. Some peasants are busy with getting in crops in the field, some of them are carrying crops to their granaries with joy.

I do like autumn season, for it is not only beautiful but also a harvest season in farming.

点评：本文用生动的语言描写秋天美丽的景色和温和怡人的气候给人们带来凉意和舒适的感觉。并描写了农村一派丰收的景象和农民们忙于秋收的情景，以及人们充满着喜悦的心情。

4. 议论文

要点提示：议论文就是讲道理，论是非，表达个人观点。它是由论点、论据和论证构成的。所谓论点就是作者的观点和主张。论据就是作者用来证明论点的理由和事实。论证就是作者运用论据证明自己的观点的逻辑推理过程。其写作特点是：1. 论点必须正确鲜明；2. 论据必须确凿、典型、恰当，有说服力，逻辑推理正确，证明自己的观点正确，一般采用归纳法。

Model 1：

Write an argumentation about "The Way to Success". In your essay, you should：

1）give an attitude to success

2）explain how one can succeed, for example

3）give the author's viewpoint

In our world, most people tried to achieve great success in their careers or in their business. But usually things turn out contrary to their wishes. Someone finally attains his/her aim while other fails, why is the reason? Some people continue their causes to the end through long period of hard struggles, but the others are lack of willpower and determination, and easily give up their goals and ideal so as to stop half-way.

It is believed that strong will, perseverance and diligence are the secret of success in one's career. A man with strong will and perseverance always has an indomitable spirit, always diligently works and studies. He also sticks to his cause no matter how tough it might be. Chairman Mao Tsetong and Premier Zhou Enlai as well as Mr. Lu Xun, Guo Moruo, etc. all are such men with great success.

I believe that where there is a will there is a way, and that a great success is always attributed to those who can suffer long years of patient toil and consistent efforts.

点评：作者首先提出对成功的态度，有的人成功，有的人失败，并揭示了原因所在，接着进一步列举许多伟人成功之道，最后的结论是：有志者事竟成，成功属于那些经过长期艰苦劳动和不懈努力的人们。

Model 2：

Write an argumentation "Try to Be a Good Student". In your essay, you should write out：

1）why to be a good student

2）what is a good student

3）how to be a good student

It has been known that we students will be the builders and reformers of our country in the near future, which is incumbent on us to make full preparations before we students leave schools to undertake such a hard and glorious task. To attain the purpose, we must put the first place of all try to be a good student.

What standards is to be a good student? It has no doubt that being a good student should be noble-minded, learned and healthy. Noble idea means having a good spirit and selfless desire in the public interests, and being ready for helping others and maintaining close relations with all schoolmates together. In anytime we must observe school discipline, public order and laws and decrees of the state, and listen to the teachers' lectures attentively and be good at thinking independently about what we learns and try to complete our homework earnestly. Besides these, we love the collective, protect state property and do not do anything harmful to the collective or others.

In order to be a good student, we should train ourselves to a high standard of morality, cultivate a good behavior or manners, devote ourselves to the shortage of various knowledge, and stick to regularly do physical exercises to be a healthy persons.

点评：作者从学生是国家未来的建设者和改革者这个角度论述做一个好学生的必要性，接着提出好学生的标准和应承担的责任，最后论述了怎样才能成为符合标准的好学生。

5. 记叙文

要点提示：记叙文是以叙事为主要内容，略带一些描写内容。记叙人的时候，则介绍人物的身世、经历和事迹等。叙事时，则描写事情发生、发展的过程以及事情发生的前因后果等，有时叙事也离不开记人。其特点是：

1）叙事文有六大要素：时间、地点、人物、事件、原因和结果；

2）记人或叙事都有一条或几条线索贯穿全文；

3）可以以人物活动的先后顺序为线索来写,亦可以以事物发展的过程为线索来写;

4）选材要典型,要有意义;

5）可以采用顺序和倒叙两种方法去写;

6）文中使用第一人称和第三人称;

7）在叙述过程中,条理清楚、层次分明、交代明白。

Model 1：

Write a narrative about narrating "Our Good Director". In your essay, you should：

1）give what calamity happened

2）narrate the whole course of this thing

3）narrate the author's feeling

In July of 2007, the mountain torrents rushed down with a devastating force, which washed away my home, the house, the furniture and all family belongings. My family became homeless. The bad news came and I was in a pain state.

"Don't be sad. Go back at once and see what to do next." Urged Li Chen, our Director, who is 40 years old.

Standing there I was silent for long, knowing what to do next.

"Don't worry about the traveling expenses. I can give you some money as the expenses." Our director, Li Chen immediately took out one thousand *yuan* note from his pocket.

"Thank you very much!"

"Now you go to the railway station to buy a ticket." And at the same time, I asked for a leave of 10 days and left for my hometown at night.

Ten days later I returned. Li Chen was the first man to meet him. I told him about the flood calamity and the relief provided by the governments at all levels and many kind people.

Li Chen added a few words, "We've collected ten thousand *yuan* and posted five thousand *yuan* to your parents yesterday. We'll give the rest to you as your living expenses."

Then I was simply at a loss what to say, being fill of limitless gratefulness in my heart, and from his shining eyes I saw real sincerity and limitless warmth.

点评:本文记叙了一位主任为作者慷慨解囊的感人事迹,热情地赞扬了主任乐于助人的优良品质。文章记叙了一系列的真实事情,歌颂了这位主任的富有爱心的伟大人格。

Model 2：

Write a narrative about narrating "A Spring Outing". In your essay, you should：

1）narrate spring scenery briefly

2）narrate the process of spring outing

Spring came to human beings with its own vitality. Its coming made the new grass expose its green color, tree leaves became green, the pretty flowers opened their blossoms. All this tempted us to go for an outing.

Today was Saturday, the 25 th of April. We four persons drove our own cars to the beautiful Zhongshan Mountain, carrying bottles of champagne, beer and bags of cakes and fruits. We slowly drove along the narrow roads by the side of the mountain, across rows of small woods and a broad meadows to come to the Central Park. We found that the various trees were green and fresh. The swallows were flying to and fro, up and down in the blue sky. The birds were singing their melodious songs in the trees, and the pretty butterflies with various colors were fluttering here and there. We happily enjoyed the beautiful scenery, breathing the fresh air deeply, laughing and talking heartily.

At 1 p. m. we parked by the roadside and began to climb up to the top of the mountain, at which, under a big tree with luxuriant foliage, we had our picnic while we took a photo of each other. We drank and ate. After the picnic we lay on grass, enjoying the fine landscape, talking about our life and studies.

At about 3 p. m. we drove back with balmy greenness and happy feeling.

点评：这是记事的记叙文,记叙了一次春游。文中既叙述了春天的美景,又记叙了作者春游的活动情况以及对春游过程的感受和愉快心情。

6. 说明文

要点提示：说明文就是用简洁的语言文字来介绍事物,解释事理。事物包括类别、性质、特点、构造、成因、关系、功用以及发展等。解释的内容包括事物运动、变化、产生、消亡过程、原理以及规律等。说明文分三类：

1) 实体事物说明文(说明书,广告,解说词,知识小品等)。

2) 事理说明文(理论性的概念解释,书文简介,教材等)。

3) 文艺性说明文(将说明对象拟人化,亦可采用编故事形式等)。

写作特点如下：

1) 文章条理清楚(顺序：空间、时间、逻辑、认识等)。

2) 写作顺序：从上到下,从外到内,从前到后,从先到后;由此及彼,由浅入深,由局部到整体,由现象到本质,由具体到抽象等。

3) 写作方法：文章采用定义法,设问法,举例法,数字图表法,比较比喻法,引用法,拟人法,描写法,分析法等。

Model 1：

Write an exposition about "Laughter and Your Heath". In your essay, you should：

1) expose the relation between laughter and health by some argumentations;

2) fear, anxiety and anger being among the greatest enemies of man;

That laughter can be a definite benefit to human health is a fact that men have realized from the beginning of human civilization.

In Holy Writ, it is recorded that "a merry heart does good like a medicine". Since that proverb was written, medical men have discoursed on the healing power of laughter. Laughter has always been not only a pleasure, but also an art. Now scientific research has thrown further light on it.

Laboratory tests the result that laughter can improve muscle tone and relax tissues, while frowning puts the body under tension and strain. Laughter has a relaxing and restful effect, even though it does vigorously exercise certain muscles organs. Physicians and surgeons continue to use all the therapeutic measures they have found to be useful; but while doing so they have known use for laughter in correction of emotional disturbances. But fear, anxiety and anger are among the most harmful enemies of men, because they're the rust and carbon that clog(阻塞)and corrode the joints of our physical and mental states. They can best be scoured off with the oil of happiness.

点评：作者论证说明他的看法：笑有利健康是有原因的，同时也说明恐惧、焦虑和气愤是有害健康的。本文采用了比较法，以理由进行了论证说明。

Model 2：

Write an exposition about "My Hobby". In your essay, you should：

1) expose your own hobby

2) expose the advantages of your hobby

I have been collecting the various information at my leisure for 15 years. I am so greatly interested in it that it has become a special hobby with which I can't part.

Information-collecting is a never-ending pleasure and great interest as well as an extra study for me. As I find a lot of information from the various newspapers, magazines and periodicals, I have obtained much knowledge including the daily life, health, food, travel, military science, technology and economy, then I begin to cut information materials out of newspapers, magazines and periodicals and stick them on a book-collecting. When I am free, I often open the book-collecting and carefully read it. Every time I would benefit from reading the book-collecting. So I always follow the hobby with great interest, which occupies a part of my spare time constructively. But I am quite ready for doing it. It makes me contented, with no time for boredom.

I will try to continually collect the various information from all aspects. I want to be an information-collecting king in my country.

点评：这篇说明文是介绍了自己的业余爱好。长时间的收集知识资料养成了一种业余爱好，并说明了这个爱好可以增长知识，给人带来很多好处。作者决心一如既往地做下去，想成为一个国内收集资料之王。

Model 3：

Write an exposition about "My University". In your essay, you should：

1) introduce its location, history and area

2) introduce its specialties, faculty and scale

3) introduce its facilities

Our university is located the southeastern suburb of Nanjing. It is an old and famous university whose origins can be traced back to 1902, when it was established as the only Zhongyang University during the Republic of China in Nanjing. Opportunity for its expansion came only after 1949, especially in the 10 years. Its expansion has reached a high tide. When a move was made to the present campus with the beauty and broadness. The campus covers about 3.8 thousand mu, with a total floor space of 1.3 thousand mu.

There are over 20 departments which offer a total of over 70 majors to more than 35 thousand on-campus students including 500 students from countries other than China. All the departments are authorized to confer B. S./B. E./B. A. and Master's degrees as well as Doctor's degrees besides the individual specialties.

The university has very fine facilities for scientific research, such as the International Online Information Retrieval Center which can connect with Dialog and BRS systems in some countries such as the United States, England, Canada and Australia, and there are many modern laboratories with the first-rate advanced facilities in it.

点评：本篇说明文采用分说法介绍了学校的位置、历史、校园面积、专业、学生情况以及办学实力等方面情况，条理清楚，语言简洁。

III. 写作练习

一、应用文写作

1. Write a letter to your teacher
2. Write an invitation to dinner
3. Write a letter for applying for a clerk
4. Write an introduction for commodities
5. Write "Self-Introduction of an Export Company"
6. Write a notice for correctness
7. Write an "Abstract of Paper"
8. Write a "Resume"

二、短文写作

1. Write an essay about the location of other countries around the country of map.

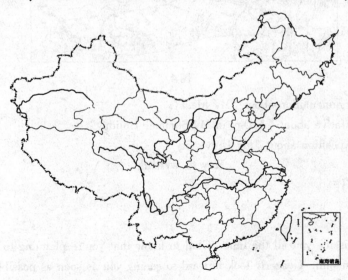

2. Write an essay according to the following statistical table abut the total amount of China's import and export.

The total amount of China's import and export

Year	Accounting by RMB (1 billion)		
	The total amount of import and export	Amount of export	Amount of import
1978	900	420	480
1982	1,060	470	590
1986	1,620	865	765
1990	1,872	986	886
1995	2,649	1,265	1,384
2000	6,489	3,245	3,244
2004	7,877	3,965	3,912
2006	8,897	4,116	4,781
2008	29,684	12,688	16,996

Note: only imitation count in above table

3. Write description about "Spring".

图 4

4. Write an argumentation about "My Ideal".

5. Write a narrative about "A Day in My Summer Holiday".

6. Write an exposition about "My University".

Key to writing

一、应用文写作

1.

Dear Mr. Li,

I have been missing you all the time. Glad to know that you're planning to come to Nanjing for a traveling this month. I eagerly look forward to seeing you as soon as possible.

I've been in Nanjing for over 10 years. I am now quite used to life here. This term I take six courses: English, history, mathematics, politics, law and physical training. I am very interested in them and they have benefited me greatly. I like them indeed.

At present I am working with several foreign teachers in our university. They are very kind to me, and often take time to help me with my English and tell me many funny things about English customs and habits. In return, I have offered to improve their Chinese. We are getting along very well with each other.

My younger brother came here to join me two months ago. He is preparing for graduate entrance examination. He intends to study English. Last Sunday, we went to Nanjing University to visit Mr. Wang, one of my uncle's friends. He showed us some interesting parts of the ancient architectures in the campus. We were deeply impressed by what we saw in it.

Are you planning to come to Nanjing to work now? I expect that you could be satisfied to realize my dream.

Yours gratefully,

Zheng Lin

2.

Dear Mr. Zhao,

My wife and I are having some good friends here for dinner on Sunday, June 1. Naturally the party wouldn't be complete without you.

We hope you can come, as we are planning to show the movies we made in New York, and we know you are thinking of going there this summer holiday.

Dinner is at six, as usual. We'll be looking for you two charming people at that time, so don't disappoint us!

Affectionately yours

3.

Dear Sir,

One of my good friends has told me that you have a vacancy for a clerk and I should like to offer myself to the post.

I am twenty-four years old and a good student of Shanghai Commercial College, where I completed four-year courses. I left college with honours, with A grade in English, and computer and book-keeping.

I am working as a secretary with Oriental Company and have spent one year happily there, but the office is too small and I wish to widen my experiences.

My former master has written the enclosed testimonial and has kindly agreed to give further details you needed. If, as I hope, you are interested in my application, you will, of course, be able to get more information about me from my present employers.

Really, I enjoy the kind of work I am doing, but wish to continue it in circumstances that offer better prospects. I shall be pleased to call for an interview at any time.

Yours faithfully,

Hao Lili

4.

Dear Sir,

We learn, through our Commercial Agency there, that you are interested in mobile phones made in China and enclose here our illustrated catalogue and pricelist.

All our mobile phones can be used with either direct or alternating current and can be supplied with or without presentation case. They are the products of the finest materials and workmanship and we offer a worldwide after-sales service.

We hope you will send us a trial order so that you can test our claim against the facts.

Yours faithfully,

Wuxi Liantong Co.

5.

Dear Sirs,

We write to introduce ourselves as one of the leading export company, from Hefei, of a wide range of Meiling freezers.

We attach a list of products we are regularly exporting and trust that some of these items will be popular in our country.

We would be interested in receiving your inquires for our freezers of different models, against which we will send you our quotation in dollars. Airlift will be arranged immediately after receipt of your L/C.

If, by chance, your corporation shouldn't deal with the import of freezers, we would be most grateful if this letter could be forwarded to the import corporation.

We expect to hear from you.

Yours faithfully,

Meiling Co.

6.

In the fifth line of the third paragraph in the left-hand column of Page 12, Chinese Translation Journal No. 4. 20... for "..." read "...".

7.

This paper discusses differences in the syntax between English and Chinese. For instance, English is an inflectional language, while Chinese is a non-inflectional language; English prefers passive voice in its articles while Chinese prefers active voice; English pays more attention to its sentence-structure, but Chinese attaches importance to its sentence meaning. Some phrases or sentences are of common in Chinese, but they are incorrect in terms of English semantic logic. Meanwhile, the paper also shows how translators use the techniques of amplification and omission in English-Chinese and Chinese-English translation when meeting those syntax differences. Translators could amplify or omit proper qualifiers, adverbials, tone words, pronouns, conjunctives and propositions or certain sentence structure.

Key words: syntax, amplification, omission

8.

Name: Wu Lin

Date of birth: August 8, 1983

Place of birth: Wuxi

Nationality：	China
Marital status：	No
Children：	No
Religion：	the Han Nationality
Party affiliation：	the Communist Party of China
Education：	Master Degree
Foreign language：	English
Work experience：	
I．	working in the Software Company
II．	being a division manager
Present address：	98 Zhong Shan Road, Guangzhou
Permanent address：	80 Jin Zhai Road, Hefei
Reference：	Professor, He Jun, Zhong Shan University

Date：2009，5

二、短文写作

1. An Essay by the Following Map of China

This is a map of China.

In the extreme northern side of this map are Russia and Mongolia. Just to the south of Russia and a little bit south is Kazakh. Almost due east of Russia lies Japan, to the eastern side of the northeast of China are N. Korea, Kirghizia, Afghanistan, Tadzhikistan, Pakistan, Philippines, and India borders the western side of China. To the southern side of China lie Nepal, Thailand, Burma and Vietnam. To the eastern side of China lies the Pacific Ocean.

2. An Essay by the Following Table

The table has shown China import and export situation since the reform and opening to the outside world. The total amount of import and expert increased steadily from 1978 to 2008. The import amount is greater than the export amount.

The foreign trade amount in 2008 was 32.91 times as much as that in 1978. The import amount in 2008 was 16,996 billion *yuan*, an increase of 31.22 fold over 1978. The import amount had been about the same as the export amount until 2000, with the exception of the trade deficit of 1 billion in 2000. 2004 saw an export surplus of 53 billion *yuan*. But the trade deficit in 2008 amounted to 4,308 billion *yuan*.

The rapid growth of the amount of China's import and export should be much attributed to the policy of the reform and opening to the outside world. So our government should continually adhere to the policy.

3. In Spring

The picture describes green spring and there are many signs that it is spring in it. There are a group of swallows flying and singing happily in the blue sky. And also it is seen that a willow with its slim branches are dancing in the wind and catkins flying in the air. Whenever people see swallows and willows, they know that spring has come.

It can be seen that there is a river in the picture, on the left side of which there are two women. One is milking a cow, and the other is shearing a sheep and milking a cow, on the right side of which there is a small village of only several houses. In front of the houses there is a large stretch of farmland with all kinds of crops.

We know that spring is a season full of vigor, of joy and of hope. All people like the beautiful spring best of all. In spring the peasants are busy with spring ploughing, and expect that there would be a bumper harvest in the year.

4. My Ideal

I believe that everyone of us should have his/her own ideal. The ideal may be a desire to reach a goal or to achieve a success, which may be a desire to do something beneficial to our society or to our human beings. Now the ideal I set for my lifetime is to be a scientist or a professor.

The ideal resulted from my knowledge about science. When I was a junior middle school student, I read a great number of all kinds of books about scientists and inventors such as Einstein, Bell, Edison, Newton, etc, and especially I was moved and greatly inspired by their achievements. By and by I knew that the great progress of mankind was brought about by their invention and creativeness such as compass, printing, seismograph, steam engine, computer, rocket, spacecraft, and that science and technology are to bring about man's civilization and progress. And I did believe that science and technology are the first productive forces and a great power to push our society forward, and that if a person made outstanding contributions to our society in science, his/her life was very worthwhile.

Since my childhood, I have been determined to work hard at my study and career, and decided to devote my whole life to science and reach the scientific peak with a strong willpower.

5. A Day in My Summer Holiday

It was very hot in summer, so I went to beach, learning to swim and enjoying the beautiful sea scenery. Besides this I always visited many places of historic interest and scenic beauty in some cities and rural areas. During the summer holiday, I, as a freshman of graduates, should know much about the curriculum, so I need my teachers' help and instruction to get more information about study in the university. Therefore, I often consult my teachers in the evenings when I meet some questions in the daytime. Sometimes I also go to the library to read other kinds of books and consult technical data, from which I have learned a lot.

In the half-days of summer holiday I still stay at my home, spending the holiday together with my parents, helping them doing some housework or going to the field to do farm work. After finishing the work, I come back to the university ahead of schedule, and look for an odd job to earn some money for paying tuition and money spent on meals.

Before I knew it two months had passed, the university begins.

6. My University

My university is located in the southern suburbs of Nanjing. It is an old, famous university whose origination can be traced back to 1902, when it was established as a Jiangsu Teacher's Institution of High Learning in Nanjing. It changed several names before 1949. Opportunity for its expansion came only after 1949. Especially in recent 30 years, it has expanded very rapidly and covers about 4,000 mu, with 3 campuses.

There are over 20 departments which offer a total of 60 majors to about 30 thousand on-campus students including about 300 students from countries other than China. All the departments are authorized to confer B. S. and B. E. degree. Master's degree courses are offered by 60 majors. In addition, doctoral programs are offered in most departments.

The university has the first-rate teachers and very fine facilities for scientific research, especially there is a prominent advantage in some majors such as civil engineering, electronics, biomedicine, communications engineering, which are very advanced at home and abroad.

参 考 文 献

Barack Obama. The audacity of hope[M]. Crown/Three Rivers Press, 2006

Daniel Reingold, Jennifer Reingold, Confessions of a Wall Street Analyst: A True Story of Inside Information and Corruption in the Stock Market[M], Collins Business, 2007

Roger Lowenstein, When Genius Failed: The Rise and Fall of Long Term Capital Management[M], Random House Trade, 2001

Thomas L. Friedman. The world is flat: A Brief History of the Twenty-First Century [M], Farrar, Straus and Giroux, 2005

丹. 莱因戈尔德,珍妮弗. 莱因戈尔德著. 华林煦,张德让,张静,翟红梅译. 华尔街顶级证券分析师的忏悔[M]. 南京:译林出版社, 2007

郭建中. 我们在太空中的使命[J]. 中国翻译, 2007, (6)

罗选民,王璟,尹音译. 奥巴马自传:无畏的希望:重申美国梦[M]. 北京:法律出版社, 2008

罗杰·洛温斯坦著;孟立慧译. 长期资本管理公司的崛起与陨落:拯救华尔街[M]. 广州:广东经济出版社,2009

杨自伍. 英国文化选本[M]. 上海:华东师范大学出版社,1996

杨振富,潘勋译. 世界是平的[M]. 台北:雅言文化出版股份有限公司,2005

叶子南. 梵·高 [J]. 中国翻译, 2007, (3)

本书编写组. 2009 年全国硕士研究生入学统一考试:英语考试大纲分析(非英语专业). 北京:高等教育出版社,2008. 7

王福林. 如何提高四、六级作文应试能力. 北京:中国科技大学出版社等,1991. 3

陈多佳等. 英语导学. 上海:上海交通大学出版社,1996. 11

张立民等. 应用文大全. 南京:江苏科学技术出版社,1984. 1

徐广联,梁为祥等. 英语写作精华. 北京:兵器工业出版社,1994. 5

2009 年全国硕士研究生入学统一考试英语试卷

考生注意事项

1. 考生必须严格遵守各项考场规则。

2. 答题前,考生应按准考证上的有关内容填写答题卡上的"考生姓名"、"报考单位"、"考生编号"等信息。

3. 答案必须按要求涂写或填写在指定的答题卡上。

(1) 英语知识运用和阅读理解 A 节、B 节的答案用 2B 铅笔涂写在答题卡 1 上。如要改动,必须用橡皮擦干净。

(2) 阅读理解 C 节(英译汉)的答案和作文必须用蓝(黑)色字迹钢笔、圆珠笔或签字笔写在答题卡上。字迹要清楚。

4. 考试结束,将答题卡 1、答题卡 2 及试题一并装入试题袋中交回。

Section I   Use of English

Directions:

Read the following text. Choose the best word(s) for each numbered blank and mark A, B, C or D on ANSWER SHEET 1. (10 points)

Research on animal intelligence always makes us wonder just how smart humans are.

____1____ the fruit-fly experiments described by Carl Zimmer in the *Science Times*. Fruit flies who were taught to be smarter than the average fruit fly ____2____ to live shorter lives. This suggests that ____3____ bulbs burn longer, that there is a(n) ____4____ in not being too bright.

Intelligence, it ____5____, is a high-priced option. It takes more upkeep, burns more fuel and is slow ____6____ the starting line because it depends on learning—a(n) ____7____ process—instead of instinct. Plenty of other species are able to learn, and one of the things they've apparently learned is when to ____8____.

Is there an adaptive value to ____9____ intelligence? That's the question behind this new research. Instead of casting a wistful glance ____10____ at all the species we've left in the dust I. Q. - wise, it implicitly asks what the real ____11____ of our own intelligence might be. This is ____12____ the mind of every animal we've ever met.

Research on animal intelligence also makes us wonder what experiments animals would ____13____ on humans if they had the chance. Every cat with an owner, ____14____, is running a small-scale study in operant conditioning. We believe that ____15____ animals ran the labs, they would test us to ____16____ the limits of our patience, our faithfulness, our memory for locations. They would try to decide what intelligence in humans is really ____17____, not merely how much of it there is. __18__ , they would hope to study a(n) __19__ question: Are humans actually a-ware of the world they live in? __20__ the results are inconclusive.

1. A) Suppose   B) Consider   C) Observe   D) Imagine
2. A) tended   B) feared   C) happened   D) threatened
3. A) thinner   B) stabler   C) lighter   D) dimmer
4. A) tendency   B) advantage   C) inclination   D) priority
5. A) insists on   B) sums up   C) turns out   D) puts forward
6. A) off   B) behind   C) over   D) along
7. A) incredible   B) spontaneous   C) inevitable   D) gradual
8. A) fight   B) doubt   C) stop   D) think
9. A) invisible   B) limited   C) indefinite   D) different
10. A) upward   B) forward   C) afterward   D) backward
11. A) features   B) influences   C) results   D) costs
12. A) outside   B) on   C) by   D) across
13. A) deliver   B) carry   C) perform   D) apply
14. A) by chance   B) in contrast   C) as usual   D) for instance
15. A) if   B) unless   C) as   D) lest
16. A) moderate   B) overcome   C) determine   D) reach
17. A) at   B) for   C) after   D) with
18. A) Above all   B) After all   C) However   D) Otherwise
19. A) fundamental   B) comprehensive C) equivalent   D) hostile
20. A) By accident   B) In time   C) So far   D) Better still

Section II Reading Comprehension

Part A

Directions:

Read the following four texts. Answer the questions below each text by choosing A, B, C or D. Mark your answers on ANSWER SHEET 1. (40 points)

Text 1

Habits are a funny thing. We reach for them mindlessly, setting our brains on auto-pilot and relaxing into the unconscious comfort of familiar routine. "Not choice, but habit rules the unreflecting herd," William Wordsworth said in the 19 th century. In the ever-changing 21 st century, even the word "habit" carries a negative implication.

So it seems paradoxical to talk about habits in the same context as creativity and innovation. But brain researchers have discovered that when we consciously develop new habits, we create parallel paths, and even entirely new brain cells, that can jump our trains of thought onto new, innovative tracks.

Rather than dismissing ourselves as unchangeable creatures of habit, we can instead direct our own change by consciously developing new habits. In fact, the more new things we try—the more we step outside our comfort zone—the more inherently creative we become, both in the workplace and in our personal lives.

But don't bother trying to kill off old habits; once those <u>ruts</u> of procedure are worn into the brain, they're there to stay. Instead, the new habits we deliberately press into ourselves create parallel pathways that can bypass those old roads.

"The first thing needed for innovation is a fascination with wonder," says Dawna Markova, author of *The Open Mind*. "But we are taught instead to 'decide', just as our president calls himself 'the Decider'." She adds, however, that "to decide is to kill off all possibilities but one. A good innovational thinker is always exploring the many other possibilities."

All of us work through problems in ways of which we're unaware, she says. Researchers in the late 1960s discovered that humans are born with the capacity to approach challenges in four primary ways: analytically, procedurally, relationally (or collaboratively) and innovatively. At the end of adolescence, however, the brain shuts down half of that capacity, preserving only those modes of thought that have seemed most valuable during the first decade or so of life.

The current emphasis on standardized testing highlights analysis and procedure, meaning that few of us inherently use our innovative and collaborative modes of thought. "This breaks the major rule in the American belief system—that anyone can do anything," explains M. J. Ryan, author of the 2006 book *This Year I Will...* and Ms. Markova's business partner. "That's a lie that we have perpetuated, and it fosters commonness. Knowing what you're good at and doing even more of it creates excellence." This is where developing new habits comes in.

21. In Wordsworth's view, "habits" is characterized by being _____.

    A) casual   B) familiar

    C) mechanical   D) changeable

22. Brain researchers have discovered that the formation of new habits can be _____.

    A) predicted   B) regulated

    C) traced   D) guided

23. The word "ruts" (Line 1, Paragraph 4) is closest in meaning to _____.

    A) tracks   B) series

    C) characteristics   D) connections

24. Dawna Markova would most probably agree that _____.

    A) ideas are born of a relaxing mind

    B) innovativeness could be taught

    C) decisiveness derives from fantastic ideas

    D) curiosity activates creative minds

25. Ryan's comments suggest that the practice of standardized testing _____.

    A) prevents new habits from being formed

    B) no longer emphasizes commonness

C) maintains the inherent American thinking mode

D) complies with the American belief system

Text 2

It is a wise father that knows his own child, but today a man can boost his paternal (fatherly) wisdom—or at least confirm that he's the kid's dad. All he needs to do is shell out $30 for a paternity testing kit (PTK) at his local drugstore—and another $120 to get the results.

More than 60,000 people have purchased the PTKs since they first became available without prescriptions last year, according to Doug Fogg, chief operating officer of Identigene, which makes the over-the-counter kits. More than two dozen companies sell DNA tests directly to the public, ranging in price from a few hundred dollars to more that $2,500.

Among the most popular: paternity and kinship testing, which adopted children can use to find their biological relatives and families can use to track down kids put up for adoption. DNA testing is also the latest rage among passionate genealogists—and supports businesses that offer to search for a family's geographic roots.

Most tests require collecting cells by swabbing saliva in the mouth and sending it to the company for testing. All tests require a potential candidate with whom to compare DNA.

But some observers are skeptical. "There's a kind of false precision being hawked by people claiming they are doing ancestry-testing," says Troy Duster, a New York University sociologist. He notes that each individual has many ancestors—numbering in the hundreds just a few centuries back. Yet most ancestry testing only considers a single lineage, either the Y chromosome inherited through men in a father's line or mitochondrial DNA, which is passed down only from mothers. This DNA can reveal genetic information about only one or two ancestors, even though, for example, just three generations back people also have six other great-grandparents or, four generations back, 14 other great-great-grandparents.

Critics also argue that commercial genetic testing is only as good as the reference collections to which a sample is compared. Databases used by some companies don't rely on data collected systematically but rather lump together information from different research projects. This means that a DNA database may have a lot of data from some regions and not others, so a person's test results may differ depending on the company that processes the results. In addition, the computer programs a company uses to estimate relationships may be patented and not subject to peer review or outside evaluation.

26. In Paragraphs 1 and 2, the text shows PTK'S _____.

    A) easy availability   B) flexibility in pricing

    C) successful promotion   D) popularity with households

27. Skeptical observers believe that ancestry testing fails to _____.

    A) locate one's birth place

    B) promote genetic research

    C) identify parent-child kinship

D) choose children for adoption

28. Skeptical observers believe that ancestry testing fails to _____.
    A) trace distant ancestors
    B) rebuild reliable bloodlines
    C) fully use genetic information
    D) achieve the claimed accuracy

29. In the last paragraph, a problem commercial genetic testing faces is _____.
    A) disorganized data collection
    B) overlapping database building
    C) unreliable computer program
    D) difficult sample selection

30. An appropriate title for the text is most likely to be _____.
    A) Fors and Againsts of DNA Testing
    B) DNA Testing and Its Problems
    C) DNA Testing Outside the Lab
    D) Lies Behind DNA Testing

Text 3

The relationship between formal education and economic growth in poor countries is widely misunderstood by economists and politicians alike. Progress in both areas is undoubtedly necessary for the social, political, and intellectual development of these and all other societies; however, the conventional view that education should be one of the very highest priorities for promoting rapid economic development in poor countries is wrong. We are fortunate that it is, because building new educational systems there and putting enough people through them to improve economic performance would require two or three generations. The findings of a research institution have consistently shown that workers in all countries can be trained on the job to achieve radically higher productivity and, as a result, radically higher standards of living.

Ironically, the first evidence for this idea appeared in the United States. Not long ago, with the country entering a recession and Japan at its pre-bubble peak, the U. S. workforce was derided as poorly educated and one of the primary causes of the poor U. S. economic performance. Japan was, and remains, the global leader in automotive-assembly productivity. Yet the research revealed that the U. S. factories of Honda, Nissan, and Toyota achieved about 95 percent of the productivity of their Japanese counterparts a result of the training that U. S. workers received on the job.

More recently, while examining housing construction, the researchers discovered that illiterate, non-English-speaking Mexican workers in Houston, Texas, consistently met best-practice labor productivity standards despite the complexity of the building industry's work.

What is the real relationship between education and economic development? We have to suspect that continuing economic growth promotes the development of education even when governments don't force it. After all, that's how education got started. When our ancestors were hunters and gatherers 10,000 years ago, they didn't have time to wonder much about anything besides finding food. Only when humanity began to get its food in a more productive way was there time for other things.

As education improved, humanity's productivity potential increased as well. When the competitive environment pushed our ancestors to achieve that potential, they could in turn afford more education. This increasingly high level of education is probably a necessary, but not a sufficient, condition for the complex political systems required by advanced economic performance. Thus poor countries might not be able to escape their poverty traps without political changes that may be possible only with broader formal education. A lack of formal education, however, doesn't constrain the ability of the developing world's workforce to substantially improve productivity for the foreseeable future. On the contrary, constraints on improving productivity explain why education isn't developing more quickly there than it is.

31. The author holds in Paragraph 1 that the importance of education in poor countries _____.

    A) is subject to groundless doubts   B) has fallen victim of bias

    C) is conventionally downgraded   D) has been overestimated

32. It is stated in Paragraph 1 that the construction of a new educational system _____.

    A) challenges economists and politicians

    B) takes efforts of generations

    C) demands priority from the government

    D) requires sufficient labor force

33. A major difference between the Japanese and U. S. workforces is that _____.

    A) the Japanese workforce is better disciplined

    B) the Japanese workforce is more productive

    C) the U. S. workforce has a better education

    D) the U. S. workforce is more organized

34. The author quotes the example of our ancestors to show that education emerged _____.

    A) when people had enough time

    B) prior to better ways of finding food

    C) when people no longer went hungry

    D) as a result of pressure on government

35. According to the last paragraph, development of education _____.

    A) results directly from competitive environments

    B) does not depend on economic performance

    C) follows improved productivity

    D) cannot afford political changes

Text 4

The most thoroughly studied intellectuals in the history of the New World are the ministers and political leaders of seventeenth-century New England. According to the standard history of American philosophy, nowhere else in colonial America was "so much importance attached to intellectual pursuits". According to many books and articles, New England's leaders established the basic themes and preoccupations of an unfolding, dominant Puritan tradition in American intellectual life.

To take this approach to the New Englanders normally means to start with the Puritans' theological innovations and their distinctive ideas about the church—important subjects that we may not neglect. But in keeping with our examination of southern intellectual life, we may consider the original Puritans as carriers of European culture, adjusting to New World circumstances. The New England colonies were the scenes of important episodes in the pursuit of widely understood ideals of civility and virtuosity.

The early settlers of Massachusetts Bay included men of impressive education and influence in England. Besides the ninety or so learned ministers who came to Massachusetts churches in the decade after 1629, there were political leaders like John Winthrop, an educated gentleman, lawyer, and official of the Crown before he journeyed to Boston. These men wrote and published extensively, reaching both New World and Old World audiences, and giving New England an atmosphere of intellectual earnestness.

We should not forget, however, that most New Englanders were less well educated. While few craftsmen or farmers, let alone dependents and servants, left literary compositions to be analyzed, it is obvious that their views were less fully intellectualized. Their thinking often had a traditional superstitious quality. A tailor named John Dane, who emigrated in the late 1630s, left an account of his reasons for leaving England that is filled with signs. Sexual confusion, economic frustrations, and religious hope—all came together in a decisive moment when he opened the Bible, told his father that the first line he saw would settle his fate, and read the magical words: "Come out from among them, touch no unclean thing, and I will be your God and you shall be my people. " One wonders what Dane thought of the careful sermons explaining the Bible that he heard in Puritan churches.

Meanwhile, many settlers had slighter religious commitments than Dane's, as one clergyman learned in confronting folk along the coast who mocked that they had not come to the New World for religion. "Our main end was to catch fish. "

36. The author holds that in the seventeenth-century New England _____.

A) Puritan tradition dominated political life

B) intellectual interests were encouraged

C) politics benefited much from intellectual endeavors

D) intellectual pursuits enjoyed a liberal environment

37. It is suggested in Paragraph 2 that New Englanders _____.

A) experienced a comparatively peaceful early history

B) brought with them the culture of the Old World

C) paid little attention to southern intellectual life

D) were obsessed with religious innovations

38. The early ministers and political leaders in Massachusetts Bay _____.

A) were famous in the New World for their writings

B) gained increasing importance in religious affairs

C) abandoned high positions before coming to the New World

D) created a new intellectual atmosphere in New England

39. The story of John Dane shows that less well-educated New Englanders were often _____.

A) influenced by superstitions

B) troubled with religious beliefs

C) puzzled by church sermons

D) frustrated with family earnings

40. The text suggests that early settlers in New England _____.

A) were mostly engaged in political activities

B) were motivated by an illusory prospect

C) came from different backgrounds

D) left few formal records for later reference

Part B
Directions:

In the following text, some segments have been removed. For Questions 41—45, choose the most suitable one from the list A—G to fit into each of the numbered blanks. There are two extra choices, which do not fit in any of the blanks. Mark your answers on ANSWER SHEET 1. (10 points)

Coinciding with the groundbreaking theory of biological evolution proposed by British naturalist Charles Darwin in the 1860s, British social philosopher Herbert Spencer put forward his own theory of biological and cultural evolution. Spencer argued that all worldly phenomena, including human societies, changed over time, advancing toward perfection. ___41___.

American social scientist Lewis Henry Morgan introduced another theory of cultural evolution in the late 1800s. Morgan helped found modern anthropology—the scientific study of human societies, customs and beliefs—thus becoming one of the earliest anthropologists. In his work, he attempted to show how all aspects of culture changed together in the evolution of societies. ___42___.

In the early 1900s in North America, German-born American anthropologist Franz Boas developed a new theory of culture known as historical particularism. Historical particular-

ism, which emphasized the uniqueness of all cultures, gave new direction to anthropology.
___43___.

Boas felt that the culture of any society must be understood as the result of a unique history and not as one of many cultures belonging to a broader evolutionary stage or type of culture. ___44___.

Historical particularism became a dominant approach to the study of culture in American anthropology, largely through the influence of many students of Boas. But a number of anthropologists in the early 1900s also rejected the particularist theory of culture in favor of diffusionism. Some attributed virtually every important cultural achievement to the inventions of a few, especially gifted peoples that, according to diffusionists, then spread to other cultures. ___45___.

Also in the early 1900s, French sociologist Emile Durkheim developed a theory of culture that would greatly influence anthropology. Durkheim proposed that religious beliefs functioned to reinforce social solidarity. An interest in the relationship between the function of society and culture became a major theme in European, and especially British, anthropology.

A) Other anthropologists believed that cultural innovations, such as inventions, had a single origin and passed from society to society. This theory was known as diffusionism.

B) In order to study particular cultures as completely as possible, he became skilled in linguistics, the study of languages, and in physical anthropology, the study of human biology and anatomy.

C) He argued that human evolution was characterized by a struggle he called the "survival of the fittest", in which weaker races and societies must eventually be replaced by stronger, more advanced races and societies.

D) They also focused on important rituals that appeared to preserve a people's social structure, such as initiation ceremonies that formally signify children's entrance into adulthood.

E. Thus, in his view, diverse aspects of culture, such as the structure of families, forms of marriage, categories of kinship, ownership of property, forms of government, technology, and systems of food production, all changed as societies evolved.

F. Supporters of the theory viewed culture as a collection of integrated parts that work together to keep a society functioning.

G. For example, British anthropologists Grafton Elliot Smith and W. J. Perry incorrectly suggested, on the basis of inadequate information, that farming, pottery making, and metallurgy all originated in ancient Egypt and diffused throughout the world. In fact, all of these cultural developments occurred separately at different times in many parts of the world.

Part C
Directions:

Read the following text carefully and then translate the underlined segments into Chinese. Your translation should be written clearly on ANSWER SHEET 2. (10 points)

There is a marked difference between the education which every one gets from living with others and the deliberate educating of the young. In the former case the education is incidental; it is natural and important, but it is not the express reason of the association. (46) It may be said that the measure of the worth of any social institution is its effect in enlarging and improving experience, but this effect is not a part of its original motive. Religious associations began, for example, in the desire to secure the favor of overruling powers and to ward off evil influences; family life in the desire to gratify appetites and secure family perpetuity; systematic labor, for the most part, because of enslavement to others, etc. (47) Only gradually was the by-product of the institution noted, and only more gradually still was this effect considered as a directive factor in the conduct of the institution. Even today, in our industrial life, apart from certain values of industriousness and thrift, the intellectual and emotional reaction of the forms of human association under which the world's work is carried on receives little attention as compared with physical output.

But in dealing with the young, the fact of association itself as an immediate human fact, gains in importance. (48) While it is easy to ignore in our contact with them the effect of our acts upon their disposition, it is not so easy as in dealing with adults. The need of training is too evident and the pressure to accomplish a change in their attitude and habits is too urgent to leave these consequences wholly out of account. (49) Since our chief business with them is to enable them to share in a common life we cannot help considering whether or not we are forming the powers which will secure this ability. If humanity has made some headway in realizing that the ultimate value of every institution is its distinctively human effect we may well believe that this lesson has been learned largely through dealings with the young.

(50) We are thus led to distinguish, within the broad educational process which we have been so far considering, a more formal kind of education—that of direct tuition or schooling. In undeveloped social groups, we find very little formal teaching and training. These groups mainly rely for instilling needed dispositions into the young upon the same sort of association which keeps adults loyal to their group.

Section Ⅲ Writing

Part A

51. **Directions:**

Restriction on the use of plastic bags have not been so successful in some regions. "White Pollution" is still going on.

Write a letter to the editor(s) of your local newspaper to

1) give your opinions briefly, and

2) make two or three suggestions.

You should write about 100 words on ANSWER SHEET 2.

Do not sign your own name at the end of the letter. Use "Li Ming" instead.

Do not write the address. (10 points)

Part B

52. **Directions:**

Write an essay of 160—200 words based on the following drawing. In your essay, you should

1) describe the drawing briefly,

2) explain its intended meaning, and then

3) give your comments.

You should write neatly on ANSWER SHEET 2. (20 points)

（插图）

参考答案和评分参考

Section I Use of English(10 points)

1. B 2. A 3. D 4. B 5. C 6. A 7. D 8. C 9. B 10. D 11. D 12. B 13. C 14. D 15. A 16. C 17. B 18. A 19. A 20. C

Section II Reading Comprehension(60 points)

Part A(40 points)

21. C 22. D 23. A 24. D 25. A 26. A 27. C 28. D 29. A 30. B 31. D 32. B 33. B 34. C 35. C 36. B 37. B 38. D 39. A 40. C

Part B(10 points)

41. C 42. E 43. A 44. B 45. G

Part C(10 points)

46. 虽然我们可以说衡量任何一个社会机构价值的标准是其在丰富和完善人生方面所起的作用,但这种作用并不是我们最初动机的组成部分。

47. 人们只是逐渐地才注意到机构的这一副产品,而人们把这种作用视为机构运作的指导性因素的过程则更为缓慢。

48. 虽然在与年轻人的接触中我们容易忽视自己的行为对他们的性情所产生的影响,然而在与成年人打交道时这种情况就不那么容易发生。

49. 由于我们对年轻人所做的首要工作在于使他们能够在生活中彼此相融,因此我们不禁要考虑自己是否在形成让他们获得这种能力的力量。

50. 这就使我们得以在一直讨论的广义的教育过程中进一步区分出一种更为正式的教育形式,即直接讲授或学校教育。

Section III Writing(30 points)

51. (10 points) (略)
52. (20 points) (略)